More Praise for *How to Reach and Teach Children with Challenging Behavior*

"Finally, someone has cut through the jargon and told it like it is! Most teachers don't have time to read research-heavy guides for the classroom—they need real-world advice they can use on Monday morning. Otten and Tuttle take complicated ideas and make them practical for the everyday teacher to use with any student. This book is comprehensive enough to cover practically everything teachers need to know to decrease behavior challenges in the classroom. It should be required reading for every classroom teacher, new or experienced."

—*Matt McNiff, behavior specialist, Beatrice, Nebraska*

"By sharing their own experience and expertise, Otten and Tuttle help educators use reflective practices to make data-driven decisions about behavior plans that work for their students. This book reads like a conversation between the authors and yourself about the students you teach!"

—*Dr. Staci M. Mathes, director, student support services, Raytown, Missouri*

"Accessible, usable, and engaging. Otten and Tuttle provide direct guidance for educators with examples and practical insights across a wide array of topics. They provide interventions that can be adapted to students with a wide variety of diagnoses, cognitive abilities, ages, and developmental levels. The information on the escalation cycle and using physical restraint and seclusion represent the latest thinking on these topics—topics which are often overlooked or underemphasized in other resources. This is the best summary of current programming and intervention ideas I have seen in some time!"

—*Reece L. Peterson, professor, special education and communication disorders, University of Nebraska-Lincoln*

"Teachers who work with behaviorally challenged children will benefit immensely from reading this book written by teachers who have been in classrooms just like ours with students who display some of the most challenging behaviors. The book is well organized, easy to read, full of resources, and covers everything you need to know to help you and your students successfully deal with behavior issues in a school setting."

—*Sandy Smith, resource teacher, emotional and behavioral disorders, Gardner, Kansas*

Titles in the Jossey-Bass Teacher
Reach and Teach Series

HOW TO REACH AND TEACH CHILDREN WITH ADD/ADHD: PRACTICAL TECHNIQUES, STRATEGIES, AND INTERVENTIONS, SECOND EDITION
Sandra F. Rief • ISBN 978-0-7879-7295-0

HOW TO REACH AND TEACH CHILDREN AND TEENS WITH DYSLEXIA
Cynthia M. Stowe • ISBN 978-0-13-032018-6

HOW TO REACH AND TEACH ALL CHILDREN IN THE INCLUSIVE CLASSROOM: PRACTICAL STRATEGIES, LESSONS, AND ACTIVITIES, SECOND EDITION
Sandra F. Rief and Julie A. Heimburge • ISBN 978-0-7879-8154-9

HOW TO REACH AND TEACH ALL CHILDREN THROUGH BALANCED LITERACY: USER-FRIENDLY STRATEGIES, TOOLS, ACTIVITIES, AND READY-TO-USE MATERIALS
Sandra F. Rief and Julie A. Heimburge • ISBN 978-0-7879-8805-0

How to Reach and Teach Children with Challenging Behavior

Practical, Ready-to-Use Interventions That Work

Kaye L. Otten and Jodie L. Tuttle

JOSSEY-BASS
A Wiley Imprint
www.josseybass.com

Published by Jossey-Bass
A Wiley Imprint
One Montgomery Street, Suite 1200, San Francisco, CA 94104-4594—www.josseybass.com

Jossey-Bass books and products are available through most bookstores. To contact Jossey-Bass directly call our Customer Care Department within the U.S. at 800-956-7739, outside the U.S. at 317-572-3986, or fax 317-572-4002.

Jossey-Bass also publishes its books in a variety of electronic formats. Some content that appears in print may not be available in electronic books.

Library of Congress Cataloging-in-Publication Data

Otten, Kaye L., 1969-
  How to reach and teach children with challenging behavior: practical, ready-to-use interventions that work / Kaye L. Otten and Jodie L. Tuttle.
     p. cm.
  Includes bibliographical references and index.
  ISBN 978-0-470-50516-8 (pbk.)
  ISBN 978-0-470-87289-5 (ebk.)
  ISBN 978-0-470-87290-1 (ebk.)
  ISBN 978-0-470-87291-8 (ebk.)
  1. Problem children—Education—United States. 2. Problem children—Behavior modification—United States. 3. Children with mental disabilities—Education—United States. I. Tuttle, Jodie L., 1968- II. Title.
  LC4802.O88 2010
  371.93—dc22

                                                                    2010026642

Printed in the United States of America
FIRST EDITION
PB Printing   11

Jossey-Bass Teacher

Jossey-Bass Teacher provides educators with practical knowledge and tools to create a positive and lifelong impact on student learning. We offer classroom-tested and research-based teaching resources for a variety of grade levels and subject areas. Whether you are an aspiring, new, or veteran teacher, we want to help you make every teaching day your best.

From ready-to-use classroom activities to the latest teaching framework, our value-packed books provide insightful, practical, and comprehensive materials on the topics that matter most to K–12 teachers. We hope to become your trusted source for the best ideas from the most experienced and respected experts in the field.

About This Book

How to Reach and Teach Students with Challenging Behavior was written by two special education teachers who together have nearly forty years of experience working with students with behavior challenges of all age, ability, and severity levels. They describe practical strategies for managing problem behavior using a three-tiered system of intervention rooted in the philosophies of positive behavior support and functional behavioral assessment. The interventions offered in this book are organized into four overall categories (instruction, prevention, reinforcement, and undesirable consequences) with a focus on teaching skills and lessons needed for success in life and on preventing problems from occurring rather than being reactive and punitive. Provided throughout are ample illustrations, examples, and case studies for clarification of concepts and how they can be applied in the classroom. In addition, issues surrounding the controversy over seclusion and restraint are examined from the viewpoint of experienced practitioners. This book provides educators faced with the overwhelming task of teaching our nation's students with the most challenging behaviors with the information they need to maximize their success and build their confidence.

About the Authors

Kaye L. Otten, M.Ed., Ph.D., has worked with children with behavioral challenges for nearly twenty years. She has teaching credentials in early childhood, elementary, and special education in several states and is a behavioral and autism specialist for the Lee's Summit School District in Missouri. In her current position, Otten consults with educators who support preschool- through high school–aged students with challenging behaviors. She presents throughout the United States on topics related to teaching students with challenging behaviors, autism, and related issues. Otten may be reached at kayeotten@mac.com.

Jodie L. Tuttle, M.Ed., worked as a teacher of students with severe behavior problems for thirteen years and at an alternative middle/high school for four years. She currently works as a behavior specialist for the Green Hills Area Education Agency in Iowa, consulting with educators on students with challenging behaviors at the preschool to high school levels. Tuttle holds teaching certificates in elementary education, special education, and behavior disorders and has presented numerous times at local, national, and international conferences. She has also served as a private behavior consultant for several school districts around the United States. Tuttle was the recipient of the 2005 Midwest Symposium for Leadership in Behavior Disorders Educator of the Year Award. She can be reached at jtuttle68@cox.net.

To all the students we taught in our program at Ezra Elementary School in Millard, Nebraska, and their courageous and inspirational families. You taught us more than any book or any class ever could, changed our lives for the better, and gave us purpose. We think of you often.

Acknowledgments

We thank John Maag for supporting us over the years as a professor, advisor, and colleague. We could not have survived some of the tough situations we have faced in the classroom without his immense knowledge of complex ideas that he made so easily understandable in his unique and entertaining way. We also thank all of the professionals who supported us during our years of teaching together at Ezra Elementary School, especially Pat Rhodes, Paula Larson, Molly Foster, Patrice Feller, Nancy Marron, Evelyn Headen, and Carol Beaty, and all our wonderful paraprofessionals: Mary Perry, Karen Bates, Virginia Cook, Gail Gosnell, Rebecca Irwin, Joan Dobmeier, Janet Bolte, Marilyn Lord, and Beth Tapprich. The accepting, inclusive culture created by all of the speech pathologists, occupational therapists, special class teachers, and general educators who embraced our students and our program so enthusiastically was truly powerful. Thanks to Staci Mathes and Matt McNiff for reading and providing feedback on the early drafts of this book and always providing wise insight and much-needed comic relief that keeps us going in a field that is so prone to burnout.

Kaye: I thank Richard Simpson for his advice and support during my doctoral program and throughout the years since. I greatly admire your humble leadership in this challenging field of emotional and behavioral disorders. My friend and colleague, Sonja deBoer: your advice throughout this process was invaluable. Great appreciation also goes to my extremely talented colleagues in the Lee's Summit R-VII School District who were so willing to share their expertise and real-life examples and provide me with daily inspiration and encouragement, especially Stacey Martin, Kelly Lee, Stephanie Campbell, Chaelah Jenkins, Amy Kempfe, Leigh Wittmeyer, Shannon Check, Ryan Rostine, and Amy Ulrich. To my current supervisor, Jerry Keimig, thanks for always being willing to listen to and support my never-ending ideas, no matter how "out of the box" they may seem. To my family and friends, thank you for your constant support and encouragement, especially this last year of "the book." Mom, I wish you could have celebrated this accomplishment with me but know you are here in spirit. And last but certainly not least, I thank my coauthor and good friend, Jodie Tuttle. The day I met you, I knew I had found a kindred spirit, and there is no way I would have made it even one day during our Ezra years without you. Thanks for always being up for the next adventure I drag you into.

Jodie: I thank, first and foremost, my friend, coauthor, teaching partner, copresenter, and colleague, Kaye Otten. You were the first to convince me that we had something to share with other educators. You inspired me to step beyond the classroom, and I have grown with every opportunity. I have greatly appreciated those I have worked with over the years. I especially note the Valenti family for working with me early in my career and teaching me so much. Thanks to Donna Moss, who led me in the world of special education for years and gave me my first opportunity as a consultant. Thanks also to Kathie DeTour, who helped me through my first experience in alternative education; to my Middle School Alternative Program colleagues Carmen Worick, Cheryl Heimes, Janet Pelster, and Jill Anderson who taught me everything about middle school; and to Becky Zorn, Terri Bush, and my behavior team colleagues in Area Education Agency 13 in Iowa who continue to teach me and have faith in me as I continue my journey in the world of challenging behavior. Finally, I thank my parents and the rest of my family, who have supported me throughout the years.

Contents

PART THREE

Preventing Challenging Behavior

PART FOUR
Reinforcing Desired Behavior

PART FIVE
Using Undesirable Consequences

PART SIX

Putting It All Together

16   Example Success Stories   **210**

Reproducible Tools

Foreword

One of the most perplexing and vexing issues facing teachers today is managing students with challenging behaviors. What should teachers do when a student misbehaves and has been kept in for recess, eats lunch alone, is sent to the hall or principal's office, and has been given both in-school and out-of-school suspensions—yet continues to misbehave. Clearly something else should be tried. But what? Kaye Otten and Jodie Tuttle have written this book, *How to Reach and Teach Students with Challenging Behavior*, for this very purpose: to provide different strategies from those associated with traditional disciplinary measures that have also accumulated a healthy evidence base.

In order to understand the need for and importance of this book, we first must understand exactly who students with challenging behaviors are. Put simply, they are students for whom traditional techniques have failed. If they didn't fail, we would not consider these students to be a challenge. Consequently, these students are defined not so much through their behavior but more as the failure of our behavior—our techniques that did not work. This is not to say that the teacher is a failure. Rather it simply means that the techniques were ineffective, and a different approach is required. Kaye and Jodie provide the tools and techniques for different, effective, and evidence-based approaches.

I have been a professor in the Department of Special Education and Communication Disorders at the University of Nebraska-Lincoln for over twenty years, where I specialize in the education and treatment of children with emotional and behavioral disorders. I have published numerous journal articles and textbooks that deal extensively with issues surrounding these students. I also teach classes in behavior management. It was in that last capacity that I met Jodie Tuttle and Kaye Otten in the spring of 1998 when they were graduate students taking a seminar I taught on issues related to students with emotional and behavioral disorders. Kaye and Jodie also taught together in the same school district. I have been in contact with them since then in the capacity of teacher, advisor, mentor, and colleague. What impressed me most was their curiosity in terms of what was out there that may work better for students with challenging behaviors. They were not afraid to try and fail, and consequently they experienced many successes. Kaye and Jodie have worked collaboratively to develop programs in their district, and they have presented the results at national conferences. They are a rare blend of scholars who are grounded in practice. If anyone could take established behavioral principles and techniques and make them user friendly, accessible, and valued for teachers, I knew it was Kaye and Jodie.

My admiration of Kaye and Jodie was not disappointed when I read this book. It is practitioner friendly and relevant. I am honored that they have cited so much of my work. However, it is their ability to take various techniques, put their unique spin on them, and provide a relevant context for their use that is so noteworthy. One example is their description of setting events and antecedents for challenging behavior. Most professionals in the field often consider these to be synonymous. However, Kaye and Jodie have elucidated the difference and explore how each can be used to identify triggers for misbehavior and remove them to prevent future outbursts. Another example is their conceptualization of teachers who set limits for students. Everyone would agree that setting limits is as necessary as establishing classroom rules. However, teachers sometimes give up too quickly when students with challenging behaviors are either slow to respond or in fact get worse. Jodie and Kaye creatively and correctly point out that students' worsening behavior—what they describe as "behavioral bursts"—in fact indicates that the limit setting is working. These are just a few of the many ways this book is unique and helpful to teachers.

The integrative approach Kaye and Jodie take will make this book a "must-have" desk reference for teachers who encounter students with challenging behaviors. These students have always existed in schools, and they always will; it's just a fact of normal human variation in behavior, personality, and temperament. Kaye and Jodie have added to the literature a guide for reaching and teaching students with challenging behavior by using positive, evidence-based, and user-friendly techniques.

John W. Maag, Ph.D.
University of Nebraska-Lincoln

Preface

If you are reading this book, you are most likely working with one or more students who exhibit behavior that frequently poses problems in your classroom. Welcome to our world! *How to Reach and Teach Children with Challenging Behavior* is the product of nearly forty years of our combined experiences as both general and special educators working with students of all age and ability levels with a wide range of challenging behavior. We developed many of the philosophies and interventions set out in this book while we were teaching partners in an elementary program for students with severe emotional and behavioral challenges. This program served students from kindergarten through fifth grade of all ability levels. We worked with students with severe autism, those with below-average cognitive abilities, academically gifted students with attention and hyperactivity challenges, students with Asperger's syndrome, conduct disorders, oppositional defiant disorders, and many others. The common denominator was that these students' behavior interfered so much with their daily school functioning that they needed intensive intervention. We experienced a great deal of success during that time together and remain in touch with many of the families whose children were in our program.

Major Influences

During our five years as teaching partners, we also earned our master's degrees together in special education with an endorsement in behavior disorders from the University of Nebraska in Lincoln under the advisement of John Maag. Maag's classes on behavior management and ongoing advisement in our everyday teaching practices had an immeasurable influence on our professional lives. Much of the content of this book in Part Two on instruction, specifically incorporating functional behavioral assessment, self-management, and identifying replacement behavior, are based on his work.[1] In addition, during this time, we discovered the work of Ginger Rhode, William R. Jenson, H. Kenton Reavis, and Daniel P. Morgan in their Tough Kid book series, which also had a profound effect on our daily practices. Their work, in addition to Maag's, is heavily embedded throughout this book, specifically in Part Four.[2]

Evidence Base

No Child Left Behind (NCLB) strongly prefers educational programs grounded in scientifically based research and requires that evidence-based interventions be used whenever possible. Positive behavior support and functional behavioral assessment practices provide the foundation for this book and are firmly grounded in applied behavioral analysis, an area of scientific study supported by over thirty years of research. We are very aware that many times educators are bored and frustrated by "research talk." Therefore, in this book, we sought to bridge that research-to-practice gap by providing research support where applicable and appropriate in common, easy-to-understand language. We attempted to minimize the number of text citations in this book by referencing several of our major influences above. However, we feel strongly that we need to credit researchers for their work on which the various interventions included in this book are based and that educators need to be able to easily locate any research support for the interventions they use. Therefore, we provide original sources of information that we adapted or built on for our daily classroom use and recommend various other resources that we have found helpful in our careers, many which may include interventions similar to the ones described in this book. The fact that multiple, experienced practitioners have developed very similar intervention provides strong qualitative evidence that these types of interventions are indeed effective.

Because of the complexity of educational research and human behavior, as problem behaviors become more challenging, ensuring that interventions are always evidence or research based, using the ideal of empirical validation through experimental methods with random assignment and control groups becomes difficult. We have taught and consulted on the cases of several students that we describe as being an "N of one." By this, we mean that due to their unique characteristics and the complexity of their conditions, typical research-based interventions did not work for them. For example, we worked with a student who had multiple significant language, cognitive, and psychological impairments. Over time we determined through ongoing functional behavioral assessment that one of the triggers to his aggressive behavior was receiving praise from adults he was not familiar with. We were never able to determine why this was, and it certainly was unusual, but nonetheless it was the trigger. Praise is a behavioral intervention well supported by research, but it did not work for this student, who fell outside the normal range of human behavior.

Although the main foundation of positive behavior support is that of the traditional gold standard of quantitative experimental research, it also embraces flexibility with respect to scientific practices, valuing more qualitative research methods such as observations and case studies that would be appropriate in cases such as the one described above. The key is that there is a systematic data source that is used to evaluate and guide intervention.[3] The evidence for some of the interventions that we describe in this book are based on our observations, experiences, and student case studies. If these interventions are used with students, systematic data collection becomes of utmost importance to provide evidence that the intervention is indeed effective in individual cases. This is a large focus of Chapter Fourteen.

Overview of the Contents

This book is divided into seven parts. Part One addresses the common frustrations we hear from educators every day who face the daunting task of managing challenging behavior in their classrooms and provides an overview of positive behavior support, functional behavioral assessment, and our intervention model. The overall framework of our intervention model has four components: instruction, prevention, reinforcement, and undesirable consequences. We have found that each of these components is essential; leave one out, and you miss a key piece of effective behavior management. Each of Parts Two through Five focuses on one of these four components in detail. Part Six outlines an effective and efficient process for designing individual behavior intervention plans based on functional behavioral assessment and provides a template and several case studies to guide that process. Part Seven addresses the reality that dangerous behavior may still occur despite our best prevention and intervention efforts; it discusses how to manage crises and provides important and timely information regarding the controversy surrounding the use of seclusion and restraint.

Since our days of teaching together, we have both moved on to other jobs in the behavior management field but have been able to apply the lessons we learned and interventions we developed during that time to students we serve in various situations. In this book, we have set out the interventions and strategies that we have found to be the most effective in addition to being realistic for educators to implement in their already overwhelming daily lives. We share stories of students we have worked with throughout the book to illustrate how various interventions and concepts have been successfully implemented and applied, and we also provide a number of reproducible tools that you are welcome to copy and use with the students you teach or support. Reaching and teaching children with behavior challenges is a tough job, but it is full of immeasurable rewards. We sincerely hope that you find this book invaluable as you help the students you serve reach their full potential.

Kaye L. Otten and Jodie L. Tuttle

Part One

A Positive, Proactive Approach to Behavior Management

Our Model of Intervention

Instruction

↓

Prevention

↓

Reinforcement

↓

Undesirable Consequences

Chapter 1

A Case for Change

What's wrong with kids today? "What happened to the good old days when students behaved themselves in school?" "I didn't sign up for this when I decided to become a teacher!" "These kids with behavior problems should just be suspended!" "Punishment worked on me and works for me!"

As behavior specialists working in the public school system, we hear similar questions from and attitudes expressed by educators almost every day. Educators are facing immense difficulties as the number of students with social, emotional, and behavioral challenges increases dramatically while at the same time public education is more closely monitored and held accountable for high academic outcomes, especially since passage of No Child Left Behind in 2002. Our training to be educators did not adequately expose us or prepare us to deal with these difficulties, and our guess is that yours didn't either, or you would not be reading this book. In fact, teachers in both general and special education have repeatedly identified behavior management as a priority in-service need, and student behavior has been in the top five teacher concerns in Gallup polls for the past thirty years. Our sincere hope is that by reading this book and applying its concepts with the students you teach, you will find behavior management less overwhelming and your confidence and belief that you can meet these challenges will greatly increase. Let's start by addressing each of these common questions and attitudes set out in the first paragraph of the chapter.

What's Wrong with Kids Today?

There is no doubt that increasing numbers of students in public schools have behavior challenges. Between 1976 and 2004, the number of students between the ages of three and twenty-one served in the emotional disturbance category doubled from 283,000 to 489,000.[1] The number of students served under the educational autism category, who also often experience behavioral challenges, has also increased dramatically—according to the Centers for Disease Control and Prevention, from 22,664 to 211,610 between 1994 and 2006.[2] In addition, many students receiving special education services under other eligibility categories such as other health impairments and learning disabilities, as well as students in general education, also exhibit challenging behaviors. It is no wonder that educators are overwhelmed. In fact, according to one survey, students with emotional and behavioral challenges are the primary reason that general educators leave the profession.[3] If you are feeling frustrated in your efforts to reach and teach students with behavioral challenges, you are certainly not alone.

What Happened to the Good Old Days?

Our response to this question is always, "How good were those days *really*?" First, where were many children with significant behavioral challenges, especially those with multiple, severe, or misunderstood disabilities if they were not in public schools? The honest answer is that they were at home with minimal learning experiences or interaction with others, either because parents did not send them to school or schools kicked them out, or they were residing in underfunded and understaffed institutions too often receiving poor care and being subjected to abuse and/or neglect. The closing of many institutions in the late 1970s and early 1980s and passage of federal legislation such as the Civil Rights of Institutionalized Persons Act of 1980 and the Education for All Handicapped Children Act in 1975 ended these widespread practices. Now, every child, even those with the most severe limitations, has the right to a free and appropriate public education and dignity and respect for all individuals is now highly valued and modeled.

Second, adults no longer model submissiveness and obedience, and this is a good thing. One of the largest influences on our behavior management philosophy is the book *Positive Discipline* by Jane Nelson, which discusses how various historical events such as the women's and civil rights movements led people to question and challenge government and authority in general and not just submissively accept the direction of those in power.[4] Children see these attitudes and behaviors modeled and also challenge authority, including teachers and administrators. They want a rationale for their curriculum, question the decisions of school personnel, and test boundaries, which drives those of us who grew up in the "because I said so" and "children should be seen and not heard" era crazy. But is challenging authority and holding leaders accountable a bad thing if we teach students to do so respectfully? Is this not a life skill we value in the current culture of transparency and accountability for those in authority? Whose behavior needs to change?

Nelson sets out three main approaches of adult-child interaction. The first is strictness, a punitive approach characterized by excessive adult control, no choices by the child, and the attitude of "You do it because I said so." This often leads to rebellion on the part of the child, who avoids or attempts to manipulate adults to get what he or she wants. Children do not learn why it isn't in their best interest to do something or not do something, only that they may be punished if they do not comply with adult directions, so they often end up making poor choices when the punishing adult is not present. The second approach is permissiveness, the exact opposite of strictness. Adults who are permissive with children fail to set limits, giving them complete freedom to do anything they want, which often leads to an attitude of entitlement and lack of personal responsibility for choices. The third approach, positive discipline, results in the most productive outcomes of responsibility and life skill development, the ultimate goal of public education. In this approach, adults are kind but firm, providing choices within appropriate limits based on mutual respect.

I Didn't Sign Up for This!

Educators we work with often express the belief that their job is solely to teach academic skills and that teaching behavioral skills is not their responsibility. However, research clearly shows a co-occurrence between academic and behavioral problems. Although the direction of this relationship is not clear, it appears complex and influenced by a variety of factors.[5] What we do know is that as social and behavioral skills improve, academic achievement also increases.[6] Preventive behavior management is one of best academic instructional support strategies and vice versa.[7]

> As social and behavioral skills improve, academic achievement also increases.

In addition to teaching academic skills, the purpose of public schools is to help young people develop into productive, contributing members of society. Individuals with poor social and behavioral skills are at risk for a wide range of problems that have a negative impact on society: school dropout, depression, anxiety, substance abuse, gang membership, low self-esteem, social maladjustment, medical problems, employment difficulties, aggression, delinquency, incarceration, higher death and injury rates, and lifelong dependency on the welfare system.[8] Social skills deficiency in childhood, in fact, is the single best predictor of significant problems in adulthood.[9]

Teachers have long identified behavioral management as an area where they need more training and support in order to increase their efficiency. National surveys of topics that are considered of great importance by general educators consistently identify discipline and safety as a high priority. Clearly behavior management is part of every teacher's job. (You actually did sign up for this; you just didn't know it.) Fortunately, good teachers have the skills they need to teach behavioral and social skills because social and academic behavior is governed by the same principles of learning and responds to the same types of intervention.[10]

Just as some students have reading difficulties, some students have difficulty selecting and using the appropriate social and behavioral skills. The difference is that traditionally academic instruction has been proactive, while behavioral instruction has been reactive.[11] Teachers would never test a student on long division before teaching him or her how to do it, but many times they "test" students on behavioral skills before teaching them. For example, teachers often hold students accountable for knowing how to get attention or help appropriately in the classroom before ever directly teaching this skill. Because many students seemingly teach themselves social and behavioral skills through observing the behaviors of those around them, educators tend to expect all students to do this. The problem with this expectation is that some students may not be exposed to appropriate models prior to and outside public education, and some may have disabilities that interfere with this learning process.

> Fortunately, good teachers have the skills they need to teach behavioral and social skills because social and academic behavior is governed by the same principles of learning and responds to the same types of intervention.

Students with Behavior Problems Should Just Be Suspended!

For many students with chronic behavior problems, suspension is not the meaningful consequence it is intended to be and often does not result in the student's changing his or her behavior for the better upon return to school. Many students do not want to be in school, which for them is synonymous with rejection and failure; for them, suspension is actually reinforcing the problem behavior. The reality is that many times, students are not adequately supervised outside school and therefore spend their time engaging in their preferred activities such as watching television or playing video games. Time away from the educational environment certainly does not facilitate the progress of at-risk students who are already academically and socially disengaged from school. When they return, they've missed even more instruction and have fallen further behind academically. These kids, viewed as troublemakers, certainly are not the ones their peers typically want to hang out with—unless they are other at-risk students in search of a peer group.

Many administrators we work with say that parents of other students in their school complain and put pressure on them to suspend students with behavior problems so that their child's learning environment is not disrupted. "My child's education should not suffer and he shouldn't have to put up with that" is a common opinion we hear. The fact is that schools using only punishment strategies such as suspension have increased rates of vandalism, aggression, truancy, and school dropout, which actually promote antisocial behavior.[12] These same parents complain when these type of problems increase in their neighborhood. In addition, part of preparing students for real life is exposing them to and teaching them to deal with all of the problems they will eventually face in society, including peers who exhibit challenging behavior.

Even if suspension is a meaningful and undesirable consequence for a student with behavior challenges, it still may not be an appropriate intervention. Although it may in some cases decrease an undesirable behavior, it does not teach a more appropriate behavioral response. The student may learn to fear or dislike the person giving the punishment (educators) and the place associated with it (school), certainly not the intended outcome. So in actuality, suspension does little more than provide educators with temporary relief from an uncomfortable and frustrating situation. This may be needed at times, but then it should be called what it is—a break for the school staff—and not be considered effective behavior management. In fact, "there is currently no evidence that suggests suspension or expulsion changes the behavior of difficult students. Rather, for troublesome or at-risk students, the most well-documented outcome of suspension appears to be further suspension and eventually school drop-out."[13]

Clearly suspension is not supported by common sense or research, and in an era of mandated evidence-based practices, it should be used sparingly.

Punishment Works for Me!

We know what you are thinking: "But kids shouldn't be this way." "I'm already overwhelmed, overworked, and underpaid." "My punitive behavior management practices have worked well for me for [fill in the blank] years." We hear you.

Kaye Says . . .

I come from a long line of educators who firmly believed in the traditional "don't smile until Christmas" philosophy and had a low tolerance for any inappropriate behavior, which they typically responded to with a punitive discipline approach. I started my career with that belief also, and in the small rural Nebraska town where I grew up and in my early teaching experiences in schools without many students with chronic behavior challenges, that approach did suppress problem behavior. Therefore, I mistakenly believed it was effective—just as many of you do.

The truth is that punitive approaches will work for about 80 to 90 percent of the student population as far as controlling behavior. But they do not develop personal responsibility or teach life skills and simply do not work for students at risk for or those who already have chronic behavioral challenges.

What Can We Do?

So far we have pointed out that increasing numbers of students exhibit chronic behavioral challenges in schools, behavior management is an important part of every educator's job, and traditional punitive approaches to behavior management that many educators typically use and are comfortable with, such as suspension, don't work in the long run. The situation may appear hopeless, but it isn't. Here is what you can do as a start.

> Punitive approaches will work for about 80 to 90 percent of the student population as far as controlling behavior. But they do not develop personal responsibility or teach life skills and simply do not work for students at risk for or those who already have chronic behavioral challenges.

Remove the Words *Should* and *Shouldn't* from Your Vocabulary

"Parents should teach their kids how to behave." "Students shouldn't be this way." "This shouldn't be part of my job." Guess what? Many times parents don't teach their kids how to behave, students are how they are, and it *is* part of your job. Period. We hate to be so blunt, but frankly if you can't let this go, we suggest you start looking through the want ads because it isn't going to change any time soon.

Limit the Time Spent "Admiring the Problem"

Many times when we are called to be a part of a problem-solving session for a student with chronic behavioral challenges, we start by staying quiet, listening, and watching the time. We hear comments from our fellow educators like, "This is so sad," "My heart breaks for this kid," and "I just want to take him [or her] home with me." Although there is a valid need to vent and dealing with these issues can be emotionally difficult, too many times, thirty to forty-five minutes or more go by with no conversation focusing on what to do about it. If we are really so short on time, we need to use it wisely, focusing more time on problem solving than problem admiring.

Strive to Understand the Perspectives of All Team Members and Stakeholders

We truly believe that a vast majority of parents sincerely care about their children and want what is best for them and that a vast majority of all educators entered the profession to help students learn and become productive and contributing members of society. Remember this when conflict arises. We all have the same goals; we just have different ideas about the best way to get there and different variables influencing our attitudes and behaviors as adults. We need to understand everyone's perspective and work together to meet the needs of teaching students with behavior challenges. We have worked with several parents who were challenging the district, calling in advocates, and threatening legal action. These moves certainly can be intimidating. When we took the time to get to know the parent, listen to and validate their concerns and build a positive relationship with them, these situations often resolved themselves.

Jodie Says . . .

One particular parent I recall was especially intimidating. She pretty much had the superintendent on speed-dial, wrote frequent letters to the editor regarding services in the schools, and generally struck fear in the hearts of school personnel. In one of our first meetings planning for the education of her child, the conversation was heated and combative. In a tense moment, I interjected, "I know I am the newest member of your child's team, but as the person who is going to teach your child every day, I want to tell you I admire you for advocating for your child. Many parents don't get involved in their child's education. Parents are such valuable members of the team because you know your child better than any of us. I want you to know that our goals are the same. We both want your child to be successful at school. We may not always agree with how to do that, but I am optimistic that we can work together to benefit your child." The conversation stopped momentarily, and when it resumed, it was more collaborative and less combative.

After the meeting, the parent stopped me and told me that no one from the schools had ever acknowledged her advocacy as a good thing and said she really looked forward to working with me. After that, we had a positive, working relationship, and we could problem-solve, compromise, and even agree to disagree. Our collaboration definitely benefited her child.

Let Go of the Old Way of Doing Things

Traditional punitive approaches to behavior management do not result in the intended outcomes and need to change. As Einstein once wisely said, "Insanity is doing the same thing over and over again and expecting different results."

Expand Your Behavior Management Toolbox

Abraham Maslow once stated: "If the only tool you have is a hammer, you tend to see every problem as a nail." However, every behavior problem is not a nail. Many of these problems have varied and complex causes. As educators, we need to increase the number of tools in our intervention toolbox because different types of problems have different types of solutions. A growing body of research is showing that alternatives to punitive practices have decreased inappropriate behavior and increased both social skills and academic achievement in many school districts. As a whole, educators need to shift their behavior management paradigm from focusing on punishment to focusing on prevention and early intervention.

Welcome to the world of positive behavior support and functional behavioral assessment. We spent a great deal of time and money learning how to implement these principles in public school settings. Let us give you the quick and cheap training in this book. With the right attitude, it can be a lot of fun and can lead to amazing progress in your students. We promise.

Key Points to Remember

- The number of students with challenging behaviors in our schools is on the rise.

- Our society promotes an attitude of scrutiny. Students today are more likely than in the past to challenge authority and question school staff.

- Traditional reactive and punitive interventions for behavior do not develop personal responsibility or teach life skills to any student and do not work with students who present chronic behavior challenges.

- Schools must work collaboratively with parents, teachers, specialists, and the administration to design positive preventive approaches to manage challenging behaviors.

- Teachers need to be provided with more information and training on effective programming for students with challenging behaviors.

- Prevention and early intervention are essential components of positive, effective behavior management for students with challenging behavior.

Discussion Questions

1. We all have had students in our classrooms who have challenging behaviors. What are some of the behaviors that they exhibit that make it difficult to teach them? What are some ways we can directly teach these students the behavioral skills they lack?

2. Suspension is one of the most frequently used behavioral consequences in schools today even though research says that it is not effective with at-risk students and students with chronic behavioral problems. Nevertheless, schools do need to address aggressive and dangerous behaviors, and they have an obligation to keep all students safe. How can we address these serious behaviors, ensure student safety, and make consequences meaningful to students with challenging behaviors? What alternatives to suspension might work in your school?

3. Parents are important members of student educational teams. What are some barriers to a positive relationship between teachers and the parents of students with challenging behaviors? What are some techniques and approaches you can use with a combative parent? What are some ways you could get an uninvolved parent more involved?

Chapter 2

Positive Behavior Support and Functional Behavioral Assessment for Educators

Y ou no doubt have run across the terms *positive behavior support* and *functional behavioral assessment* in your career. But what do they really mean for educators on a day-to-day basis? First, it is important to understand that functional behavior assessment is considered a positive behavior support: the two go hand in hand. When we refer to positive behavior support throughout this book, we are including the ongoing process of considering the function of behavior, that is, functional behavioral assessment.

Positive behavior support is overwhelmingly viewed as best practice by leaders in the educational field. In addition, it is highly favored and possibly on the verge of being required by federal law when No Child Left Behind (NCLB) and the Individuals with Disabilities Education Act (IDEA) are reauthorized. Lawmakers are increasingly aware that if academic outcomes are to improve, behavior needs to improve and that the punitive practices used in many of our nation's schools are highly ineffective, if not damaging to students. IDEA currently requires that positive behavioral interventions, strategies, and supports be "considered" for students whose behavior impedes their learning or the learning of others.

In the American Recovery and Reinvestment Act of 2009, the U.S. Department of Education encourages local education agencies to use these funds for professional development in reading, math, writing, and science and for positive behavior support.[1]

What Exactly Is Positive Behavior Support?

Positive behavior support is a major initiative that has developed over the past decade in order to shift the focus of behavior management away from reactive, negative approaches to more proactive, positive ones. Positive behavior support is not simply providing rewards or incentives to students for behaving appropriately. It is a much broader concept with multiple applications in the educational setting. The Office of Special Education's Technical Assistance Center on Positive Behavioral Interventions and Supports officially defines *positive behavior support* as "an application of a behaviorally-based systems approach to enhance the capacity of schools, families and communities to design effective environments that improve the link between research-validated practices and the environments in which teaching and learning occurs."[2] Two key points in this definition are research-validated practices and enhancing the capacity of all environments. We will focus on each of these key points in turn.

Research-Validated Practices

NCLB strongly prefers educational programs grounded in scientifically based research and requires using only evidence or evidence-based interventions whenever possible. Positive behavior support and functional behavioral assessment practices are firmly grounded in applied behavioral analysis, an area of scientific study supported by over thirty years of research confirming the effectiveness of various antecedent and consequence strategies, data collections, graphing, and monitoring.[3] The main research foundation of positive behavior support is that of the traditional gold standard of quantitative experimental research. However, educational research is complex, and many important topics do not lend themselves well to traditional research techniques. Therefore, positive behavior support embraces flexibility with respect to scientific practices, valuing the information gained by qualitative research methods such as naturalistic observations and case studies. A systematic data source is invaluable to evaluate and guide intervention.[4]

Enhancing the Capacity of Environments

By focusing on the "environments in which teaching and learning occurs," including "schools, families and communities," the goal of positive behavior support is not just on "fixing" the student with behavioral challenges but also on "fixing" aspects of the learning environment that contribute to the problem behavior. This includes increasing the prevention and early intervention skills of the adults rather than continuing to allow them to react only after behavioral problems have occurred. A reactive, punitive-only approach does not work. The positive behavior support movement has given birth to the idea that the best time to intervene is when the problem behavior is not even occurring.[5] Just as safety laws prevent and reduce accidents and preventative medicine prevents and reduce illness, positive behavior support prevents and reduces behavioral problems.

> The best time to intervene is when the problem behavior is not even occurring.

A Three-Tiered Model

Positive behavior support is a systematic three-tiered model in which all students get universal intervention (this is the foundation); some students who do not respond adequately to universal intervention receive more intensive intervention; and a few students receive intensive intervention.

Research increasingly is demonstrating that three-tiered models pairing evidence-based interventions at each level of support are effective in reducing the number of students identified for expensive and intensive special education support and help educators to work smarter, not harder. Most educators who work with students with chronic behavior challenges want to focus on the top of the triangle: interventions targeting the most challenging students. In addition, school districts and buildings often implement only hit-and-miss strategies with students with behavior challenges rather than taking a systematic approach. These are huge mistakes. The entire positive behavior support pyramid needs to be built from the ground up because it works exponentially. That is, the interventions at the top of the triangle have a much more powerful effect if the interventions at the foundation are firmly in place.

> The entire positive behavior support pyramid needs to be built from the ground up because it works exponentially. That is, the interventions at the top of the triangle have a much more powerful effect if the interventions at the foundation are firmly in place.

Having interventions in place at all levels also cuts down on more minor behavior problems, thus leaving more resources in terms of time, energy, and finances to allocate to the upper levels. Providing a strong foundation at the first level of positive behavior support benefits all students and is essential to the goal of reaching and teaching students with behavioral challenges. Universal, or first-tier, interventions prevent the onset of problem behavior among low-risk students and sustain improvements made as a result of second- and third-tier interventions over time.[6]

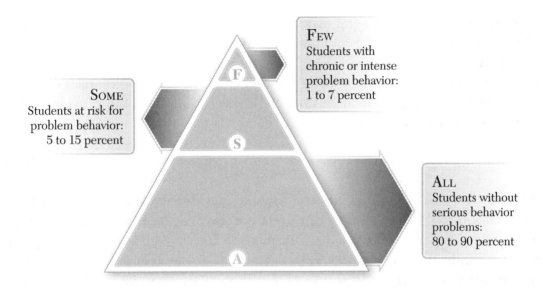

Figure 2.1 Positive Behavior Support Triangle

What Exactly Is Functional Behavioral Assessment?

Functional behavioral assessment (FBA) examines why problem behaviors occur in order to guide prevention and intervention efforts, thereby increasing efficiency and effectiveness. Functional behavioral assessment is one of the most misunderstood processes in education. This is largely because at the time it was mandated as part of the amendments to IDEA in 1997, practice exceeded the research base. That is, there was no consensus among researchers regarding the essential components and processes of FBA in the educational environment,[7] and the techniques traditionally researched were originally designed for students with severe development disabilities in clinical settings.[8]

As educators, we are keenly aware that the variables that exist in a public school setting (such as individual teaching styles, academic and social demands, and sensory stimulation) are much more complex than the fairly controllable environments in clinical settings, and therefore the practice of FBA has not translated well to the education field. This confusion has resulted in the development of several common myths that surround functional behavioral assessment in the educational setting:

Myth: Functional behavioral assessment is a paperwork process conducted by highly trained and skilled behavior analysts or school psychologists that only exists in special education.

The reality: Some FBAs can be quite simple. For example, if an administrator believes that a student behaved inappropriately with the goal of being suspended so he or she could escape the aversive school environment and go home to a preferred or more reinforcing environment and activity, the administrator may choose to instead give the student in-school suspension. No data were taken, and no formal plan was written. Other forms of FBA can be quite complex, involving specialists, multiple observations, and various forms of data collection and analysis. Although FBA was developed with developmentally delayed individuals in clinical settings, a more third-tier intervention, it should provide guidance throughout all three tiers of intervention.[9]

Myth: There is only one way to conduct an FBA, and it requires using specific data collection tools.

The reality: Not all individuals are comfortable and fluent using certain assessment and intervention tools. Instead, they can use a process that results in the most helpful information for designing effective behavioral interventions in their situation. For example, we have both conducted multiple functional behavior assessments at all levels of complexity and neither of us have ever used a scatter plot. Although a scatter plot is an excellent tool for some, it is not one that we prefer using.

Myth: A formal FBA needs to be conducted and an individualized behavior intervention plan (BIP) designed and implemented for every problem behavior that students exhibit. These plans need to be included in each student's individual education plan (IEP), and the IEP team needs to reconvene every time the plan is changed.

The reality: At the time of the 1997 mandate, we were coteaching in a program for students with severe and chronic behavior challenges and felt that we had a pretty good handle on considering functions of problem behaviors and having that guide our interventions. Our supervisors at the time informed us that we needed to do what is stated in this myth, and our first response was *"What!!"* Although we agree this is ideal, it is often not realistic. Our reply at the time was that the IEP team may as well set up camp in our classrooms because we would be meeting every day, if not multiple times a day, in order to meet this requirement. Anyone who has worked on a daily basis with students with chronic, severe behavior problems in the public school setting knows that functions of behavior can change very quickly, that different behaviors can serve the same function, and that the same behavior can serve different functions based on many environmental variables that are constantly interacting and changing.

> Anyone who has worked on a daily basis with students with chronic, severe behavior problems in the public school setting knows that functions of behavior can change very quickly, that different behaviors can serve the same function, and that the same behavior can serve different functions based on many environmental variables that are constantly interacting and changing.

Experts in the field acknowledge that the content, intensity, and complexity of functional behavioral assessment activities will vary.[10] Some problems are much simpler than others and in many cases conducting a lengthy and complex formal FBA would be a waste of valuable educator time. Clearly, the public school environment is much different from a clinical environment, and we need to develop more school-friendly, efficient, and effective FBA processes than what has traditionally been used in the clinical world.[11] We hope this book will do just that.

Three Key Concepts of FBA

Becoming proficient in determining the functions of behavior begins with a clear understanding of three key concepts: setting events, triggering antecedents, and maintaining consequences. These concepts, especially setting events and maintaining consequences, are often misunderstood because the everyday use of these terms in an educational setting tends to mean something quite different from what they mean in the world of FBA. Let's clear up this confusion.

Setting Events

Educators typically think of the word *setting* as meaning where something happens, like the setting in a fictional story. In the world of functional behavioral assessment, however, setting events mean something quite different. We call this, "You know it is going to be a bad day when _____." Fill in the blank thinking about a student you work with or have worked with who exhibited problem behaviors:

> We call this, "You know it is going to be a bad day when _____."

> You know it is going to be a bad day <u>when he spent the night at Dad's rather than Mom's.</u>

> You know it is going to be a bad day <u>when there is a special activity such as a holiday party or field trip.</u>

> You know it is going to be a bad day <u>immediately after a weekend or long break.</u>

We find that once they get to know their students, many educators often instinctively know these things; they just don't realize they are identifying setting events. Setting events exaggerate the likelihood that the problem behaviors will occur or makes them worse. These events do not always mean that the problem behaviors will occur, but the behaviors are more likely to happen, and happen at a higher intensity, when these variables are present.

Triggering Antecedents

We call triggering antecedents "the straw that broke the camel's back." Often when there is a setting event present, or more than one, the student is experiencing negative emotions such as anxiety, anger, or disappointment. Then something happens, and the student exhibits problem behavior seemingly out of nowhere. Maybe you give the student an academic task that involves writing, which tends to be hard for him (this is a common trigger); or maybe there is a sudden change in the schedule, a loud noise, a strong smell, or other sensory input that he finds aversive. Triggering antecedents can be internal too—a negative memory evoked by something in the story being read or suddenly not feeling well. Identifying these events

> We call triggering antecedents "the straw that broke the camel's back."

can be challenging, especially with students who are nonverbal or have language difficulties. (Strategies for minimizing the influence of setting events and triggering antecedents are the focus in Part Three of this book.)

Maintaining Consequences

The third key concept in FBA is maintaining consequences, that is, what happens after the problem behavior that contributes to its occurrence and maintenance. Educators typically think of punishment in connection with the word *consequences*—something they "give" students to try to discourage them from repeating the problem behavior. However, in the FBA world, maintaining consequences refers to what naturally happens after the behavior that reinforces it. We call it the "payoff," or "what the student gets

> We call [maintaining consequences] the "payoff" or "what the student gets out of it."

out of it." Is the student getting attention or a reaction from others in the environment, either adults or their peers? Are they able to escape from an undesirable task or environment even temporarily? Are they getting some sort of desired sensory input? The student may or may not be aware that he or she is doing it for this reason because it is often subconscious.

If you can identify what is serving as the natural reinforcer in the environment, you have come a long way toward intervening effectively by minimizing that reinforcer and providing an alternative, more powerful reinforcer for the desired replacement behavior. (We explore maintaining consequences in more detail in Part Four.)

Common Functions of Problem Behavior

When we make presentations to special and general educators of students at all ages and ability levels around the United States, we often ask, "What are the two most common functions of inappropriate behavior?" Almost without fail, educators quickly respond with "attention" and "escape or avoidance," and they are exactly right. Educators usually know their students well and often instinctively know what the function of the problem behavior is. However, they don't always react in the most effective and efficient way based on this knowledge. The most common traditional approaches to behavior management are lecturing (attention), time-out (escape or avoidance), and suspension (more escape or avoidance). Clearly we need a larger toolbox of interventions and a problem-solving process for choosing which ones to use when. The rest of this chapter discusses other common functions of problem behaviors, and the entire book provides a framework for matching responses and interventions to these functions.

The classic text *Applied Behavior Analysis for Teachers* categorizes functions of behavior as attention seeking and escape and avoidance.[12] Others divide all possible functions into positive and negative reinforcement.[13] Yet still others suggest that some functions cannot be classified into these two categories and have identified various other possible functions, such as power or control, affiliation (belongingness), justice, gratification, and revenge.[14] Clearly there is no universally accepted list of possible functions of behavior.

As educators attempting to use FBA in the school environment, we never found dividing functions into broad categories to be very helpful. Rather, in our daily practices, we have come up with the following categories in our attempt to understand the common functions of students' problem behavior and use them to guide the development of effective responses and interventions:

- To get attention or a reaction from peers and adults

- To get something tangible

- To get power or control

- To meet a sensory need

- To communicate feelings, wants, and needs

- As a result of a lack of understanding

- To escape or avoid something

We will look briefly at each of these.

To Get Attention or a Reaction

The most common mistake teachers make when attempting to intervene with students with behavior challenges is they forget about or underestimate the power of attention or reaction as a reinforcer. As we will discuss in depth in Chapter Nine, whether something acts as a reinforcer is the effect it has on behavior, not the intent of the educator. Although you may think that lecturing, reprimanding, and repeatedly giving long explanations for why behavior is inappropriate will cause the student to reflect on and decrease her inappropriate behavior, the opposite is often true for many students with chronic behavior problems. Many of these individuals are not stellar students who are involved in lots of school activities, and they rarely get any attention when they are behaving appropriately. For these students, negative attention is better than none at all. In addition, many of these students are miserable at school: they face enormous academic and social challenges and see educators as the deliverers of their miserable circumstances. When educators react negatively to these students' behavior, even by doing something as seemingly slight as rolling their eyes or tensing their bodies, the students see evidence that their inappropriate behavior is making educators uncomfortable or upset and are actually reinforced by this. They may think, "Well, if I am miserable, everyone else might as well be too." We all know the old saying that misery loves company.

To Get Something Tangible

We have found that many students have obsessive interests or needs that they will pretty much do anything to get access to. We have worked with several students with Prader-Willi syndrome, a chromosomal disorder partially characterized by a chronic feeling of hunger. Access to food is often a common function for a variety of inappropriate behaviors for these individuals. Students on the autism spectrum often have such intense interests that they will engage in all types of interesting and potentially inappropriate and disruptive behaviors to gain access to their current fixation.

To Obtain a Sense of Power or Control

Nothing is more frustrating to educators than students who engage in countercontrol: situations in which adults attempt to change the behavior of a student and the student responds by trying to change the adult's behavior because of resentment at being controlled.[15] These individuals are often described as manipulative, oppositional-defiant, stubborn, rebellious, and noncompliant. It is amazing at times the lengths they will go to simply to do the opposite of what adults tell them to do. When you say *up*, they say *down*. When you say *black*, they say *white*. You give them a line, and they will put their toe across it and look at you as if to say, "What are you going to do about it?" You give them a time limit and they comply the second *after* the time is up.

To Meet a Sensory Need

Hypo- or hyperprocessing in one or more of the sensory systems is common for students on the autism spectrum and others who commonly exhibit challenging behavior. Many students seek movement, deep pressure, or tactile stimulation, resulting in all kinds of potentially odd or disruptive behavior. Finding acceptable, more socially appropriate alternatives is key when meeting this function.

To Communicate Feelings

A majority of children with behavioral and social challenges also demonstrate problems in receptive and/or expressive language.[16] Considering how complex human interaction is, think about how stressful daily life must be for individuals in an environment where academics and social interaction are the main focus, both requiring a great deal of expressive and receptive language skills, and how difficult it must be for these individuals to be able to communicate their feelings appropriately when they struggle with the language skills that most people simply take for granted.

As a Result of a Lack of Understanding

Many students with challenging behavior struggle with an area of language called pragmatics. This is particularly true of students with Asperger's syndrome, a type of autism spectrum disorder. *Pragmatics* refers to the social rules of language—for example:[17]

- Using language for different purposes (greeting, requesting, information)
- Changing language according to the needs of the listener or situation (speaking differently with close friends versus strangers)
- Following conversational rules (taking turns, eye contact)

These individuals also typically have theory-of-mind deficits, which cause them to have difficulty understanding their emotions and mental states, as well as the emotions and mental states of others.[18] Students with deficits in this area commonly have the following types of problems:

- Understanding and predicting their own emotions and behaviors
- Understanding and predicting the emotions and behaviors of others
- Taking others' perspective
- Inferring others' intentions
- Understanding that their behavior has an impact on how others think and feel

These deficits can make understanding the complexities of interpersonal interaction and behavioral expectations in various contexts difficult, even impossible. This is often called the "hidden curriculum," which refers to social rules that are usually not directly taught but rather are assumed to be known because most people pick them up naturally through observation or social learning. Lack of understanding becomes a common function of problem behavior for these students in many cases.

To Escape or Avoid Something

Educational environments are often aversive to students for a variety of reasons. Some students are behind academically and the tasks presented are difficult for them.

Some students lack social skills, and with so many peers present, their learning environment can become highly stressful for them. Some students are overwhelmed by the sensory input that often accompanies loud and crowded hallways and the cafeteria. Due to their difficulties with pragmatic language and understanding the hidden curriculum, school is a difficult environment for some students. It is understandable that many of these students simply want a way out.

The Bottom Line on Functional Behavioral Assessment

The whole idea behind FBA is that behavior is rarely simply behavior. Usually some basic biological or emotional need underlies the behavior that the student does not know how to express appropriately. Think of student behavior as an attempt to communicate with you and you as the detective trying to break the communication code.

> Think of student behavior as an attempt to communicate with you and you as the detective trying to break the communication code.

Considering the function of the behavior or why it is happening will lead to much more effective responses, improved behavior, and less frustration for everyone.

Our Model of Intervention

Once the functions of problem behavior are identified, educators need to design an intervention that encourages students to meet that function in a more socially acceptable way. We have developed a model of intervention, shown in Figure 2.2, that provides the foundation for the remainder of this book.

Educators tend to want to jump to the bottom of this flowchart when responding to inappropriate behavior and immediately provide undesirable consequences. This is how many of today's educators were raised and what they experienced in school (we did too), and therefore it is what has been modeled for us and what most of us are comfortable using. We are not "always" or "never" thinkers and believe there is a place for undesirable consequences when managing behavior, a topic that we address in detail in Part Five. However, we also strongly believe, and research clearly supports, that effective intervention begins with instruction and prevention, which can be done only when the functions of the behavior have been identified and their complexity understood. Once students learn appropriate skills, the performance of these skills should be encouraged through high levels of reinforcement until they become fluent. Only after these three steps have been tried and found to be inadequate should undesirable consequences be considered.

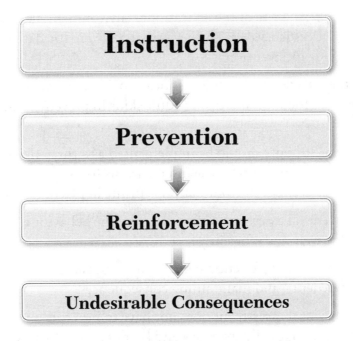

Figure 2.2 Model of Intervention

Consistent with positive behavior support and functional behavioral assessment, all the components of our intervention model (instruction, prevention, reinforcement, and undesirable consequences) are to be implemented as part of a three-tiered *all, some, few* process shown in Figure 2.1. Many teachers will say that they have no control over whether a three-tiered philosophy is adopted and implemented at the district or schoolwide level, and to some extent this is true. However, regardless of the practices of the larger system, individual teachers can often choose to adopt these practices in their classroom and can also provide their supervisors with research-based information that supports a three-tiered intervention model.

Key Points to Remember

- Positive behavior support is highly favored and may be on the verge of being required by federal law when No Child Left Behind and the Individuals with Disabilities Education Act are reauthorized.

- Two key points of positive behavior supports are using research-validated practices and enhancing the capacity of all environments.

- No Child Left Behind strongly prefers educational programs grounded in scientifically based research and implies that only empirically validated interventions should be used whenever possible.

- Due to the complex nature of the educational environment, flexibility with respect to scientific practices is needed. The key is that a systematic data source is used to evaluate and guide intervention.

- To enhance the capacity of the child's educational environment to support positive behavior, we must focus on increasing adult skills in prevention and early intervention.

- Positive behavior support should be implemented as a three-tiered model, which benefits all students; in addition, the interventions for more challenging students are much more effective if the foundation is firmly in place.

- Functional behavioral assessment considers why the behavior is occurring in order to respond effectively and efficiently.

- The three key concepts of functional behavioral assessment are setting events, triggering antecedents, and maintaining consequences.

- Functional behavioral assessment does not have to be a complicated process requiring multiple pages of paperwork and school psychologists or other behavior specialists. It should be an ongoing, fluid process that occurs daily.

- There are multiple ways to conduct functional behavior assessments, and they vary in intensity and complexity.

- The functions of challenging student behavior can change quickly. Different behaviors can serve the same function, and the same behavior can serve different functions based on many environmental variables that are constantly interacting and changing.

Discussion Questions

1. Data collection and progress monitoring are crucial components of any well-run behavioral intervention plan. Knowing what data to collect, monitoring those data, and deciding when to change interventions is a common challenge for many teachers. How can behavior intervention teams work through this process effectively?

2. Thinking of functional behavioral assessment as more of a regular problem-solving process and less of a formal paperwork process is crucial to designing, monitoring, and adapting behavioral intervention programs. What can you do to make this an ongoing process instead of a once-a-year consideration?

Part Two

Social Skills Instruction

Instruction

Chapter 3

Teaching Social Skills: The Basics

This book began by discussing how important it is that students develop appropriate behavioral skills if they are to become productive members of society and why behavioral skills instruction is partially the job of the public school system. Behavioral and academic learning are governed by the same principles and respond to the same types of intervention. Just like academic instruction, behavioral instruction requires careful planning and implementation. Throughout the chapters in Part Two, we often use the terms *behavior* and *social skills* interchangeably because they are closely related and often refer to the same thing. In this chapter, we use the term that is most common in the research literature, *social skills instruction,* and focus on effective and teacher-friendly planning and implementation.

Traditional Approaches to Social Skills Instruction

Social skills instruction has traditionally taken place in a combination of ways: (1) incorporated with large groups of students by embedding it into daily routines and academic instruction schoolwide and/or classwide, (2) small groups of students who have been identified as struggling with certain social skills are taken aside and provided instruction, and/or (3) individual students are taught on the spot as problems arise throughout the school day, which is often referred to as *incidental teaching*.[1] Research has shown that these traditional approaches to social skills instruction have some positive effects.[2] However, their effectiveness is limited by a number of problems, the most prominent being lack of individualization to specific student deficits[3] and lack of generalization of social skills taught to new situations and environments.[4]

The traditional focus of social skills instruction has been on targeting appropriate behaviors and attempting to increase their occurrence with no understanding of why the problem behavior is occurring. Appropriate behavior will not increase and generalize across environments if the need or want behind the behavior still exists—in other words, if the function has not been met. Therefore, a more effective approach to teaching social skills is to identify the function the problem behavior serves for each individual and teach that individual a specific replacement behavior that meets that function for him or her. Because this differs in each situation, teaching replacement behavior does not lend itself solely to the traditional approaches of social skills instruction. Therefore, we agree with those who advocate incorporating functional assessment into social skills instruction with the goal of individualizing and generalizing skills across environments.[5] A three-tiered model that includes individualized social skills instruction for each student is needed to accomplish these goals.

> Appropriate behavior will not increase and generalize across environments if the need or want behind the behavior still exists—in other words, if the function has not been met.

A Three-Tiered Approach to Social Skills Instruction

Social skills instruction is most effective when it is embedded throughout all three tiers of the positive behavior support triangle and incorporates functional behavioral assessment (see Figure 3.1). Tier 1 is schoolwide and/or classwide large group instruction, which directly teaches school and/or classroom expectations and routines, setting the stage for overall prosocial behavior in addition to increasing positive peer modeling and the probability that desired skills will be naturally elicited and reinforced. Tier 2 is more traditional small group social skills instruction, and tier 3 is systematic individualized replacement behavior training which is the most challenging to implement.

At all levels, social skills instruction is a process of (1) providing direct instruction of the desired skills, (2) having opportunities to see models of the skills, (3) practicing the skills through role playing and other activities, (4) receiving corrective feedback, and (5) having opportunities to practice the skills in a variety of settings.[6] Table 3.1 provides a social skills

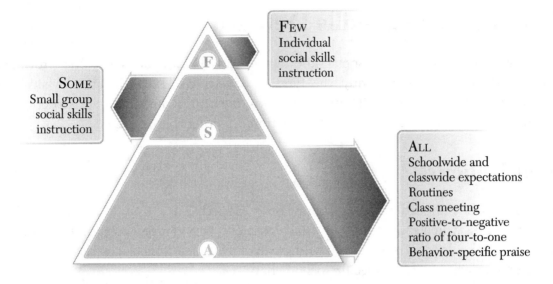

Figure 3.1 Three-Tiered Social Skills Instruction

Table 3.1 Eight-Step Social Skills Lesson Plan

1. Break the desired skill into specific steps.

2. Describe each step. (What does it look like? What does it sound like?)

3. Provide a rationale for the importance of the skill for each student specifically based on his or her personal goals.

4. Provide modeling through video or role plays.

5. Provide guided practice through additional role plays and activities.

6. Give specific feedback.

7. Put the student in situations, natural or created, where the skill can be applied and generalized.

8. Highly reinforce the student for exhibiting the skill.

instructional format that is similar to a traditional academic lesson plan; it includes and further specifies the components of the social skills instructional process. Of course, all of these steps may not happen on the same day or even in a specific order. Rather, they provide a framework within which teaching and learning take place.

Types of Social Skills Deficits

Researchers have broken down social skills deficits into the categories of skill, performance, and fluency deficits.[7] Identifying the type of deficit that exists in specific situations is important because this will guide decisions regarding the type of instruction and instructional settings that are most effective for correcting these deficits.

Skill Deficits

Students with skill deficits don't know how to perform the skill or have difficulty discriminating which skills to use in what situation. This can be exceedingly challenging because social rules are complex and vary greatly based on context. That is, a specific social behavior can be appropriate in one environment and inappropriate in another. Skill deficits are often referred to as a "can't do" and can be addressed in large group, small group, and/or individual settings. Intervention is focused on breaking the skills into steps, directly teaching each step, and practicing each step through role playing its appropriate use in appropriate situations.

> Skill deficits are often referred to as a "can't do."

Kaye Says . . .

I had a first-grade student with Asperger's syndrome who had problems with being silly in class. I taught him how to be serious, explained why it was important to be serious at school, and practiced this skill with him in the classroom. He proceeded to go out to recess and walked around and told all of the other students (much to their annoyance) that we needed to be serious at school and that they should stop laughing and having fun. Obviously he had mastered how to perform the skill but was having difficulty discriminating when it was appropriate to use it at school.

Performance Deficits

Performance deficits exist when the student knows how to perform the skill and can discriminate which skills to use in what situations but fails to do so at acceptable levels

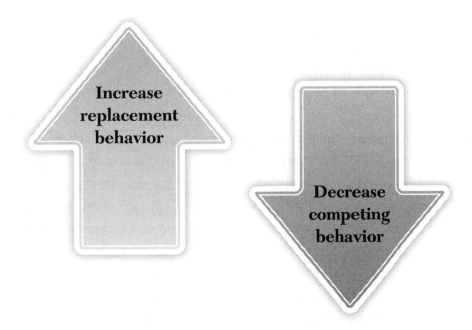

Figure 3.2 Correcting Performance Deficits by Increasing Replacement Behavior and Decreasing Interfering or Competing Behavior

for a variety of reasons. Performance skills deficits are often referred to as a "won't do"; however, it is important to be extremely careful that we do not automatically assume this is because the student is being stubborn or oppositional (although this is sometimes the case). Often there are interfering

> Performance skills deficits are often referred to as a "won't do."

and/or competing factors or behaviors that need to be addressed. Sometimes internalizing factors such as anxiety or depression or externalizing problems such as impulsivity interfere with the student's ability to access these skills when needed. In other cases, the student may have a more developed competing behavior that is easier to perform and leads to more immediate and reliable reinforcement. A common example is a student calling out rather than raising her hand when she has something to share. Many times calling out is a much easier and quicker way to get the teacher's attention than raising one's hand and waiting patiently for a turn. Another example of this appears in the "Jodie Says" box in this section. Whatever the interfering and/or competing factors and behaviors are, the result is that the skill is there, but the student has difficulty accessing it. Intervention is most effective when it is individualized to meet the needs of the specific student and focused on both decreasing the reliability and efficiency of competing behaviors and increasing the reliability and efficiency of desired social skills or replacement behaviors (see Figure 3.2).

Jodie Says . . .

In a middle school alternative program, one of my students was the class clown. She felt reinforced by her peers when she disrupted class with inappropriate, although humorous, comments and actions. In middle school, peer acceptance is always the highest priority. Our team sat down with her, talked about her behaviors, and helped her see that they were attention seeking. We were also able to help her understand that while she obtained attention on the spot by making her friends laugh, the bottom line was that she was hurting herself by not progressing through the levels of the program, which was keeping her from social activities that were contingent on reaching that level. In addition, she was in more trouble at home and was grounded as a result, which restricted her access to more social activities. Over the long term, her relationships with peers were suffering because she was missing out on social events. They were moving on and finding other people to hang out with. In the end, we were able to get her motivated by helping her realize her behaviors were preventing her from meeting her goal of more time with and therefore more attention from peers. Once she saw this connection, she began increasingly using positive attention-seeking skills (with frequent coaching from staff at first), and the competing behavior of inappropriate class disruption faded.

Fluency Deficits

Fluency deficits exist when the student knows how to perform the skill and performs it at acceptable levels but is awkward and unpolished when exhibiting the skill. This can be compared to students who are able to decode and comprehend reading passages but are slow and choppy when reading aloud. Many students on the autism spectrum have mastered skills and are able to perform them, but they are so awkward that their performance leads to problematic outcomes, such as peer rejection. A classic example of this is learning the "steps" to greeting peers, but going about it in an overly formal and robotic (and possibly not age-appropriate way) that actually makes peers uncomfortable.

Fluency deficits are difficult to address, and intervention needs to happen through immersing students in environments where they have appropriate models, there are plenty of opportunities to practice, and they are reinforced consistently and at a high rate. It is

Table 3.2 Social Skills Deficits and Instructional Approaches

Type of Deficit	Instructional Approach
Skill: "Can't do"	Large group, small group, or individual
	Break the skill into steps, and directly teach and practice each step
Performance: "Won't Do"	Individualized
	Decrease the reliability and efficiency of the competing problem behavior
	Increase the reliability and efficiency of the replacement behavior
	Increase motivation through support and reinforcement
Fluency: Unpolished	Immerse in appropriate models
	Provide plenty of opportunities to practice
	Give high levels of reinforcement
	Involve peers

extremely important that peers are educated and involved when a classmate is attempting to improve his or her fluency deficits. Table 3.2 summarizes the three types of social skills deficits and the most effective instructional approaches for each.

Self-Management: The Ultimate Goal

The ultimate goal of all social skills instruction is for students to eventually manage themselves without needing external instruction, cuing, or reinforcement. Self-management is based on cognitive behavioral theory, which focuses on the interdependent relationship of the environment, behavior, and thinking and is based on three assumptions: (1) an individual's thinking affects his or her behavior, (2) an individual's thinking may be monitored and altered, and (3) desired behavior change may be affected through these changes in thinking.[8] Individuals who successfully learn to self-manage carry with them the internal cues and reinforcement they need to engage in appropriate social behavior. There are several types of self-management we commonly use, which we define in Table 3.3.

As educators, our ultimate goal is to teach students to manage their own behavior, rather than relying on external controls, so that they continue to be successful when we are not with them. Self-management encourages students to take greater responsibility for their own behavior, which gives them a sense of ownership and control that is inherently reinforcing and may make it less

> Teaching students to self-manage increases the likelihood that appropriate behavior will last over time and generalize to various settings.

Table 3.3 Types of Self-Management

Type	Description
Self-monitoring	Students become aware of their behavior and make a tangible mark to keep track of it.
Self-evaluation	Students compare their performance against some criteria.
Self-reinforcement	Students give themselves a positive consequence.
Self-graphing	Students make a visual representation of their performance.

likely that they will try to control the teacher's behavior. Teaching students to self-manage increases the likelihood that appropriate behavior will last over time and generalize to various settings and allows teachers to spend more time teaching and less time trying to control behavior. In addition, the defining, measuring, graphing, and evaluating involved in various types of self-management give meaningful practice for other parts of the curriculum.[9] Self-management techniques have commonly been used with individual students to improve behavioral skills such as staying on task and paying attention. However, group behavioral management programs can also incorporate self-management principles.

Developing social skills across the skill and performance domains to the point that students are able to self-manage these skills and eventually become fluent is the focus of this book. Strategies to help develop self-management skills are integrated into each of the four components of the model (instruction, prevention, reinforcement, and undesirable consequences).

Key Points to Remember

- Social skills have typically been taught with a combination of large group instruction of routine behaviors, small skill groups, and individual incidental teaching.

- The most effective way to teach replacement behaviors is to combine functional assessment and individual social skills instruction.

- Evidence-based social skills instruction includes direct instruction, modeling, practicing the skill through role plays, practicing the skill across settings, and receiving feedback on performance of the skill.

- Teachers need to consider whether the student has a skill deficit, a performance deficit, or a fluency deficit when designing effective social skills instruction.

- The ultimate goal of all social skills instruction is for the student to eventually self-manage without needing external instruction, cuing, or reinforcement.

- Throughout this book, we incorporate self-monitoring, self-evaluation, self-reinforcement and/or self-graphing into each one of the four overall intervention components of instruction, prevention, reinforcement, and undesirable consequences.

Discussion Questions and Activities

1. With the three-tiered positive behavior support triangle in mind, what are some social skills instruction activities that would occur for tier 1? Tier 2? Tier 3?

2. Billy is a student with anger control issues. Frequently when playing with peers or when a consequence is given and he perceives something as unfair, he "blows." Knowing that there are three types of social skills deficits (skill, performance, and fluency), brainstorm some ways to discern which kind of social skill deficit this child has. What kinds of things would help you decide which kind of deficit he has? What kinds of questions do you need to ask?

3. Give an example of how you could use each type of self-management strategy defined in this chapter: self-monitoring, self-evaluation, self-reinforcement, and self-graphing.

Chapter 4

Group Social Skills Instruction

Group social skills instruction can take place schoolwide and classwide (tier 1) or in targeted small groups (tier 2). There are many ways to embed group instruction into the everyday structure already in place in the school environment.

Schoolwide and Classwide Social Skills Instruction

Schoolwide and classwide social skills instruction provides the foundation for addressing basic skill deficits. It is extremely important (and often overlooked) that behavioral expectations at this level need to be clearly defined and taught. Many times educators will say, "Oh yes, we teach the rules. We have them posted in the school and the classroom."

Simply posting rules is not the same as teaching the expected skills, however. It is important to schedule time for teaching the expected behaviors to all students and practicing them regularly rather than simply hoping that it will just happen. When you walk into your classroom on the first day of school, assume that none of your students

> Simply posting rules is not the same as teaching the expected skills.

know how to behave appropriately in a school environment, and have a plan for embedding social skills instruction into your school day.[1]

Class Meetings

Holding class meetings is an effective way to embed social skills instruction classwide and involve students in a democratic problem-solving process. Class meetings serve as a forum for students and teachers to discuss issues, set goals, and participate in peaceful conflict resolution. Class meetings should be held regularly (ideally at least once a week), and not only when problems arise. Teachers need to provide structure for class meetings, determining who can request one and when they will be scheduled. Some teachers allow class meetings to be called by anyone at any time and any place, and others have certain days and times they are regularly scheduled. It is important that the topic of the meeting is determined at the beginning and that the meeting stays on topic.[2]

Mini-Lessons

Daily lessons should always have at least two main objectives—one academic and one social. For example, at the beginning of a math lesson on division, the teacher may describe to students how to appropriately get her attention by raising a hand before calling out, discuss why this is important, and practice this skill by doing a brief role play. During the lesson the teacher can give specific verbal feedback to students who are and are not exhibiting this skill, and at the end of the lesson she can provide reinforcement to those who have successfully exhibited this skill.

Frequent Positive Feedback

Frequent positive feedback provides social skills instruction by frequently letting students know exactly what behaviors are expected. Two concepts are important in providing frequent positive feedback: positive-to-negative ratio and behavior-specific praise.

Positive-to-Negative Ratio

Although there are critics of giving students praise,[3] a large research base supports its effectiveness with improving student behavior.[4] In addition, there is really no excuse not to use this extremely simple intervention: it is free and requires no extra time or preparation. Although the exact positive-to-negative ratio in the research literature varies slightly, a four-to-one or five-to-one is fairly common.[5] Paying attention to your positive-to-negative ratio will not only provide social skills instruction to students, but it will also ensure that your learning environment feels encouraging and positive, even when redirection needs to be given at times.

As adults we don't like to be around people who point out only the bad things we do. Imagine what your job would be like (or maybe is like) if you get mostly negative feedback from your supervisor. Most people are not productive or motivated in this type of environment, and students are no different. If you are unsure of your positive-to-negative ratio, consider asking a colleague to observe your classroom and take data or videotape yourself for a day and take the data yourself. Reproducible 1 can be used for this purpose.

Kaye Says . . .

When I was teaching, I always started the year very enthusiastically, giving lots of positives. About October, I would start wondering, "What happened to all those well-behaved students who entered my classroom at the beginning of the year?" I blamed the downturn in their behavior on the upcoming holiday season, a full moon, a change in the weather, or anything else I could think of. However, when I started focusing on increasing my positive-to-negative ratio, student behavior almost always improved. Whose behavior did I change? That of the only person I could truly control: myself.

Behavior-Specific Praise

Positive feedback or praise that is immediate (or as immediate as possible without seriously interrupting the flow of your instruction), frequent, enthusiastic, and clear is most effective. Feedback should be given about the specific behavior that was appropriate rather than using general statements.[6] For example say, "I really like the way you are standing patiently in line" rather than, "Good job!" to increase the likelihood that students will recognize exactly what they are doing right and repeat that behavior.

Schoolwide and Classwide Expectations or Rules

Most educators set their individual classroom rules at the beginning of the school year. The most important thing to remember here is that classroom expectations should (1) be limited to three to five general expectations that cover all common behavior problems, (2) involve students in making them whenever possible because this promotes student buy-in, (3) be stated positively in terms of what the students should do instead of what they should not do ("walk in the hallway" versus "don't run"), and (4) be posted in multiple places where they can easily be referred to. We recommend that written classroom expectations be accompanied by pictures for students who are not able to or have difficulty reading.

The classroom rules that we typically use are

1. Be safe.

2. Respect others.

3. Follow adults' directions.

4. Do your best.

Being safe at school is always the most important rule. "Respect others" targets common problem behaviors such as using appropriate language at school and keeping hands off peers. "Follow adults' directions" is self-explanatory and is an important one for most educators. "Do your best" refers to skills that are important to academic learning, such as staying on task and putting forth maximum effort.

Various programs positively state common school expectations or rules in different ways, and one is not necessarily better than the other. The key is that they follow the four guidelines listed above and are taught and reinforced consistently. Ideally, the same expectations would be used throughout the entire school (or, even better, the entire district) to send the message that all of the adults have the same expectations and are in agreement on the rules. Students often have difficulty realizing that Mr. Jones has different expectations from Ms. Castro and struggle to simply master the behavioral skills needed to be successful in one environment, much less the more complicated skill of changing their behavior based on the different expectations of different teachers. Think of how many problems could be prevented or avoided (and how much time would be saved) if every adult in the environment (including office, lunch, and recess staff) consistently expected, reinforced, and held students accountable for the same behaviors.

> Think of how many problems could be prevented or avoided (and how much time would be saved) if every adult in the environment (including office, lunch, and recess staff) consistently expected, reinforced, and held students accountable for the same behaviors.

Schoolwide and Classwide Routines

In addition to overall schoolwide and classwide expectations, the first part of the social and behavioral curriculum at the start of a school year is to teach school and classroom routines. Teachers often make the mistake of assuming students enter their classroom knowing basic classroom routines such as how to line up, listen in groups, walk in the hall, and hand in papers. Just like basic behavior expectations, educators need to provide direct instruction of classroom routines using the basic lesson plan components provided in Table 3.1. Students should be highly reinforced for practicing the routine, especially over the first few weeks of school, with reinforcement fading over time as the students

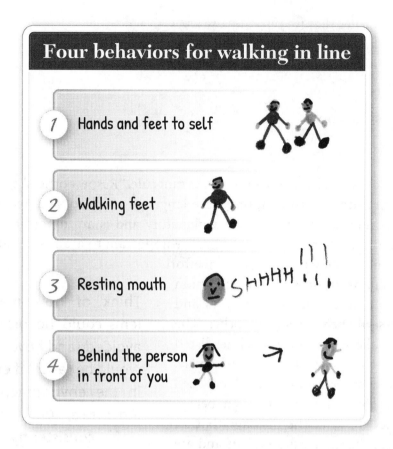

Figure 4.1 Four Behaviors for Walking in Line

demonstrate mastery of the skill. Teachers may also choose to precorrect for desired behaviors by providing students with opportunities to practice or with prompts about expected behavior before they enter situations in which displays of problem behaviors are likely.[7] For example, if a class typically has difficulty in line, students could be asked to recall the four expectations for acceptable behavior in line immediately before lining up. Figure 4.1 provides a student-illustrated task analysis of this common routine.

All classrooms have their own routines so we can't assume that a student who is successful in one teacher's classroom will automatically be successful in the next. Classroom routines need to be taught at the beginning of the school year, and then reviewed and practiced regularly throughout the year when behaviors surface that communicate that this is needed. The book *Teaching Effective Classroom Routines* by Joe Witt, Lynn LaFleur, Gale Naquin, and Donna Gilbertson is an excellent resource for this purpose. Table 4.1 provides a list of common classroom routines that students should be directly taught.

Recommended Resource

Teaching Effective Classroom Routines, by Joe Witt, Lynn LaFleur, Gale Naquin, and Donna Gilbertson (Longmont, CO: Sopris West, 2004).

How to Reach and Teach Children with Challenging Behavior

Table 4.1 Common Classroom Routines

How the teacher should get students' attention

How students should get the teacher's attention

Starting the school day

How and where to get supplies

Lining up

Walking in the hallway

Where and when to pass in papers

Making corrections to assignments

Working in a small group

What to do during free time

Ending the school day

Field trip behavior

Substitute teacher behavior

Recess behavior

Lunchroom behavior

Bathroom behavior

Assembly behavior

Evacuating the classroom

How to behave with classroom visitors

Important Schoolwide and Classwide Lessons

Later in this book, we will be encouraging you to use a variety of prevention and reinforcement techniques for individual students and are already anticipating the common protest, "What about the other students? Why should the problem student get special treatment?" We all have people in our lives with social and behavioral problems. The following schoolwide and classwide lessons will teach all students important life lessons for dealing with these individuals and will reduce the common protests, "Why does he or she get that and I don't?" and "It's not fair!" that you may hear from students when they perceive that you are giving students with challenging behavior special accommodations and reinforcements:

Lesson One: Everyone has strengths and weaknesses. It is crucial for students to realize that absolutely everyone has strengths and weaknesses, and we all would prefer that others build on and appreciate our strengths and ignore or help us overcome our weaknesses. Some students have weaknesses in reading, some in athletics, some in musical ability and some in social skills.

Lesson Two: Fair is not equal. Life isn't fair. It isn't fair that many students with social and behavioral challenges have language or neurological disorders. It isn't fair that some of them come from less-than-optimal homes and family lives. Fair is not giving everyone the same thing; it is giving everyone what they need. Not everyone wears glasses, not everyone needs hearing aids, not everyone needs their assignments in braille, and not everyone needs extra behavioral support. If students don't need extra behavior support, they are most likely already way ahead when it comes to things being "fair."

Lesson Three: Ignore others who are making poor choices. Despite best efforts, there will be times that some students make poor choices and behave inappropriately. The purpose of teaching their classmates to ignore them during these times is to minimize the reinforcement that may be provided by peer attention and to encourage others not to join in. It is amazing how on task students can be even in the presence of some pretty unusual or extreme behavior if they are taught to ignore others who are making poor choices and are highly reinforced for doing so.

Lesson Four: Evacuating the classroom. Most schools directly teach their students and regularly practice how to handle crises such as fires, tornados, and bomb threats. Simply add handling behavior crises to these routine procedures. Students should know a code word for initiating this process, independent learning activities and packets that they can take with them, and a predetermined location to go where there is an adult who has been informed ahead of time about what to do in this situation. This ensures that the school day of all students stays as productive and uninterrupted as possible when a behavior crisis occurs.

Taking care of teaching these concepts at the beginning of the school year will save hard feelings, time, and effort when difficult situations emerge later. Being proactive is the key.

If you teach students the above skills and why they are important, our experience is that a vast majority of them understand that peers with behavior challenges are sometimes part of the school day and accept it. In fact, we have yet to teach these lessons to a classroom of students who were not understanding and accepting. Well-informed students who are taught how to support their peers with behavior or social challenges and how to respond if these students disrupt the learning environment often become your best helpers and have a powerful impact on the lives of these individuals. Don't underestimate them.

> Well-informed students who are taught how to support their peers with behavior or social challenges and how to respond if these students disrupt the learning environment often become your best helpers and have a powerful impact on the lives of these individuals. Don't underestimate them.

Small Group Social Skills Instruction

Small group social skills instruction provides another layer of intervention for addressing skill deficits. Often small numbers of students are at risk for or have difficulties mastering the same skill and can be grouped together for efficiency and provided additional instruction. We recommend several resources for structuring small

group social skills instruction. Topping our list is *Social Skills Training for Children and Adolescents with Asperger Syndrome and Social-Communication Problems* by Jed Baker.[8] Baker includes not only teacher-friendly lessons and activities but also helpful advice for structuring the sessions, managing behavior during them, individual student assessment for determining what social skills to work on and what instructional strategies are most effective, and many reproducible forms.

Choosing Curricula: A Case Study

Some of my colleagues and I (Kaye) went through a process of rating social skills curricula for the purpose of choosing the most cost-effective program to purchase for use in a public school district that others may find helpful when making similar decisions. We chose six curricula to review: (1) Connecting with Others, (2) Getting to Know You, (3) Second Step: Violence Prevention, (4) Skillstreaming, (5) PATHS, and (6) Super Skills. Five of them were chosen because they had been previously reviewed by the Heartland Area Education Agency 11 in Johnston, Iowa (www.aea11.k12.ia.us) to determine if they were supported by research and given either a gold, silver, or "promising" rating. The sixth curriculum was chosen because it was specifically designed for students on the autism spectrum. Most publishing companies send educators a copy of their curricula to preview for four to six weeks at no cost.

We created a rubric (Table 4.2) for the purpose of rating each curriculum, and five experienced behavior and autism specialists completed the rubric in six areas: (1) preassessment, (2) direct instruction activities, (3) guided practice activities, (4) video examples, (5) generalization activities, and (6) supporting children/youth literature. Results of their rating are shown in Table 4.3, and general information, including price and where to order each curriculum, is shown in Table 4.4. Other resources and curricula that we have found helpful for small group social skills instruction (and many would also be helpful for individual replacement training that we will focus on in the next chapter) are listed in Table 4.5.

Table 4.2 Social Skills Curriculum Rating Rubric

Rating	Description
0	Area is not included.
1	Area is included but of poor quality, very general, or brief. An educator would need to do extensive additional preparation, creation of reproducibles, and so on.
2	Area is included but of marginal quality and fairly general. An educator would need to do some additional preparation, creation of reproducibles, and so on.
3	Area is of excellent quality, comprehensive and specific. Ready to use with very little additional preparation needed.

Table 4.3 Average Ratings Given to Social Skills Curricula

	Preassessment	Direct Instruction	Activities	Video Examples	Generalization Activities	Supporting Literature
Connecting with Others	0	3	3	0	2	3
Getting to Know You	2	3	2	0	1	0
Second Step	0	3	3	3	3	3
Skillstreaming	2	3	1	0	1	0
PATHS	0	3	2	2	2	3
Super Skills	3	3	3	0	2	0

Children's literature provides an effective avenue to opening up discussions about various social situations and captures student interest. Over the years, we have developed a large collection of children's literature on various social skills topics, which is provided in Table 4.6 at the end of this chapter.

Table 4.4 General Information on Social Skills Curricula

Curriculum	Publisher and Date	Grade Levels	Research Support	Price
Connecting with Others	Research Press, 2001 http://www.Researchpress.com	K–12	Promising	$149.25
Getting to Know You	Educational Media Corp, 1998 http://www.educationalmedia.com	1–9	Promising	$104.85
Second Step: Violence Prevention	Committee for Children http://www.cfchildren.org	PreK–9	Silver	$2,217
Skillstreaming	Research Press, 2003 http://www.Skillstreaming.com	PreK–12	Promising	$150.80
PATHS	Developmental Research and Programs, 1994 http://www.channing-bete.com	K–6	Gold	$699
Super Skills	Autism Asperger Publishing Company http://www.asperger.net	Not identified	Not reviewed	$39.95

Table 4.5 Other Recommended Social Skills Resources

Title	Author	Publisher
Social Skills Training for Children and Adolescents with Asperger Syndrome	Jed Baker	Autism Asperger Publishing Company, 2007 http://www.asperger.net
The Stop & Think Social Skills Program	Howard M. Knoff	Sopris West, 2001 www.sopriswest.com
Social Skills Activities for Secondary Students with Special Needs	Darlene Mannix	Jossey-Bass, 1998 www.josseybass.com
Social Skills Activities for Special Children	Darlene Mannix	Jossey-Bass, 1993 www.josseybass.com
Let's Talk Emotions	Teresa A. Cardon	Autism Asperger Publishing Company, 2004 http://www.asperger.net
Thinking, Feeling, Behaving	Ann Vernon	Research Press, 1989 www.researchpress.com
Navigating the Social World	Jeanette McAfee	Future Horizons, 2002 www.futurehorizons-autism.com
The PREPARE Curriculum	Arnold P. Goldstein	Research Press, 1999 www.researchpress.com

Key Points to Remember

- Schoolwide and classwide social skills instruction provides the foundation for addressing basic skill deficits. It is imperative that behavioral expectations be directly taught.

- Social skills instruction can be embedded into the school day in several ways through class meetings, mini-lessons, and planned feedback.

- Frequent positive feedback provides social skills instruction by frequently letting students know exactly what behaviors are expected.

- Shoot for a ratio of at least four positives to every negative or redirection to encourage a positive, encouraging learning environment.

- Any feedback given should be specific to the behavior being performed to be meaningful and effective.

- Classroom rules should (1) be limited to three to five general expectations that cover all common behavior problems, (2) involve students in the making of them whenever possible as this promotes student buy-in, (3) be stated positively in terms of what the students should do instead of what they should not do, and (4) be posted in multiple places where they can easily be referred to.

- Teachers need to provide direct instruction, reinforcement, and precorrections for common classroom and schoolwide routines.

- Students with similar behavioral skill deficits can be grouped together for small group social skills instruction.

- Children's literature can be a valuable resource to illustrate prosocial behaviors in social skills lessons.

Discussion Questions and Activities

1. Holding regular class meetings is one way to embed social skills instruction into the school day. Give examples of issues that could be discussed in a class meeting. How could class meetings be used to resolve conflicts?

2. In this chapter, some guidelines for setting up school or class rules were outlined. What are your classroom rules? Do they meet the criteria outlined in this chapter? What do you like about your rules? How could you improve them?

3. Many examples of classroom routines that need to be taught were given. Identify some routines specific to your classroom or school that need to be directly taught but were not included as examples.

4. Think of a children's literature book that is familiar to you. Are positive behaviors modeled in that book? How could you use the book in a social skills lesson on those behaviors?

Table 4.6 Children's Literature for Social Skills Instruction

Topic	Title	First Author	Description
Accepting "no"/anger	I Was So Mad	Mayer	A boy gets mad when told "no"
ADHD	Sit Still!	Carlson	A hyperactive kid learns how to cope
Anger	When Sophie Gets Angry—Really, Really Angry	Bang	Dealing with anger
Anger	Let's Talk About Feeling Angry	Berry	Feelings are OK
Anger	From Mad to Worse	Boulden	How to express oneself (worksheets)
Anger	Mad Me	Boulden	Like Mad to Worse (grades K–2)
Anger	Mean Soup	Everitt	Getting out anger
Anger	Tristan's Temper Tantrum	Formby	Anger can alienate friends
Anger	How I Feel Angry	Leonard	Identify and understand anger
Anger	A Volcano in My Tummy	Whitehouse	Stories, games, and activities
Apology	Franklin Says Sorry	Bourgeois	Franklin learns how to apologize
Attention—needing	Let's Talk About Needing Attention	Berry	How to get attention appropriately
Attitude	Some Days Other Days	Petersen	A boy doesn't want to get up if it will be a bad day
Attitude	Alice and Greta	Simmons	A good witch and a bad witch
Autism	Ian's Walk: A Story About Autism	Lears	Explains autistic behavior
Bad friends	Double Trouble	Boulden	Following poor role models
Bad friends	Hard Choices	Boulden	Following poor role models
Blaming	The Blame Game	Berenstain	Blaming others for our mistakes
Blaming	Ebb & Flo and the Greedy Gulls	Simmons	Ebb gets blamed for something she didn't do
Bossiness/taking turns	Franklin Is Bossy	Bourgeois	Not always having your own way
Bossiness/taking turns	Crabby Gabby	Cosgrove	Fun more important than winning

Topic	Title	Author	Description
Bossiness/taking turns	The Rat and the Tiger	Kasza	Be bossy—lose friends
Bossiness/taking turns	Me First	Lester	Hazards of always being first
Bossiness/taking turns	Deep in the Jungle	Yaccarino	Lyon learns his lesson about being bossy
Bullies	It's Not Okay to Bully	Anderson	Coloring book solutions
Bullies	The Bully	Berenstain	Handling a bully
Bullies	Playground Push-Around	Boulden	Workbook and discussion
Bullies	Push and Shove	Boulden	Bully and victim
Bullies	How to Handle Bullies, Teasers . . .	Cohen-Posey	Activities and role-plays
Bullies	Bully Trouble	Cole	Two boys stand up to a bully
Bullies	The Ant Bully	Nickle	Dealing with a bully
Cafeteria	Cafeteria Lady from the Black Lagoon	Thaler	Fun tie-in for cafeteria behavior
Cheating	Arthur and the True Francine	Brown	Cheating and blaming someone else
Complaining	A Children's Book About Complaining	Berry	Appropriate complaints
Compliance	A Children's Book About Disobeying	Berry	Importance of being obedient
Compliance	Saying No	Berry	When saying no is OK and when it's not
Compliance	The Tale of Peter Rabbit	Potter	Peter ignores instructions and puts himself in danger
Compliance	Come Along Daisy	Simmons	A duck doesn't mind mother and ends up in danger
Conflict	Berenstain Bears Get in a Fight	Berenstain	Fighting interferes with friendship
Conflict	Give and Take	Boulden	Making choices
Differences/tolerance	Franklin's New Friend	Bourgeois	A new friend who is "different"
Differences/tolerance	Franklin's Secret Club	Bourgeois	Including all kids
Differences/tolerance	The Braids Bully	Canfield & Hansen	Need for love and acceptance

(continued)

Table 4.6 (*continued*)

Topic	Title	First Author	Description
Differences/tolerance	*Stellaluna*	Cannon	Birds and a bat learn to be friends despite differences
Differences/tolerance	*Verdi*	Cannon	A snake fights growing up and turning green
Differences/tolerance	*Big Al*	Clements	Fish aren't friends with Big Al because he looks scary
Differences/tolerance	*Leo the Late Bloomer*	Kraus	A little tiger learns to do things later than others
Differences/tolerance	*Three Cheers for Tacky*	Lester	Penguins learn to appreciate Tacky, a clumsy penguin
Differences/tolerance	*Just a Little Different*	Mayer	Tolerance
Differences/tolerance	*Extraordinary Friends*	Rogers	Being friends with different kinds of people
Differences/tolerance	*Why Am I Different?*	Simon	All kinds of differences in kids
Fables	*Fables*	Lobel	Twenty fables with social skills tie-in
Fear	*Wemberly Worried*	Henkes	Worrying too much
Fear	*The Lion Who Lost His Roar*	Nass	Being afraid
Feelings	*Feelings and Faces*	Aliki	Little stories about feelings
Feelings	*Feelings and Faces*	Boulden	Feelings activities
Feelings	*Franklin's Bad Day*	Bourgeois	Franklin takes bad mood out on others and friend moves away
Feelings	*Franklin Goes to the Hospital*	Bourgeois	Franklin has operation
Feelings	*Arthur's Underwear*	Brown	Embarrassing situations
Feelings	*Arthur Goes to Camp*	Brown	Arthur is scared to go to camp

Topic	Title	Author	Description
Feelings	How Are You Feeling Today?	Creative Therapy	Chart and guidebook
Feelings	Today I Feel Silly	Curtis	Exploring moods
Feelings	The Hurt	Doleski	Need to get feelings out
Feelings	My Many Colored Days	Dr. Seuss	Moods
Feelings	What Was I Scared Of	Dr. Seuss	Discusses fears
Feelings	How Are You Peeling?	Freymann & Elffers	Fruits and veggies with feelings
Feelings	Frog in the Middle	Gretz	Three friends work out their problems with jealousy
Feelings	The Knight Who Was Afraid of the Dark	Hazen	A knight is afraid of the dark and overcomes it
Feelings	The Very Noisy Night	Hendry	A mouse is afraid of noises at night
Feelings	The Leaving Morning	Johnson	Feelings when one is moving
Feelings	The Hyena Who Lost Her Laugh	Lamb-Shapiro	Negative thinking
Feelings	How I Feel Happy	Leonard	Things that make you feel happy
Feelings	How I Feel Scared	Leonard	Being scared is OK sometimes
Feelings	There's a Nightmare in My Closet	Mayer	A boy is afraid of the dark and overcomes it
Feelings	Loving	Morris	What people do for us when they love us
Feelings	Thunder Cake	Polacco	A grandma helps a girl overcome her fear of thunder
Feelings	Jenny's Journey	Samton	A girl feels lonely after her friend moves away
Feelings	Spinky Sulks	Steig	How to respond to teasing
Feelings	The Bus Driver from the Black Lagoon	Thaler	A boy is afraid what new bus driver will be like

(continued)

Table 4.6 (continued)

Topic	Title	First Author	Description
Feelings	The Music Teacher from the Black Lagoon	Thaler	A boy is afraid what new music teacher will be like
Feelings	The Teacher from the Black Lagoon	Thaler	A boy is afraid what new teacher will be like
Feelings	The Hating Book	Zolotow	Angry at a friend
Feelings/differences	A Porcupine Named Fluffy	Lester	A young porcupine is embarrassed by his name
Forgetfulness	Busy Bea	Poydar	Bea forgets everything
Forgetting	I Just Forgot (two copies)	Mayer	A little critter forgets a lot
Friends	Bootsie Barker Bites	Bottner	Getting along with a mean friend
Friends	Fun with Friends	Boulden	How to be a friend (grades K–2)
Friends	Getting Along	Boulden	I statements
Friends	Franklin's New Friend	Bourgeois	Moose is new in school
Friends	How to Be a Friend	Brown	Guide to making and keeping friends
Friends	The Very Lonely Firefly	Carle	Feeling lonely
Friends	How to Lose All Your Friends	Carlson	Things to do wrong
Friends	Don't Need Friends	Crimi	Importance of friendship
Friends	Two Is Company	Delton	Getting along with three friends
Friends	What Are Friends For?	Grindley & Dann	Two friends fight and make up
Friends	Chester's Way	Henkes	A new girl arrives in the neighborhood
Friends	The Rat and the Tiger	Kasza	Be bossy—lose friends
Friends	I'm Sorry	McBratney	Quarreling and making up with a friend
Friends	Making Friends	Petty & Firmin	How to make friends and be one

Topic	Title	Author	Description
Friends	Rainbow Fish to the Rescue	Pfister	The group includes new fish in their play
Friends	The Rainbow Fish and the Big Blue Whale	Pfister	Friends make up after a fight
Friends	A Friend for Dragon	Pilkey	Dragon has trouble making friends
Friends	Peace Begins with You	Scholes	Resolving conflicts
Friends	Rosie and Michael	Viorst	What a friend is
Friends	Ira Sleeps Over	Waber	Two boys figure out they both sleep with teddy bears
Kindness	Sassafras	Cosgrove	Kindness is better than sarcasm
Kindness	The Buckethead Families	Epperly	Givers and takers
Kindness	Wilfrid Gordon McDonald Partridge	Fox	A boy is kind to an elderly lady who has lost her memory
Kindness	Hey, Little Ant	Hoose	Should he squish the ant?
Kindness	Somebody Loves You, Mr. Hatch	Spinelli	How kind acts change people
Kindness	Mufaro's Beautiful Daughters	Steptoe	Kindness wins
Kindness	Pooh Helps Out	Zoehfeld	Helping each other
Kindness/attitude	Jubal's Wish	Wood	Positive versus negative attitudes
Listening	Listen Buddy	Lester	Silly mistakes due to not listening
Listening	The Conversation Club	Stanley	Listening is easier if we don't all talk at once
Lost	Franklin Is Lost	Bourgeois	Lost playing hide and seek
Lost	The Bear That Heard Crying	Kinsey-Warnock	A lost girl is protected by bear
Manners	Manners Matter	Brown	Being polite to others
Manners	Perfect Pigs	Brown	Variety of good manners
Manners	The Grumpling	Cosgrove	A big bear is taught manners
Middle school	How to Survive Junior High	Hodgman & Marx	Everything about junior high

(continued)

Table 4.6 (*continued*)

Topic	Title	First Author	Description
Misbehavior	*The Name-Game*	Ludwig	Lots of bad behaviors and solutions
Moving	*Boomer's Big Day*	McGeorge	A dog's view of moving
Neatness	*Franklin Is Messy*	Bourgeois	Franklin can't find anything in his messy room
Parents	*Trouble with Grownups*	Berenstain	How it feels to be parent or a kid
Peer pressure	*Monkey See, Monkey Do*	Schwartz	Follow your feelings instead of your friends
Problem solving	*It's Up to You . . . What Do You Do?*	Humphrey	Problems to solve
Problem solving	*Win or Lose by How You Chose*	Judge Judy	Problems to solve with multiple-choice answers
Problem solving	*What Would You Do?*	Schwartz	Problems to solve with multiple-choice answers
Problem solving	*What Would You Think?*	Schwartz	Tons of problems to solve
Promises	*A Children's Book About Breaking Promises*	Berry	Keep promises if you want others to keep theirs
Promises	*Arthur's Promise*	Brown	Keeping promises
Relaxation	*A Boy and a Bear*	Lite	Lesson in relaxation
Relaxation	*Cool Cats, Calm Kids*	Williams	Stress management
Respect	*D.W. Saves the Day*	Brown	Respecting nature
Responsibility	*Three Little Kittens*	Galdone	Kittens learn to be responsible for their mittens
Responsibility	*Responsible Rascal*	Schwartz	Following through on tasks
Rules	*Playing the Game*	Firmin	Learn why rules are important
Rumors	*Rumor and Revenge*	Boulden	Chapter book for older students
Safety	*Officer Buckle and Gloria*	Rathmann	A dog helps teach safety
Self-esteem	*Leo the Lop*	Cosgrove	You are okay the way you are

Topic	Title	Author	Description
Self-esteem	I Wish I Were a Butterfly	Howe	A cricket wants to be a butterfly instead
Self-esteem	Stick Up for Yourself!	Kaufman	Instructional book for being more assertive/confident
Sharing	Fun to Share	Boulden	Interactive workbook
Sharing	It's Mine!	Lionni	Sharing is more fun than arguing
Sharing	We Share Everything	Munsch	Kindergartners learn to share
Sharing	The Rainbow Fish	Pfister	Sharing makes fish happy
Silliness	How I Feel Silly	Leonard	When silliness is OK and when it's not
Sportsmanship	Clifford's Sports Day	Bridwell	Clifford joins in on field day
Sportsmanship	Tiggers Hate to Lose	Gaines	Tigger loses a game and has a tantrum
Stranger danger	Don't Talk to Strangers, Pooh!	Zoehfeld	Pooh practices the "stay safe" rules
Study skills	How to Be School Smart	James & Barkin	Ideas and activities
Study skills	How to Do Homework Without Throwing Up	Romain	Homework tips
Tattling	Telling Isn't Tattling	Hammerseng	Differences between telling and tattling
Tattling/telling the truth	Armadillo Tattletale	Ketteman	Armadillo tells a stretched version of what others say
Teamwork	Franklin Plays the Game	Bourgeois	More to the game than winning
Teamwork	I Can't Said the Ant	Cameron	Ants and spiders work together to get a job done
Teamwork	Swimmy	Lionni	Small fish work together to escape a big fish
Teamwork	The Turnip	Morgan	Teamwork helps pull out a big turnip
Teasing	Too Much Teasing	Berenstain	Helping a friend being teased

Table 4.6 (continued)

Topic	Title	First Author	Description
Teasing	The Meanest Thing to Say	Cosby	How to respond to teasing
Teasing	Chrysanthemum	Henkes	First day of school teasing
Teasing	Marvin and the Mean Words	Kline	Mean words can really hurt
Teasing	But Names Will Never Hurt Me	Waber	A girl is teased about her name
Teasing/differences/tolerance	Angel Child Dragon Child	Surat	Kids make fun of a new student
Telling the truth	The Dog Who Cried "Woof!"	Barkly	Crying wolf
Telling the truth	Oh, Brother! Someone's Fibbing	Birney	Pooh learns about fibbing
Telling the truth	Franklin Fibs	Bourgeois	Franklin's story gets bigger and bigger
Telling the truth	I Did It, I'm Sorry	Buehner	Honesty, dependability, and consideration
Telling the truth	Finders, Keepers	Crary	What to do when you find a wallet
Telling the truth	The Empty Pot	Demi	A boy's honesty is rewarded
Telling the truth	Fibber E. Frog	Newman	Frog learns he doesn't have to fib to have friends
Telling the truth	The Boy Who Cried Wolf	Ross	Not telling the truth
Telling the truth	A Big Fat Enormous Lie	Sharmat	A lie stays with you
Telling the truth/keeping promises	Clifford and the Big Leaf Pile	Page	Clifford breaks a promise to a friend
Trying new things	Picky Mrs. Pickle	Schneider	A woman tries new things and likes them

Chapter 5

Individualized Social Skills Instruction

Individualized social skills instruction, including teaching replacement behavior based on the function of the problem behavior, is crucial for successful skill development that generalizes across environments and is maintained over time. The key to success is to specify what problem behaviors will be targeted and what replacement and other desirable behaviors will be taught, who will provide the instruction, when it will be embedded into the students' school day, and how it will be delivered in terms of both instructional strategies and content.

What Behaviors Should Be Focused on During Individualized Instruction?

In individualized social skills instruction, the first step is to start with the "what": What problem behavior does the student frequently exhibit that needs to be replaced? First, make sure that this behavior is truly a problem. If you cannot come up with a true reason for why the behavior needs to change, this is a sure sign that you need to let it go.

"So What?" Behavior

You can determine if the behavior is truly a problem by applying the "so what" test. Many educators choose to fight battles that frankly *do not need to be fought*, and this leads to unnecessary power struggles.

Behaviors pass the "so what" test if they are harmful in any way (socially, physically, emotionally, or academically) to the student exhibiting the behavior or to others.[1]

> Many educators choose to fight battles that frankly *do not need to be fought,* and this leads to unnecessary power struggles.

The 3 D's: Behavior That Is Dangerous, Destructive, or Seriously Disruptive

Behaviors that are dangerous to the students or others, destructive to the environment, or seriously disrupt the operation of the learning environment obviously need to be replaced. The key word here is *seriously*. Does it really bother other students, or is it simply you, as the adult, trying to exert your power and control over them? Think about this. Many adults want children to do things only "because we said so" even if there is no valid reason. Is this left over from childhoods of hearing that from parents and teachers and wanting a turn? Does this make any sense? It's time to break the cycle. Unnecessary power struggles usually create more problems and take up more time than they are worth. Some common behavior battles that educators often pick but should reconsider include these:

- Using a specific writing utensil. (One of your students hates to write and will do so only with a purple glittery pen. Let her. You can pick that battle later if needed.)

- Using a specific organizational system or binder. (Do you use the same system that all of your colleagues do? How would you feel if you were forced to?)

- Sitting still at a desk to work. (As long as they are working, does it matter if they stand?)

- Doodling during teacher-directed instruction. (This actually helps some people concentrate.)

- Making eye contact. (Some people, specifically those on the autism spectrum, can't look and listen at the same time.)

- Using "proper" handwriting. (When was the last time you used perfect penmanship? If others can read it, does it really matter? Many of us would be out of job if this was truly needed for life success.)

- Following adult directions the first time. (Maybe they need processing time or a reminder.)

Behaviors That Cause Others to View the Student Negatively or Invite Bullying

These behaviors are "maybe" behaviors. Deciding whether to attempt to change them should be based on the feelings and individual goals of the student and his or her family. It may not be a priority for them, and trying to change it may simply be too stressful. An example may be trying to get immature students to not wear certain characters on their shirt or bring certain "babyish" items with them to school. Other things such as hygiene problems may be more important, but again, it may not be a priority if the student is working on changing other more problematic behaviors.

Jodie Says . . .

Middle school is tough for many students. Kids can be brutal to each other at this stage. When I taught in a middle school alternative setting, we had a student who was sent to the program for school-phobic behaviors. This young man was very intelligent, but he had some behaviors and habits that called negative attention to him. He was constantly teased and at times bullied to the point where he could hardly enter the front door of his middle school by the fourth week of his sixth-grade year. He was upset, and his parents were beside themselves because he had loved school in his elementary years.

His team decided a smaller setting would be better for him while he adjusted to the tough transition from elementary school to middle school. Once he was in our program, he seemed more at ease. I was his homeroom teacher, and he seemed okay coming to me with any issues or problems he was having. The first few months went well, but then everyone started to get comfortable with each other, and some of the teasing resumed. He never got to the point of not wanting to come to school, but he definitely was upset. Since we had an established relationship, our team decided it was time to sit down and talk with him. We talked about some of his clothing choices. He often wore juvenile characters like Lightning McQueen from the Disney movie *Cars* and a T-shirt with cute kitties on it. We talked about how this set him apart from his peers. We stressed that it was never okay for other students to tease and bully him, but we talked about how he could be proactive. We also talked with his parents. They

(continued)

agreed that those shirts would be best worn when he was at home. His mom had an older sibling go with him to buy some more age-appropriate shirts for him to wear to school. He felt more confident, and although it didn't stop all teasing, it certainly made it more tolerable for him. He became more assertive when being teased, which also helped to reduce his negative incidents at school.

Identifying Replacement Behavior

How do we make sure the skills we are teaching actually replace the problem behavior, that is, they meet the same (or if this is impossible a similar) function? The key to doing this is to follow three rules: the potato or dead man's rule, the fair pair rule, and the matching rule.[2]

The Potato or Dead Man's Rule

The basic guideline for this rule goes back to teaching students what you want them to do rather than telling them what you don't want them to do. That is, the replacement behavior should be stated in terms of action. If a potato or a dead man can do it, there is no action involved and the rule is not being followed. For example, "Don't run" would not follow the rule because a potato or dead man can certainly not run. "Walk in the hallway" may be a better way to state the desired behavior.

> The basic guideline for this rule goes back to teaching students what you want them to do rather than telling them what you don't want them to do. That is, the replacement behavior should be stated in terms of action. If a potato or a dead man can do it, there is not action involved and the rule is not being followed.

The Fair Pair Rule

Replacement behavior must be desired by or acceptable to the teacher and serve the same (or similar) function as the problem behavior, or the students will just come up with a new (and most likely still inappropriate) way to meet that function. For example, if a student has a tantrum to escape an unpreferred task and is given an undesirable consequence for the tantrum, he or she may start to ask to go to the bathroom or nurse's office frequently to escape the task. Teaching that same student to take a short, appropriate break would serve the same function and be acceptable to the teacher although possibly not desired. Table 5.1 gives several examples of teaching different replacement behaviors for the same problem behavior based on function.

Table 5.1 Examples of Replacement Behavior

Problem Behavior	Function	Replacement Behavior
Calling out	Getting the teacher's attention	Raise hand and wait to be called on
	Escaping work by being sent to time-out	Ask for a short break from or help with work
Hitting	Communicating that someone is crowding personal space	Communicate with words, icons, or gestures
	Expressing anger	Use words to express feelings

The Matching Rule

Students will engage in behavior that leads to the highest level of reinforcement and is the most efficient. If the inappropriate behavior continues to be reinforced at a higher level than the replacement behavior, it will not result in a decrease in the problem behavior or an increase in the replacement behavior. For example, teachers often tell students to raise their hand and wait to be called on before giving an answer or making a comment. We cannot tell you how many times we have seen an enthusiastic student raising a hand patiently and not getting recognized by the teacher. These students finally call out and immediately get the response, "I told you to raise your hand." Was raising a hand or calling out a more efficient and effective way to getting the teacher's attention? Of course, teachers can't always call on a student right away. However, when they begin to teach this skill, they should at least acknowledge the student is raising his or her hand ("Thank you for raising your hand. I'll be with you in a second") as quickly as possible in a positive way, providing some immediate feedback and reinforcement.

> If the inappropriate behavior continues to be reinforced at a higher level than the replacement behavior, it will not result in a decrease in the problem behavior or an increase in the replacement behavior.

Other Target Behaviors

There may be other prosocial target behaviors that may not serve the same or similar function as the problem behavior (and therefore are not replacement behaviors) yet are important to teach. For example, if a student hits to express feelings of anger, we need to teach him how to express these feelings by using words (replacement behavior) and to keep his hands to himself (other target behavior). Another example is students who don't follow the teacher's instruction because following that instruction (such as "Get out your journal") would result in an unpreferred task (having to write) that they want to escape or avoid. In this case, they need to be taught how to take breaks to temporarily escape tasks (replacement behavior) and follow the teacher's instructions (other target behavior).

Who Should Provide Individualized Instruction?

Any available adult can serve as the "who" as long as he or she is also clear about the "what" and "when," is provided with the "how" by a supervising certified teacher, and is held accountable for following through. We have designated this responsibility to unlikely or often overlooked candidates such as health aides, copy clerks, or recess aides, in addition to the more obvious and logical school personnel such as speech and occupational therapists, classroom teachers, paraprofessionals, and special educators.

Many schools are hiring and training extra personnel to serve solely in this capacity. The Check and Connect program uses monitors who function as individual student mentors, providing intervention that involves problem solving and social skills development, including replacement behavior training.[3] These positions are staffed by graduate students and community members with bachelor's degrees in human services–related fields or equivalent experience. We highly recommend that schools consider allocating some financial resources to creating similar positions to provide the much needed extra set of hands to provide consistent and high-quality individualized social skills instruction without disrupting the flow of classwide academic instruction. These individuals need not have an advanced professional degree but can be taught and supervised by those with specialized training in behavior management.

> **Recommended Resource**
>
> More information about Check and Connect can be found at www.ici.umn.edu/checkandconnect.

When Should Individualized Instruction Take Place?

Providing individualized social skills instruction does take some time. We know that teachers' plates are already full and time is very limited. However, we also know that embedding this instruction into the existing structure of the school day with very few additional time demands is possible if educators think creatively.

Embedded into Existing Structures and Therapies

Many students with behavioral challenges receive individualized therapies such as speech and language, occupational therapy, and counseling. Collaborating with these service providers to provide replacement behavior training is an easy way to embed it into a student's typical school day.

Check-In

Brief one-on-one check-in meetings with the student can be done first thing in the morning and throughout the day as natural breaks occur. This should be done with a staff member whom the student has developed a positive, trusting relationship. During these meetings, the adult provides direct instruction or review of the skills needed to have a successful day, anticipates problems that may occur during the day based on known settings events and triggering antecedents and formulating solutions, and simply gets to know the student and provides an outlet for expressing his or her feelings, wants, and needs.

Precorrection

Precorrections function as reminders by providing students with opportunities to practice or be prompted concerning expected behavior immediately before they enter situations in which displays of problems behaviors are likely.[4] We discussed the use of precorrection as a classwide instructional strategy in Chapter Four, but it can also be used to target the specific skills of individual students. For example, an adult can talk to a student who typically has problems of standing patiently in line immediately before lunch to review why this skill is important in the cafeteria and quickly practice the skill through a brief role play.

Behavior Tutoring Sessions

Just as students who have not mastered reading skills may have tutoring sessions before or after school or during free-time activities, students who do not master behavioral skills may need additional behavior tutoring sessions. This can also be structured as an undesirable consequence to help determine whether the student truly has a skill deficit (can't do) and needs extra instruction or is exhibiting a chosen performance deficit (won't do simply because she doesn't want to). We discuss this further in Chapter Thirteen.

Incidental Teaching

Incidental teaching refers to taking advantage of the teachable moments that occur naturally throughout a student's school day as situations occur. For example, a student who gets in an argument with another student at recess over taking turns on the swing can be pulled aside by an adult, discuss why it is important to take turns, and quickly role-play the situation again using appropriate replacement behavior. Although incidental teaching does not provide adequate direct instruction for the mastering of replacement behavior, it does support the generalization and maintenance of these skills and is a valuable part of an overall program.

How Should Individualized Instruction Be Delivered?

The same type of lesson plan format shown in Table 3.1 that is used for tier 1 (schoolwide and classwide) and tier 2 (small group) instruction can be followed for individualized social skills instruction. A few other additional direct instruction strategies that are particularly well suited for individualized instruction (although they may also be appropriate to use at the other tiers of instruction as well) are worth mentioning.

Video Modeling

In video modeling, students watch a video of themselves or someone similar engaging in the targeted problem behavior or targeted replacement behavior. This is often combined with other instructional practices such as questioning, discussion, and evaluation. Research has supported the use of video modeling with a variety of student populations to address a wide range of behavioral issues.[5] Videos can be made in real-life situations or in simulated role plays.

Social Stories

The term *social stories* is commonly used to refer to the Social Story that was developed by Carol Gray in the early 1990s.[6] Social stories use positive language and are written from a first- or third-person perspective to help students understand events and expectations that exist in a social environment and learn effective responses to those that may cause frustration. We have found social stories helpful in providing direct instruction on the complexities of social interaction specifically for students with language challenges. Social stories provide a structure to teach these skills in a way that uses consistent language across all possible instructors. Social stories can be read again and again by various adults at school, by the student themselves, in a tape recorder so the student can listen to them as often as needed, or sent home and read by parents at bedtime and in the morning before school, giving students a consistent message regardless of who is delivering the instruction.

Social stories can easily be misused as a way to tell students what to do rather than help them understand a situation and learn the appropriate response. Gray's Social Stories use six types of sentences and a specific formula so that it describes more than it directs and emphasizes student success and strengths. We include an example of a social story in Joey's success story in Chapter Sixteen. However, rather than simply start writing them on your own, we highly recommend Gray's Social Stories 10.0, which explains this instructional strategy in much more detail and can be downloaded for a fee at www.thegraycenter.org.

Commonly Overlooked Replacement Behaviors

In our experience, there are two replacement behaviors that can prevent a great deal of frustration and problem behavior, but unfortunately they are often overlooked. These are teaching students to take appropriate breaks and to negotiate assignments.

Taking Appropriate Breaks

As adults, there are many times we have overwhelming feelings that prevent us from having successful interactions with others. Having a discussion with someone at the height of our anger is almost always counterproductive to a positive outcome. Most adults have learned that they need to take a break and use calming strategies before they can successfully engage in a productive conversation with the object of their anger. Teaching students to identify when they are experiencing an overwhelming feeling and what to do to handle that feeling can significantly decrease the need for teacher intervention because they would be more likely to self-manage by taking a break before inappropriate behaviors occur.

Students can also learn to take appropriate breaks during independent academic work to prevent frustration that can escalate to problem behavior. How many times do we as adults allow ourselves to get up and move around when working simply because we need a break to regroup and refocus? Yet how many educators teach and allow students to do this?

Some educators fear that allowing students to take breaks anytime will be providing an outlet for them to escape and avoid undesirable tasks. "Won't they just ask for a break every time they are given something they don't want to do?" they ask. First, don't automatically assume students will abuse this. We have seen many students use breaks appropriately and never abuse them. Second, teach students what is a reasonable time to take a break for various purposes (calming down, regrouping, simply getting a break from a work task). For students who start abusing breaks, it is important to limit breaks in addition to teaching them that they will still be accountable for the work they missed during the break. Reproducible 2 provides a sample break pass.

Negotiating Assignments

Many times students are given assignments that are aversive to them for whatever reason but they either feel that they have no choice but to do it or express their feelings about the assignment in a disrespectful, non-teacher-pleasing way. The root of the teacher-student conflict in this situation is often that the teacher knows he or she should be differentiating instruction and providing options based on student interest and preferences (we discuss both of these in Part Three) but cannot do so for lack of time and so feels guilty about this. When a student expresses frustration in a disrespectful, inappropriate way the teacher responds defensively, and the power struggle begins.

We often teach students that if they are given an assignment that they don't like for whatever reason to negotiate an alternative assignment with the teacher. They can do this by (1) creating an alternative assignment that meets the lesson objectives but is based on their own strengths and interests, and (2) presenting the alternate assignment to the teacher in a respectful way. Suddenly the difficult and oppositional student becomes a charming and skilled negotiator who not only provides an appropriate alternative assignment for himself or herself but also other students in the classroom. Think of how much of the work involved in differentiating instruction could actually be taken care of (and off the teacher's plate) by teaching students this valuable life skill.

Key Points to Remember

- Individualized social skills instruction can be embedded into the school day.

- Many educators choose to fight unnecessary battles with students that lead to power struggles by trying to change behaviors that are not truly problems.

- Behaviors that are truly problems are those that are dangerous, destructive, seriously disruptive, or possibly those that cause the student to be seen negatively or invite bullying.

- When identifying replacement behavior, an educator should consider the potato or dead man's rule, fair pair rule, and matching rules.

- When determining who will be delivering social skills instruction to an individual student, schools can be creative. Any available adult in the school environment who has been trained by a behavior specialist or certified teacher in what content to deliver, how to deliver the instruction, and when to deliver it can provide this instruction.

- Individualized social skills instruction can be delivered throughout the day in existing therapies, scheduled check-in times, precorrections, behavior tutoring sessions, and incidental teaching opportunities.

- Individualized social skills instruction can be delivered in many formats. Two examples that have been effective are video modeling and social stories.

- Taking breaks and negotiation skills are two commonly overlooked replacement behaviors. Teaching them to students can prevent many problem behaviors.

Discussion Questions and Activities

1. When you are deciding what problem behavior to address, you should look at the 3 D's (dangerous, destructive, or seriously disruptive). Decide whether the following behaviors pass the 3 D's test. (A) A student blurts out in class approximately ten times an hour. (B) A student gets angry and colors on other

students' papers. (C) A student hits others when frustrated with an academic task. (D) A student crawls under furniture to escape undesirable tasks. (E) A student makes noises instead of working.

2. When thinking about the fair pair rule, decide which of these problem behaviors and replacement behaviors are fair pairs. (A) Problem behavior: Makes noises when frustrated with a task. Replacement behavior: Tell the child he can only make noises outside. (B) Problem behavior: Makes noises when frustrated with a task. Replacement behavior: Teach the child to hold up a card to signal the teacher she needs help with a task.

3. Brainstorm a list of staff in your school who could deliver individual social skills instruction if properly trained by a behavior specialist or certified teacher.

4. Many teachers expect that when they give an assignment, students will complete it without argument. If a student with challenging behavior has been taught appropriate negotiation skills, how could you convince a resistant teacher to be open to positive negotiations from the student?

Part Three

Preventing Challenging Behavior

Instruction

↓

Prevention

Chapter 6

Preventing Challenging Behavior: The Basics

The key to effective behavior management is to focus primarily on prevention and to begin prevention early on. Effective prevention efforts start by identifying the first two key concepts of functional behavioral assessment—setting events and triggering antecedents—which both happen before the problem behavior occurs (as discussed in Chapter Two). Setting events exist in the environment and exaggerate the likelihood that the problem behavior will occur or will make it worse than usual ("You know it is going to be a bad day . . ."), and triggering antecedents happen immediately before the problem behavior ("the straw that broke the camel's back").

Targeting Setting Events and Triggering Antecedents

Sometimes setting events and triggering antecedents can and should be controlled by removing them or modifying their influence. For example, a setting event may be that a student tends to have more problems when she is hungry, so her educators provide breakfast at school and snacks throughout the day, thereby removing the setting event. A triggering antecedent may be an unexpected change in the routine. Educators can anticipate this

71

problem and prepare the student for these changes. However, sometimes setting events and triggering antecedents cannot or should not be controlled. In this case, support may need to increase.

We cannot control the weather or many aspects of a student's home life that may serve as setting events or triggering antecedents, and we cannot change certain aspects of the curriculum. However, we can provide emotional support, accommodations, modifications, and increased levels of reinforcement. We often heard educators say, "Well, they are just going to have to learn. That's how things are in life." It is important to remember that students with behavior challenges often have significant disabilities that affect their ability to learn coping and problem-solving skills. Saying, "They are just going to have to learn," without providing increased support would be the same thing as expecting a physically injured person to just teach himself how to walk again without any physical therapy.

> Sometimes setting events and triggering antecedents can and should be controlled by removing them or modifying their influence.

> Sometimes setting events and triggering antecedents cannot or should not be controlled. In this case, support may need to increase.

Maybe the student has a meltdown every time he is asked to do any written task (and the task is truly not too difficult). We cannot take written tasks completely away in the school environment or the world we live in, so obviously this is something most individuals need to learn to do to some extent. But a student who truly finds this task extremely aversive for whatever reason may need more than the usual amount of encouragement and motivation. Maybe tangible reinforcement needs to increase, maybe he needs more frequent breaks, maybe the task can be made into a game to make it more motivating, or maybe the teacher needs to modify the assignment or check on that student more frequently. The solution will be different for each child, but the key is the same: remove or modify the influence of setting events and triggering antecedents or validate a student's frustration and provide increased levels of support. Never underestimate the power of the message "I know this is hard. I will help you."

> Never underestimate the power of the message, "I know this is hard. I will help you."

Identifying Sources of Frustration

Many variables in the educational environment can lead to frustration and serve as setting events or triggering antecedents to problem behavior—for example:

- Educators who interact with students in an overly domineering way that invites power struggles

- Lack of a valid reason to exhibit a behavior, such as following a direction or completing an academic task

- Tasks that are too easy or boring, or too difficult or complex

- Lack of understanding of expectations

All of the topics we touched on in Part Two on instruction will reduce some of this frustration, especially that caused by the lack of understanding of expectations. In addition, countless prevention strategies are available that provide additional support and further reduce frustration for students who continue to struggle. This section focuses on three areas that by themselves, or in combination, help ease student frustration and therefore prevent problem behaviors from occurring: (1) developing a positive relationship, (2) assisting with executive functioning tasks, and (3) providing appropriate and engaging academic instruction. We look at developing a positive relationship in this chapter and devote the next two chapters to, respectively, executive functioning and academic instruction.

Developing a Positive Relationship

Students tend to behave more appropriately when they have a positive relationship with the staff members they are working with. We all know teachers who seem to be able to magically get a student to do things that others cannot as a result of their relationship with the student. Developing this capability is not easy. Many times students who exhibit behavior problems have had less-than-positive experiences in schools. They have had numerous suspensions and negative consequences for behaving inappropriately, and no one has taught them what they are supposed to do instead. Lack of social skills has led to conflicts with peers, resulting in social alienation. Their behavior has interfered with their learning, resulting in poor academic results. Their parents are frustrated with them and with the schools they have attended. Together, these experiences have culminated in a general mistrust of schools, administrators, teachers, and the education system in general. What would make these students think that you will be any different? Here are some ways for you to start showing them that you are different (or certainly hope to be).

Be Consistent

We are true believers that consistency breeds trust. Students have to know that you say what you do and you do what you say. Albeit usually subconsciously, students want limits, and they want these limits to be consistently enforced. The reason educators often don't realize this is that students behave as if they want exactly the opposite, and may even say so. When limits are put into place, these students test those limits to see if you truly mean what you say. In the clinical world, this is well documented by research and referred to as a *behavioral burst*. Things often get worse before they get better as the student goes through this testing process. Therefore, we may think our consistency is not working when, in fact, the behavior burst is evidence that it is working. We just need to be patient and stand our ground.

Students have to know that you say what you do and you do what you say. A good analogy to illustrate this concept is to compare a student to a night watchman. A night watchman's job is to make sure his place of business is safe and secure. He goes around the property periodically during the night to make sure all doors are properly locked and secure, and he tries each door to make sure that this is indeed the case. He does not want them to open and may feel anxious about the thought of the door opening, but he tries them nonetheless. He is relieved when the doorknobs do not turn, and a feeling of safety returns.

Some students will test your limits for a short time until they realize that the limits are intact and they know what they can expect when they choose certain behaviors. Some students go through cycles of testing limits based on various uncontrollable variables in their lives. The bottom line is that if you do what you say and say what you do, students will be more likely to trust you, and this trust provides the essential foundational relationship that can assist the child in making behavioral progress.

Develop a Partnership

Another key to establishing a positive relationship with a student is to clearly define the roles of teacher and student. Many students with behavioral challenges have issues with authority and fight for power and control in their learning environment. Clearly an authoritative approach with this population is not effective. Rather, a partnership approach tends to minimize power struggles and lend itself to cooperation and progress.

Consider the respective jobs of teacher and student at school. The teacher's job is to teach students the academic and behavioral skills they need to succeed in life and maintain the safety of everyone in their classroom. The student's job is to learn. Any behaviors that occur in the classroom that prevent any individual from doing his or her job need to be addressed in order to maintain a productive learning environment. The teacher can't do his or her job if the students are not doing theirs, and vice versa. It is truly a partnership that must be worked on together.

> The teacher's job is to teach students the academic and behavioral skills they need to succeed in life and to maintain the safety of everyone in their classroom. The student's job is to learn.

The Teacher Is Not "The Boss"

Establish that the teacher is not the boss. (We know what you are thinking: *Are you crazy? Take away any authority I have? How can this help?*) The truth is, you are not the boss, and you cannot make anyone do anything. You can't fire a student, especially a student with disabilities in a public school system in a country that ensures that every individual will be provided a free and appropriate public education. In order to do your job, you need the students to behave appropriately by their choice if you are to be successful.

The teacher's job is to provide the structure and assistance needed to students to recognize that the choices they are making are connected to the natural and logical consequences they experience, both positive and negative. Teaching a child that he is his own "boss" and ultimately is in charge of what happens to him, at least in your classroom at school, is a powerful lesson.

We always told our students that we couldn't make them do anything; in fact, they determined what happened to them by the choices they made. Many times they would respond, "Yes, you can! You are the teacher!" We always countered that we wished we could make their choices for them. Then we would make only good choices so that only good things would happen to them, but we could not do that for them. They had to choose that for themselves.

Teaching students they are in charge of themselves is crucial in removing the teacher from the power struggles and blame games that students with behavioral issues often engage in. If they believe they are in charge of themselves and you are simply the person connecting their choices with the consequences they experience, then they no longer can shift blame onto you and are forced to look at their own personal responsibility for their life.

We Are All in the Same Boat

It is also powerful to teach students that children are not the only ones who experience the undesirable consequences of their choices. Giving them real-life adult examples of choices and undesirable consequences for those choices illustrates that we are all in the same boat and serves as an effective relationship-building tool. If a student experiences undesirable consequences for refusing to do her work and calling the teacher a nasty name, ask her what would happen to an adult if his supervisor gave him a task to do and the adult responded by refusing and calling the supervisor something profane. Most often the student will guess that the adult may be fired. The teacher can then expand this by pointing out that this would mean the adult would not get a paycheck and therefore wouldn't have enough money. He wouldn't be able to pay bills or buy food and might even lose his house.

Assist Students in Setting Goals

Another way to partner with students is to help them make short-term and long-term goals that will help them get what they want. What is it exactly that they want at school? More friends? To do better in math? Get in less trouble? Have others trust them? Be given more responsibility? Get by with doing as little homework as possible? Get them to pinpoint what they want and help them see the connection between getting what they want and their behavioral choices. Even if initially they say they want to do as little work as possible (a common response), you can work with this. Simply point out that if that is truly their goal, then to rush through their work and hand in an assignment that they have not done their best on is truly not the way to reach it: that work will be handed back to them and they will be required to complete the assignment again during their free time. Now they have not only done double the work but are missing time when they could be having fun instead of working. Of course, if you assist them in making this connection between their behavioral choices and getting what they want, it is absolutely essential that you follow through on your part and make sure they do indeed experience the undesirable consequence.

Focus on Frequent Positive Feedback

A final way to build a positive relationship is to simply and sincerely give students frequent positive feedback. We discussed the importance of this with all students when providing instruction on classroom expectations in Chapter Four. However, we feel it is worth mentioning again because this is especially important for students with chronic behavioral challenges who have often had overwhelmingly negative experiences at school. Positive feedback, or praise, has been demonstrated to have a positive effect on these students both behaviorally and academically.[1] Vigilantly keeping in mind the rule of thumb of four positives to every one negative especially with these students can help us truly make a shift in how we interact with them. Children who have already had a lot of negative life experiences have a heightened sensitivity to criticism and negativity. When they realize that you are able to see the good things they do and not just focus on the bad, partnering with them becomes exponentially easier. (Isn't this true of all human beings?)

By developing a positive relationship with your students, you show them that you are different. They see that you are there to help them make positive choices and get what they want, and they stop seeing you as someone who lives to make them work and torture them. Building this relationship is crucial, though not an easy or fast process.

Key Points to Remember

- Effective prevention efforts start by identifying the first two key concepts of functional behavioral assessment, setting events and triggering antecedents, which both happen before the problem behavior occurs.

- Some setting and triggering antecedents can be removed or their influence can be minimized.

- Some setting events and triggering antecedents cannot or should not be changed. In these cases, the teacher must modify, accommodate, provide emotional support, and increase the frequency of reinforcement to provide students with needed support in difficult situations.

- Students tend to behave more appropriately when they have a positive relationship with the staff members they are working with.

How to Reach and Teach Children with Challenging Behavior

- Consistency breeds trust. Students with challenging behavior are more likely to work for people they trust.

- A student-teacher partnership is based on the concept that a teacher's job is to teach and keep students safe, and a student's job is to learn. Neither job can be done with only one of the parties participating.

- Students can be empowered when the teacher points out she is not the boss and can't make them do anything. Students are in charge of their choices and, therefore, the positive and negative consequences that follow those choices.

- Showing students that adults also experience consequences for their choices can be a powerful tool to establishing a relationship.

- Asking students to identify what they want and then showing them the connection of their behavior choices to achieving their desires is a powerful tool in developing personal responsibility.

- Creating a positive environment through frequent positive feedback is an excellent tool to prevent negative behaviors.

Discussion Questions

1. Billy's triggering antecedent is reading. He does not like to read, and it is hard for him. Reading, however, cannot be completely removed from his school day. How can you prevent problems and increase support during reading tasks to help Billy?

2. We talk a lot about the concept of consistency in education. What are some ways that educators fail to be consistent? What are the ramifications of inconsistency? What benefits stem from consistency?

Chapter 7

Assisting with Executive Functioning Tasks

Supporting students who have difficulty with executive functioning skills is an often overlooked area of providing preventive intervention and support. *Executive functioning* refers to the mental processes that help us connect our past experience with action now. We use executive function skills when we perform such activities as planning, organizing, strategizing, and paying attention to and remembering details.[1] We count on our executive functioning skills every day to plan, set goals, and self-regulate our behavior, so difficulty with executive functioning can lead to many of the problems that students with challenging behavior commonly exhibit. Abilities that are linked to executive functioning include[2]

- Making plans

- Keeping track of time

- Keeping track of more than one thing at a time

- Meaningfully including past knowledge in discussions

- Engaging in group dynamics

- Evaluating ideas

- Reflecting on work

- Changing our mind and making midcourse corrections while thinking, reading, and writing

- Finishing work on time

- Asking for help

- Waiting to speak until called on

- Seeking more information when we need it

The Source for Executive Function Disorders by Susanne Phillips Keeley identifies the following characteristics of executive function disorders:[3]

- Difficulty with planning and organization

- Trouble identifying what needs to be done

- Problems determining the sequence of accomplishment

- Difficulty carrying out steps in an orderly way

- Difficulty beginning tasks

- Problems maintaining attention

- Trouble evaluating how one is doing on a task

- Difficulty taking feedback or suggestions

Recommended Resource

The Source for Executive Function Disorders, by Susanne Phillips Keeley (East Moline, IL: LinguiSystems, 2003).

In our experience, students with executive functioning challenges are often described as disorganized and lazy. What many teachers don't realize is that difficulty with executive functioning skills are often caused by damage to or improper development of the frontal lobe of the brain. This condition is well documented in individuals who have had a traumatic brain injury in this area. These students usually are perfectly capable academically but often receive poor grades because of difficulties with many of the skills in the preceding lists, especially in middle and high school when long, multistep projects are more common and greater independence with these skills is expected. In order to reduce their frustration related to academic tasks, it is crucial to teach them strategies that will help them develop their executive functioning skills and provide modifications and accommodations when appropriate.

Using Visual Supports

A visual support is anything that we see that helps us comprehend environmental information. Maps are an excellent example of a visual support that helps us understand how our surroundings are laid out. Speed limit signs are another example of a visual support that serves as a notification or reminder of driving expectations.[4] Although most of the research on visual supports is based on their use with students with autism spectrum disorders, we have found that these supports help many students with behavior challenges.

Visual supports play a double role in prevention: they help with executive functioning skills such as organization and attention,[5] and they clarify verbal information, which can be confusing for students with language disorders.[6] Many students with chronic behavior problems have language disorders, so it stands to reason that some behavior problems stem from these disorders and the communication difficulties they cause. Visual supports are one way of improving and supporting communication and executive functioning tasks as they clarify verbal information, are quickly and easily interpreted (the old saying, "A picture is worth a thousand words," applies here), encourage independence, and provide additional structure. In addition, visual supports stay still in time. This allows the learner to review the verbal input by looking at the visual representation of the input as often as needed.

> Visual supports play a double role in prevention: they help with executive functioning skills such as organization and attention, and they clarify verbal information, which can be confusing for students with language disorders.

Let's use the analogy of learning a foreign language to clarify this concept. If you were visiting Paris and were conversational but not fluent in French, would you rather have a native give you verbal directions, give you visual directions using a map, or pair verbal with visual directions? I think most of us would agree that we would find the verbal and visual pairing most helpful.

Many educators use the software program Boardmaker (a free trial can be downloaded at www.mayer-johnson.com) to create visual supports but we find that free computer graphics, digital photographs, or hand-drawn visual supports work just as well, and that is what we used for the visual supports provided in this book. (Free images can be found at http://office.microsoft.com/EN-US/CLIPART.) Don't let thinking that a visual support has to look perfect keep you from using them. We prefer to have students illustrate their own visual supports when possible because they can choose the visual representation that is most meaningful to them. In addition, going through the illustration process helps them comprehend the content of the visual support. Some very simple visual supports that we most commonly use to assist students are organizational helpers, behavior prompts, visual schedules, and transition helpers.

Organizational Helpers

Organizational problems are common for students who have difficulty with executive functioning tasks. Keeping track of assignments and materials and handing completed assignments in on time are frequent battles. Making lists, prioritizing items on the list, using organizational checklists, and using a planner are all crucial skills needed for getting and remaining organized. Students can use visual checklists to self-monitor while they organize, and they can also serve as a guide for an adult check when finished. Figures 7.1 and 7.2 provide two examples of visual checklists.

Behavior Prompts

Behavior prompts provide a visual representation of the replacement or appropriate behavior. These prompts can be taped to a student's desk for a continual reminder or used as a prompt as needed. Since redirection should be given with minimal attention, they are ideal for pointing to or holding up to provide guidance with limited interaction. Peer models can even be taught to provide the visual cue, or students can carry behavior prompt visuals with them in a notebook to refer to throughout the day. We prefer to use digital photographs of the actual student engaging in examples and nonexamples of the behavior or have students illustrate their own visual behavior prompts so that they are meaningful to them. Figures 7.3 through 7.7 provide examples of visual behavior prompts.

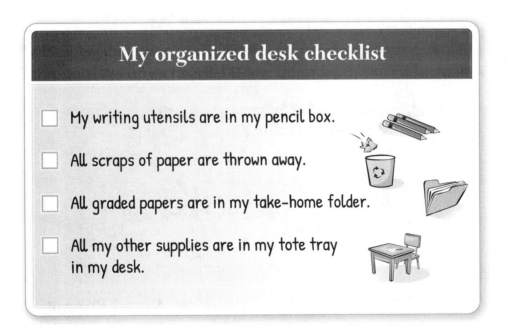

Figure 7.1 Organized Desk Checklist

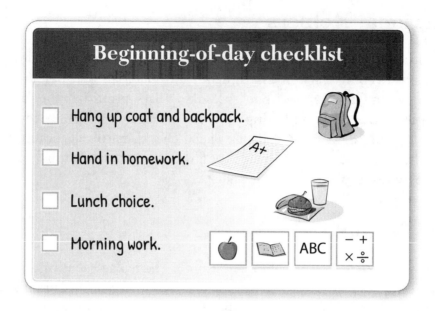

Figure 7.2 Beginning-of-Day Checklist

Figure 7.3 How to Follow Directions Visual Prompt

How to Reach and Teach Children with Challenging Behavior

Figure 7.4 How to Treat Others Nicely Visual Prompt

Figure 7.5 Sitting Properly Visual Prompt

Figure 7.6 Not Sitting Properly Visual Prompt

Figure 7.7 Calm Down Visual Prompt

Visual Schedules

Visual schedules create a picture of the order of events or activities.[7] We often use these to assist in teaching time management to students. These schedules help students anticipate and plan their day by allowing them to view the order of activities and what they should prepare for next. If there is a change in schedule due to school assemblies or special school parties, this can be included in a visual schedule to help students mentally prepare for the change.

The format of visual schedules can vary greatly. Younger children may benefit from picture schedules that use icons, drawings, or photos that are removed when certain portions of their day are finished and these types of visual schedules tend to be the ones that come to mind. Older students can also benefit from written visual schedules that they can check or cross off. Figures 7.8 and 7.9 respectively provide examples of an icon and a written visual schedule.

Transition Helpers

Many individuals with behavioral challenges have difficulty with transitions. This may be due to difficulty tracking time, accepting change, ending a more preferred activity to start a less preferred one, sensory issues or the lack of structure that often accompanies transition, or a combination of all of these. Transition helpers support students by providing structure

Figure 7.8 Icon Visual Schedule

Figure 7.9 Written Visual Schedule

and predictability, in addition to giving them all the information about what is going to happen and time to process it and become cognitively and emotionally ready to handle the change. The three transition helpers we most commonly use are five-minute countdowns, timers, and transition objects.

Five-Minute Countdown

We recommend giving students at least a five-minute warning before a transition and counting down to provide multiple reminders that the transition is coming. It is not important to do this according to the minute; the idea is to let them know that the time is getting close and they need to finish up what they are doing and prepare for the next activity. This can be done verbally, by holding up fingers, or with a visual countdown strip with numbers that can be crossed out or removed (Figure 7.10). Reproducible 4 provides multiple countdown strips.

Timers

Timers, especially if they are visual, make the abstract concept of elapsed time more concrete and quickly answer the common questions that cause confusion and anxiety in many students such as, "How much time is left of writing?" and "How much longer until recess?" "How many minutes until I can go home and see my mom?" (Figure 7.11). A variety of visual timers are available at www.timetimer.com, including an overhead timer that can be used with a large group, several sizes of individual timers, and a watch. Simple

Figure 7.10 Transition Countdown Strip

Figure 7.11 Visual Timer

kitchen egg timers that count up or down can be used (but beware of their tendency to become a triggering antecedent; their ticking can stress some students). Sand timers and a simple stopwatch on a student's desk are also options.

Transition Objects

Although transition objects (for example, stuffed animals, music, and sensory objects such as fans or things that light up) are not really visual supports, they are important to the topic of transitions. These highly preferred objects are especially helpful when students are required to make the transition from more preferred to less preferred activities such as from recess to the classroom or from the classroom to the bus. Students can carry their preferred objects with them during

> Students can carry their preferred objects with them during transitions to make the transition more reinforcing and distract the student from the not-so-reinforcing task that is coming next.

transitions to make the transition more reinforcing and distract the student from the not-so-reinforcing task that is coming next. The choice of what object to use is student specific.

A Final Word About Visual Supports

Many students with language challenges become very good at faking it (that is, acting as if they understand you when they really don't) and therefore teachers underestimate the need for and value of language support. Numerous variables affect verbal communication, so a student who understands or expresses herself clearly in one situation may not be able to do so in a different situation. There are unlimited ways that visual supports can be embedded throughout a student's school day. Always consider ways to make verbal communication visual. Excellent resources for using visual supports in a variety of areas and for a variety of skills that may affect behavior are *Solving Behavior Problems in Autism: Improving Communication with Visual Strategies* by Linda A. Hodgdon and *Making Visual Supports Work in the Home and Community: Strategies for Individuals with Autism and Asperger Syndrome* by Jennifer L. Savner and Brenda Smith Myles.

Recommended Resources

Solving Behavior Problems in Autism: Improving Communication with Visual Strategies, by Linda A. Hodgdon (Troy, MI: QuirkRoberts, 1999).

Making Visual Supports Work in the Home and Community: Strategies for Individuals with Autism and Asperger Syndrome, by Jennifer L. Savner and Brenda Smith Myles (Shawnee Mission, KS: Autism Asperger, 2000).

Assistance with Other Executive Functioning Skills

Some common executive functioning tasks that students struggle with include breaking long projects into steps, waiting to be called on, and staying on task. The following sections describe some interventions that we have found helpful in assisting students with these skills.

Breaking Long Projects into Steps

Long projects such as report writing that require a student to complete several steps and have a far-off due date are often hard for students with executive functioning problems. They tend to procrastinate or spend too much time on one part of the project and underestimate or not leave enough time for others. Providing aids that serve as a task analysis for different steps of the project and appropriate time allotments for each step is helpful in these cases. By simply breaking down the task into steps and preplanning each step, students are often able to see the big picture. For an example, see the structure given to a middle school project on biomes at the end of this chapter.

Waiting to Be Called On

An important classroom executive functioning skill for all students is raising their hand and waiting to be called on. When we taught smaller classes for students with challenging behaviors, it seemed sort of nitpicky to require students to raise their hands when we had only a group of two. However, general education teachers put shouting out in classrooms high on their list of undesired behaviors, and understandably so. Twenty-six students all shouting out at once in a classroom, for example, would be chaotic. So even in small groups of two, we taught this skill in order to prepare the students for a typical classroom environment.

Waiting to be called on seems simple enough, but this can be a difficult skill for students with executive functioning difficulties to master. These students must decide if and when they need help or would like to share something. They must control the impulse to shout out, and then wait to be called on if their teacher is busy.

Jodie Says . . .

One of my students had an especially difficult time learning to wait until he was called on. I tried everything: giving immediate reinforcement for raising his hand, putting the skill on his target behavior sheet, ignoring his shout-outs, making special contracts for the number of times he raised his hand, reading social stories about raising his hand, and providing visual prompts on his desk. The list could go on and on. One day I pulled him aside to talk about why he was having such difficulty with this skill. We reviewed the purpose for raising his hand (to share something or ask a question) and talked about why it was important and the undesirable consequences he was receiving for choosing not to raise his hand. He knew it all. He looked at me and said very sincerely that he would really try.

The next day, this second grader returned to school with a very crude-looking sign made out of poster board, duct tape, and a paint stirring stick. On one side he had written (in his second-grade scrawl), "I have a question," and the other side, "I want to share something." He informed me he was going to use this sign when either of those two situations

(continued)

occurred. I thought it might work at first but then wear off. Much to my surprise, however, it worked, and his hand-raising behavior increased dramatically. Holding the sign up over his desk—even though he didn't hold it up very high—was a marked improvement over constantly shouting out. He started experiencing all the positives that were in place for raising his hand and feeling more confident. After a couple of weeks of success, I upped the ante a little bit and explained to him that he needed to hold the sign up a little higher in order for a staff member to call on him. It took a little practice, but he started doing that on a regular basis, again feeling all the positives for performing the behavior. After a couple of more successful weeks, I required that his arm be fully extended with the sign. Within three months, we were able to fade out the sign altogether.

Staying on Task

We typically recommend using an intervention called "chart moves" as a self-monitoring system during independent work time for students who have difficulty remaining on task.

We first came across the chart moves intervention in the book *The Tough Kid Toolbox* by William R. Jensen, Ginger Rhode, and H. Kenton Reavis, which provides several examples that can be photocopied. This resource also provides many other behavior interventions that we find extremely helpful.

Recommended Resource

The Tough Kid Toolbox, by William R. Jenson, Ginger Rhode, and H. Kenton Reavis (Longmont, CO: Sopris West, 1994).

Students choose a picture of a reinforcer they would like to earn or of a special interest to increase motivation to use the system. A random cuing system such as a beep tape or MotivAider is used. Table 7.1 provides a description and ordering information for three commercially available cuing systems. When the cuing system goes off, the student self-monitors whether he is on task (after having been directly taught this skill, of course). If he is, he connects a dot. When he connects to a bigger dot, he earns a small or quick reinforcer such as a short break. And when he connects all the dots around the chart, he earns a larger reinforcer. This same system could be used for an entire class during independent work time if you do not want to single out one student as this intervention can certainly benefit many students in a classroom. See Figure 7.12 for a sample analysis of staying on task; see Figure 7.13 for a sample chart moves.

Table 7.1 Cuing Systems Information

Name	Description	Ordering Web Site	Approximate Price
Audio reinforcement reminder tones	Tapes or CD Tones can be set to play at random, variable intervals averaging 1, 2, 3, 5, 7, 10, or 15 minutes	Pyramid Education Products pyramidproducts.com	$13
MotivAider	Vibration signal can be set to cue at set or random intervals	www.habitchange.com	$50 (includes a teacher appreciation discount)
Get 'Em on Task Software: A computer signaling program to teach attending and self-management skills	CD tone signal system Instructors can determine length of intervals (or random cues), how long the program will run, and how the cues will sound	Sopris West www.sopriswest.com	$48

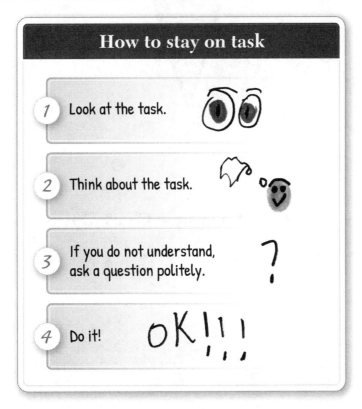

Figure 7.12 Steps for Staying on Task

Figure 7.13 Example Chart Moves

How to Reach and Teach Children with Challenging Behavior

Troubleshooting

What if a student cheats and connects dots that he did not earn? We have found that if students are not punished for temporarily not staying on task and missing a connection and highly praised for being honest, this usually does not happen. You can also add a penalty for getting caught cheating, such as erasing connections. However, we prefer to stay away from this practice if at all possible because it can trigger additional behavior problems.

Key Points to Remember

- People count on their executive functioning skills every day to plan, set goals, and self-regulate their behavior. Difficulty with executive functioning can lead to many of the problems that students with challenging behavior commonly exhibit.

- Visual supports are one way of improving and supporting communication and executive functioning tasks as they clarify verbal information and are quickly and easily interpreted.

- Organizational problems are common for students who have difficulty with executive functioning tasks. Templates, checklists, and planners can assist with this deficit.

Tricks of the Trade

Have several chart moves with popular pictures laminated and ready at all times for use with students having a hard time staying on task. Use a wipe-off marker so the charts can be used repeatedly. Reproducible 4 can be used for this. Student drawings, icons, graphics of preferred characters, or reinforcers can easily be placed in the middle.

- Behavior prompts, visual schedules, and transition helpers are tools to aid students with executive functioning deficits.

- Executive functioning deficits affect students' success on long-term projects, waiting to be called on, and staying on task. Preventive interventions can help.

Discussion Questions

1. Your student Kyle exhibits difficulties with executive functioning. He attends general education classes with behavioral support. How would you work with a teacher who resists making modifications and accommodations for Kyle because, she says, he is perfectly capable and is simply lazy?

2. Brittany is your student who has difficulty starting assignments, keeping track of them, and getting them in on time. What are some supports you could put in place to help her with these problems?

Biome Project

A biome is a large area of the earth that has its own set of conditions and living things. Using books, encyclopedias, and the Internet, you will research a biome that is of interest to you. Here are the biomes from which you may choose:

Tundra	Grasslands
Tropical Rainforest	Taiga (Coniferous Forests)
Desert	Temperate Forest

Project Summary

After researching your biome, you will create a PowerPoint presentation that informs people about your biome. You will include pictures of the landscape, animals, and plants, as well as describe the many features and conditions of your biome. You must include the following items in your project:

1. Name of the biome

2. Where it can be found in the world (all locations)

3. Geography of the area (landforms that affect life in the biome)

4. What the climate is like (temperature and rainfall for a typical year)

5. What plants and animals are found there (identify at least five of each)

   • Are there any endangered species there?

6. Human-environment interactions (positive or negative) that affect the biome

   • Does conservation affect your biome? How?

7. Interesting features and facts about your biome

   All of these items will be checked according to the attached rubric on the back of this page.

Internet Sites

1. http://earthobservatory.nasa.gov/Laboratory/Biome/

2. http://www.library.thinkquest.org/11234

3. http://enchantedlearning.com/biomes

4. http://www.ucmp.berkeley.edu/glossary/gloss5/biome/

5. http://www.cotf.edu/ete/modules/msese/earthsysflr/biomes/html

6. http://idahoptv.org/dialogue4kids/season4/ecology/biomes/html

7. http://lsb.syr.edu/projects/cyberzoo/biome.html

8. TAIGA ONLY: http://mbgnet.mobot.org/sets/taiga/

This will count as much as a test grade and will be due Tuesday, February 14.

My Biome Notes

Name: _____

Each of the following numbered areas will be one slide on your PowerPoint. You have two class periods to complete your notes. (See project time line.)

1. Name of the biome.

2. Where it can be found in the world (all locations).

3. Geography of the area (landforms that affect life in the biome).

4. What the climate is like (temperature and rainfall for a typical year).

5. What plants and animals are found there (at least five of each). Are there any endangered species there?

6. Human-environment interactions (positive or negative) that affect the biome. Does conservation affect your biome? How?

7. Interesting features and facts about your biome.

Biome Project Time Line

Name: _____

Date project assigned: Thursday, February 9

Date project due: Tuesday, February 14

Check off each bulleted activity as you complete it. If you complete more than outlined for each day, continue through the checklist until all items are checked.

Day 1

- Choose a biome, and write your choice on the list posted on the board.
- Write your name and the name of your biome on your notes page.
- Consult Web sites listed on the project assignment page and information found on your notes page. (You should complete at least three areas of your notes page today!)
- Show Ms. Tuttle how much you completed at the end of class.
- Put your notes in your science folder before you leave class.

Day 2

- Get your biome notes from your science folder.
- Continue researching your biome. Complete your notes by the end of the class period.
- Show Ms. Tuttle how much you completed at the end of class.
- Put your notes in your science folder before you leave class.

Day 3

- Get your biome notes from your science folder.
- Log onto your computer using your username and password.
- Open Microsoft PowerPoint.
- Make a title slide that includes the name of your biome and your name.
- Type the information on your notes onto slides. *All information should be typed in today!* Remember you will have at least one slide per area on your notes page. (This means a minimum of eight slides including your title slide.)

   ***Today we are inputting information. We will not be choosing slide backgrounds or fonts until *all* information is typed onto your slides!

- Save your file into your shared folder.
- Show Ms. Tuttle how much you completed at the end of class.
- Put your notes in your science folder before you leave class.

Day 4

- Get your biome notes from your science folder.
- Log onto your computer using your username and password.

- Use Google Image Search or other searches to find at least one picture for each slide. Make sure your picture matches the information on each slide.
- Once you have at least one picture per slide, you can spend the rest of the class choosing your background, adding special effects, and fonts for your text.
- Save your file into your shared folder.
- Drag and drop your finished PowerPoint presentation in the shared folder named "Tuttle Science."
- Show Ms. Tuttle your completed project before the end of class.
- Put your notes in your science folder before you leave class.

We will be practicing our presentations in partners tomorrow in class!

Chapter 8

Providing Appropriate and Engaging Academic Instruction

One common misconception about working with students with chronic behavior challenges is that academic instruction should be put on the back burner until behavior is under control. We could not disagree with this notion more, and research does not support this. We discussed the complex and interdependent relationship between academic and behavioral performance in Chapter One. Engagement in learning is clearly a proactive behavioral management strategy, with ample evidence showing that the problem behaviors of students decline when effective instruction is taking place.[1] As experienced educators, we can attest to the fact that if students are truly engaged in the learning process, they are less likely to act out. In addition, many of the problem behaviors that occur in the classroom are a result of the academic demands placed on students with challenging behavior. Thus, if you remove all academic demands from the student and focus solely on teaching behavioral skills, you will logically see a decrease in problem behaviors because the academic demands were the triggering antecedent. But the minute you reintroduce academic demands, the same behaviors will most likely resurface, and you will have lost not only precious instructional time but valuable opportunities to teach positive classroom behaviors.

For these reasons, we strongly believe in teaching behavioral skills in the context of academic instruction. This means teaching students coping skills and learning strategies to deal with the academic requirements of school and giving them an authentic context in which to practice and generalize them. If you can gain behavioral control but only in an environment where all academic demands are removed, you have not taught students anything about handling the stressors and challenges that often go along with learning. Our job as educators is to teach academic and behavioral skills simultaneously because they are so intertwined you cannot separate them. We admit that this can be extremely challenging considering the wide diversity of learning styles and ability levels that exist in a classroom. This chapter focuses on some of the academic instructional practices that we have found most helpful in meeting this challenge.

Differentiated Instruction

Most school districts have a set curriculum that is to be taught to ensure mastery of essential learner outcomes. However, students don't always fit the pace and structure of district curriculum time lines. If our curriculum map tells us to teach a particular concept, and it turns out that one or more students already know it, they will be bored and may act out. And on the flip side, if we are

> We strongly believe in teaching behavioral skills in the context of academic instruction.

Recommended Resources

Books on differentiated instruction by Carol Ann Tomlinson:

Integrating Differentiated Instruction and Understanding by Design, with Jay McTighe (Alexandria, VA: Association for Supervision and Curriculum Development, 2006).

How to Differentiate Instruction in Mixed Ability Classrooms (Alexandria, VA: Association for Supervision and Curriculum Development, 2001).

The Differentiated Classroom: Responding to the Needs of All (Alexandria, VA: Association for Supervision and Curriculum Development, 1999).

Fulfilling the Promise of the Differentiated Classroom: Strategies and Tools for Responsive Teaching (Alexandria, VA: Association for Supervision and Curriculum Development, 2003).

Differentiation in Practice: A Resource Guide for Differentiating Curriculum Grades K–5, with Caroline Cunningham Eidson (Alexandria, VA: Association for Supervision and Curriculum Development, 2002).

introducing a concept and some students have not mastered the prerequisite academic skills, they will be frustrated and may act out. Our responsibility is not only to increase student engagement in learning by using effective instructional strategies but also to meet the individual needs of each student through differentiating instruction. It is important to closely monitor student mastery and plan for reteaching activities for struggling students as well as enrichment learning opportunities for those who have already mastered the skills.

Differentiating instruction is an enormous topic that is outside the scope of this book. We highly recommend any book on this topic by Carol Ann Tomlinson.

Providing Choices

Simply giving choices to students with chronic behavior challenges can reduce problem behavior.[2] This seems like common sense because students will naturally choose things that are reinforcing to them. However, research shows that behavior improves even when both choices

> Simply giving students with chronic behavior challenges choices can reduce problem behavior.

are not or are only moderately preferred[3] or when the assignment is not preferred but the student gets to choose certain aspects of it, such as the sequence of tasks.[4] Human beings instinctively like having multiple choices, and providing choices gives students a sense of some control over their environment, which many times is the function of problem behavior. Choices can be embedded into various aspects of an academic task: the actual task or activity (a classroom can have various centers or reading workshop activities), the order of the task (the student must do spelling, phonics, and handwriting but gets to choose the order), the materials used to complete the task (students can practice spelling words with magnetic letters, typing them on the computer, or writing on the dry erase board), who will help with the task (they can choose to play a math game with a peer or the paraprofessional), the location where the task is completed (they can choose at the table or on the floor), and when the task will be completed within reason (they can choose to complete it immediately or in two minutes).[5]

Embedding Interests and Preferences

Activities and assignments that students find boring are common setting events and/or triggering antecedents to problem behavior. Embedding the interests and preferences of students into academic tasks can help increase motivation by making them more inherently reinforcing.[6] For example, math story problems can be written using actual student names and be written about NASCAR racing, or a student can choose books about dinosaurs to work on reading decoding and fluency skills.

Jodie Says . . .

In a middle school English class I taught, students were required to learn about poetry. When I introduced the unit, I heard groans from all of the students in the class, especially the boys. I had predicted this reaction, so I had planned to teach the different forms of poetry by using music that they listened to. I opened the lesson with a popular song, with the lyrics up on the projector screen. I have never seen a class of middle school students so focused in all my years of teaching. That starting activity hooked them. After teaching all the forms of poetry, their final project was to find a song that exemplified one of the types of poetry, show the lyrics, and explain what elements of the lyrics made it that type. Of course, being middle school, I had to set parameters pertaining to content of the song and language used. The kids were excited about the project, and every student presented the assignment on time.

Writing Strategies

Everywhere we go, we hear stories of students who will pretty much do anything to get out of writing. Avoiding or even escaping from written tasks is an extremely common function of problem behavior.

What makes writing so aversive? Writing involves multiple steps and skills. You have to think about what you want to write, formulate sentences, and then do the motor planning and have the fine motor skills needed to get those sentences down on paper. Writing tends to be overwhelming even for many of us who possess the needed language and executive functioning skills to complete this task, so think about how difficult it must be for those who struggle with these skills. Then think about how many of the assignments given in the classroom are paper-and-pencil tasks that involve at least some, if not a combination, of these skills.

Following are some strategies we commonly use to remove or provide additional support when the setting event or triggering antecedent to behavior problems involves written tasks.

Provide Alternatives to Writing When Possible and Appropriate

We can assess mastery of a concept in numerous ways that do not require students to complete a worksheet or put a pencil to paper, therefore removing a common trigger of problem behavior and increasing engagement in learning. Allowing students to tell you what they know about a topic verbally or through a scribe and creating multiple-choice versus short-answer or essay questions are just a few that come to mind. Be creative, and think about what you are truly trying to assess and if that can be done in another format besides using paper and pencil. Ask your student for ideas (see our discussion in Chapter Five about teaching them negotiating skills). Welcoming their thoughts also has the effect of reducing resistance and behavior problems.

Use Technology

In the rapidly advancing world of technology, computers have become a way of life for students. Social networking and gaming sites on the Internet have them hooked, and it is amazing to watch the ability of even the youngest students to use computers and access the Internet. Harnessing technology and using it to engage student is the logical thing to do.

Some students struggle with spelling. While we would never discontinue spelling instruction, letting students type a writing assignment and use the spell checker is a reasonable alternative. Many adults we know have recognized their weakness in spelling and use this tool all the time.

Having the students communicate about a concept through a teacher-created blog is a way to use get students to discuss academic concepts being focused on in class. Another idea is accessing the iTunes site, which has podcasts on a variety of academic concepts.

Make Paper-and-Pencil Tasks More Reinforcing

When a paper-and-pencil task is what you choose to assess mastery, there are ways to make the task more appealing:

- If a worksheet is used, slip it into a plastic sleeve and allow the student to complete with a wipe-off marker. If a hard copy is needed, make a photocopy before the student wipes off his or her answers.

- If the task is a reading page that requires the student to pick out the main idea and write it on lines below the passage, simply have the student highlight the main idea with a marker or use highlighting tape to determine whether the student grasps the concept.

- For assignments that focus on content objectives and not writing mechanics, such as short-answer questions, have students use "text speak"—the language commonly used to communicate via text message on a cell phone. By allowing them to communicate in a way they do with their friends on a daily basis, you have paired writing with a preferred activity, making it more interesting and reinforcing.

- For short writing activities such as writing spelling words or completing worksheets that involve limited writing, allow students to choose from among a variety of writing utensils.

Provide Structure and Assisted Practice with Longer Writing Tasks

Although we are definite believers in alternatives to paper-and-pencil tasks for assessing students' learning, we also know that if they don't learn to write, their academic careers are going to be long and painful indeed. We have worked with many students whose hatred of writing resulted in them becoming master escape artists of any written academic work. Although we often modified assignments and provided alternatives to writing when appropriate, we also required our students to journal every single day in order to get more practice with the difficult skill of writing. We provided them with a great deal of structure and support during this activity because few could experience success with writing if we had just given them a journal topic or said, "Write in your journal."

Using the following strategies, we have seen many students go from being writing haters to truly enjoying the process or at least tolerating it without any major behavioral meltdowns.

Start Small and Build Success

With extreme writing haters, start by requiring just one sentence and not requiring appropriate spelling or spacing. Once the student experiences success with the one sentence, advance to requiring appropriate spacing, then correct spelling, and then increasing sentence length and number of sentences per entry. The key is setting your expectation just slightly above where the student

> With extreme writing haters, start by requiring just one sentence and not requiring appropriate spelling or spacing.

is currently successful and building slowly from there so the student continues to feel successful and therefore increasingly confident.

Kaye Says . . .

I had a fourth-grade student who moved into our district halfway through the school year. The first day we met, he informed me that he needed level 5 special education services (which were the most intensive services in the state he had moved from) because he was highly distractible, was prone to fits of rage, and that written tasks triggered his anger. The first few days in the program, I didn't ask much of him and allowed him to do a lot of preferred activities while he adjusted to the new educational setting.

About the fourth day, I asked him to write one sentence. He waved me over and whispered, "Remember, I don't write. It triggers my anger." I asked him what he did at his old school, and he responded that sometimes he used the computer, but mostly his written work just "piled up." When I asked him if he passed his classes, he replied, "Oh yes. I can't fail. I'm on an IEP [individual education plan]." Really? He had now met the wrong teacher. I insisted that we would expect him to write at this school and he would not be going home until the one sentence was written, but we would help him and would never ask him to do anything that was too hard. That day he needed to write only one sentence, not worry about spelling or spacing, and I would write every other word.

He responded by throwing an enormous fit, crawling on the floor, making animal noises, and tearing up any paper that was in his reach. Another teacher witnessed his tantrum and asked me if the new student was "crazy." I replied that no, he had just become a master written-work avoider and that acting like that typically got a similar response to hers and teachers had reinforced this behavior for years by removing written tasks.

I waited out his behavior burst and helped him with his one sentence. Every few days I increased the demands slightly, always prepared to wait out a tantrum. Within three months, he was writing beautiful stories with legible handwriting and was fully included in his general education classroom for communication arts.

Talk Through the Idea First

Many students experience chronic writer's block, and although they can talk your ear off, they suddenly have nothing to say when it comes to putting pencil to paper. Simply starting a conversation with them by asking questions such as, "What did you do this weekend?" or "Tell me what you know about dinosaurs" (or some other area of special interest) can help get around this obstacle. After a few sentences, stop them, repeat what they said, and have them write it down on paper. You may have to repeat each sentence several times or say the sentence one word at a time and have them write the word immediately after you have said it. Another strategy is to have them talk into a tape recorder and then play it back and write their words down, rewinding when needed.

Require Sentences to Have More Than Seven Words

Students who hate to write often come up with very short, boring sentences such as, "I like dinosaurs." That's a start, but we have found that requiring more than seven words in a sentence results in the use of more descriptive and complex language such as, "I like green dinosaurs that ate plants." Once students have mastered writing sentences with seven words, you can increase the required number of words per sentence or sentences per journal entry.

Chunk and Check

When working with writing haters, never wait to give feedback until they have finished the entire assignment. Nothing is more discouraging to a student who thought she had completed a task she found excruciating than having to go back and correct it (a good example of a triggering antecedent). Break the assignment into small

> When working with writing haters, never wait to give feedback until they have finished the entire assignment.

parts and check after each part, giving feedback and requiring corrections after each chunk. A good rule of thumb is to shoot for giving feedback about every ten to fifteen minutes, so base the size of each chunk on the work pace and abilities of the individual student.

Handwriting Help

Many times students have great ideas and can get them down on paper, but their handwriting is either atrocious or they waste too much time making sure their handwriting is perfect. Of course, many times students can use a keyboard, but sometimes this is not possible.

A few basic strategies that we have found helpful is to use a "space man," a face on the end of a popsicle stick to put between words to ensure proper spacing. Students can create their own "space man," which makes using it more reinforcing. Lightly making a dot or dash between words that can later be erased is less obvious and more appropriate for older students. Various forms of raised and color-coded paper that helps with spacing and alignment are available (www.specialkidszone.com). You could also have the student say the sentence aloud to an adult or peer buddy before writing and have that person make very light boxes about the size that the words are supposed to be, have the student write the words in the boxes, and then erase the boxes. To keep math problems in proper alignment, often an issue for students with writing challenges, use graph paper.

We have also taught students to self-monitor their handwriting by having them write the three sentences shown in Figure 8.1 on lined paper appropriate for their grade level in the handwriting indicated in each sentence.

Students are not told the purpose of this activity in advance because we find they typically think it is fun and are pretty accurate when creating the examples when they are not aware they will be using it in the future to self-assess their handwriting on various assignments. The example sentences are then glued to the inside of a file folder, labeled on the front with the student's name, and laminated so it lasts the entire school year. Students are taught that best handwriting is reserved for final copies of assignments and is rarely used in this day and age of technology, everyday handwriting is used for most assignments, and sloppy handwriting is not acceptable at all for school work because it often is illegible. When there is a question or disagreement regarding the acceptability of a student's handwriting on a assignment, the student compares it to the example sentences and is highly reinforced for giving an honest assessment about which of the three handwriting categories it falls into.

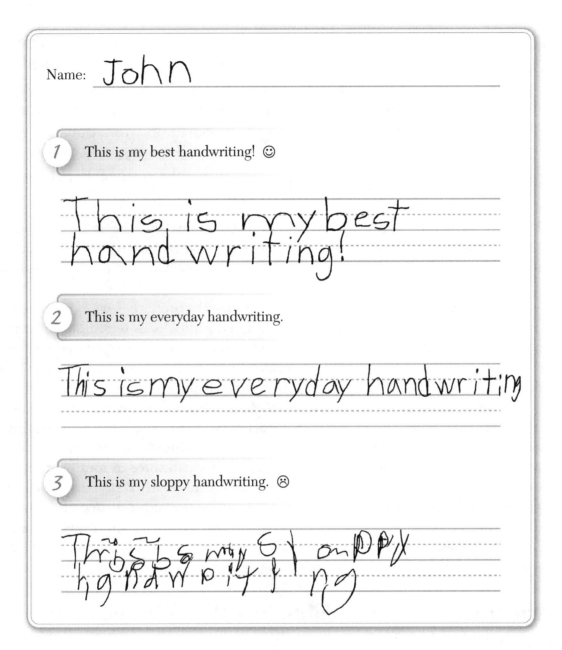

Figure 8.1 Handwriting Samples

Scheduling

Well-thought-out academic instruction has a structure. The consistency and routine of a well-planned daily schedule where students are academically engaged offer little opportunity for downtime, when students are more likely to exhibit problem behaviors. In addition, consistency provides students with the security of knowing what to expect. For these reasons, we are true proponents of having a schedule and sticking to it if possible.

Within the established schedule, it is important for teachers to be prepared and for all staff involved in instruction to have their roles and duties clearly defined. The schedule and plans should be such that if one person is called away from academic instruction to handle a crisis situation, another staff member can step in and continue instruction for students who remain on task. Admittedly, creating a detailed weekly schedule and lesson plans takes considerable time, but

> The consistency and routine of a well-planned daily schedule where students are academically engaged offer little opportunity for downtime, when students are more likely to exhibit problem behaviors.

it is always a good investment because well-thought-out plans help the entire staff work together and prevent behavior problems. It is a classic example of pay now or pay later, that is, put the time in before the week starts than during the week handling problems created by an unorganized schedule.

We are keenly aware that many teachers of students with chronic behavioral challenges teach in self-contained settings with multiple grade and ability levels served by numerous adults (paraprofessionals, speech and occupational therapists, therapists, and others) and are charged with the challenging task of managing all of this potential chaos. When we worked together, all of the students in our school district with severe behavioral challenges were placed in our program regardless of their medical or educational diagnoses or cognitive abilities. We had a true mix: students with severe autism and cognitive impairments, academically gifted students with Asperger's syndrome, and students with oppositional defiant or conduct disorders. In addition, we had three to four grade levels in a single classroom and multiple paraprofessionals to coordinate. We often likened the management of all these individual schedules to being the conductors of an orchestra.

Early-career teachers we have worked with (and sometimes even the most seasoned educators) have often said that they wished someone had provided them with training on creative scheduling in their teacher preparation program. The following sections do just that.

Learn How to Make a Table in a Word Processing Program

When we started working together, we would both draw out charts to try and organize our schedule and erase and recreate it multiple times or when there was a change. At that time, we were not fluent in technology and thought that it was just too complicated to learn. How wrong we were! Table 8.1 gives simple directions for creating a table using Microsoft Word. You will find that this skill will make your life much easier.

Schedule Things That Are Absolutely Inflexible First

In order to maximize inclusionary experiences in the general education environment, our students attended special classes (physical education, music, and art) with their same-age

Table 8.1 Getting Started Creating Tables in Microsoft Word

To create a table	Click Table-Insert-Table-Choose number of rows and columns-OK
To add a row	Click Table-Insert-Rows Above or Below
To add a column	Click Table-Insert-Columns to the Left of Right
To merge cells	Click and drag on cells wish to merge-Click Table-Merge Cells
To shade or color	Click and drag on cells wish to shade or color-Click Format-Borders and Shading-Shading-Choose color-OK

peers in addition to nonacademic social times such as lunch and recess. These were obviously areas scheduled by the school, and since these areas were things we could not control or change, we plugged them in first.

Schedule the Major Core Academic Areas

The core academic areas are reading, writing, and math. Students can't learn much in social studies, science, and other classes if they can't read and write. Nevertheless, many students are pushed through school without ever becoming proficient in these basic skills.

Since full inclusion was the ultimate goal in our program, we tried to match up the core academic areas as much as we could with each student's general education classroom. This made it easier to increase their participation in the general education environment. We always found that when we did not do this, every time a student spent more time in a general education class, our class schedule had to be completely overhauled. This was time-consuming for us and created chaos for all the students.

Use Paraprofessionals Wisely and Appropriately

Because it was impossible for us as lead teachers in the program to teach all grade levels and all subjects within those grade levels, we had paraprofessionals deliver instruction through well-designed, detailed lesson plans. We were ultimately responsible for each student's individual educational plan so we did all the planning, assessment, and evaluation of progress and regularly rotated implementing the lesson plan among the instructional groups. This ensured that all students were directly involved with the teacher and the teacher had the opportunity to observe every student's performance firsthand. Color-coding the classroom schedule (Table 8.2) so each paraprofessional's daily assignments were easily tracked and giving a copy to every adult working in the program ensured that everyone knew what they were responsible for and kept things running smoothly. (Because

Table 8.2 Example Schedule

	Joey (1st Grade)	Jack (2nd Grade)	Anthony (2nd Grade)	Ned (3rd Grade)	Tommy (4th Grade)
8:45–9:00	Pledge/Warm-Up Activity (Inclusion)	Pledge/Warm-Up Activity (Inclusion)	Pledge/Warm-Up Activity (Inclusion)	Pledge/Warm-Up Activity (Inclusion)	Pledge/Warm-Up Activity (Inclusion)
9:00–9:30	Reading/Writing	Spelling (Inclusion)	Spelling (Inclusion)	Math	Math
9:30–10:00	Reading/Writing	Specials (Inclusion)	Specials (Inclusion)	Handwriting/Phonics Drill/Speech	Journal/Spelling
10:00–10:30	Handwriting/Phonics Drill/Speech	Math (Inclusion)	Math	Specials (Inclusion)	Math Drill/Calendar/Occupational Therapy
10:30–11:05	Math	Math (Inclusion)	Math Drill/Calendar	Math Drill/Calendar/Speech	Specials (Inclusion)
11:05–11:35	Lunch	Lunch	Lunch	Reading	Reading
11:25–11:40	Recess	Recess	Recess	Lunch	Handwriting/Phonics Drill/Speech
11:55–12:35	Journal/Spelling	Writing	Writing	Recess	Lunch
12:35–1:05	Unit Studies (Inclusion)	Reading	Reading	Journal/Spelling	Recess
1:05–1:30	Social Skills	Social Skills/Occupational Therapy	Social Skills	Social Skills	Social Skills
1:30–2:00	Math Drill/Calendar	Handwriting/Phonics Drill/Journal/Speech	Handwriting/Phonics Drill/Journal/Speech	Writing	Writing
2:00–2:20	Recess (Inclusion)	Recess	Recess	Recess	Recess
2:20–2:50	Specials (Inclusion)	Unit Studies (Inclusion)	Unit Studies	Unit Studies	Unit Studies
2:50–3:10	Reinforcement Time	Reinforcement Time	Reinforcement Time	Reinforcement Time	Reinforcement Time

Note: blue = Mrs. Tuttle; green = Mrs. Perry; yellow = Mrs. Cook; white = all supervise.

this book is printed in black and white, we have provided a legend showing possible color assignments at the bottom of Table 8.2.)

Make Sure You Get a Planning Time

In order to have adequate time to create these detailed, complex plans you must schedule your own plan time. Schools are full of teachers who do not adequately plan, saying that they have to be with the students all the time or chaos will ensue. Be aware that inadequate plan time will never result in program improvement, and you will eventually burn out. We can attest to the fact that, although not easily done, even teachers of students with the most severe behavior challenges can consistently get their planning time. In order to do this, paraprofessionals must be able to independently supervise students, even if a certified teacher is physically present. This can be done when students are engaged in routine activities requiring skills they have mastered or nearly mastered. Traditional activities that are appropriate for paraeducator supervision include calendar activities, math drills or games, silent reading, reading aloud, special classes, recess, lunch, spelling practice, journal, and any independent practice of academic concepts being taught. We also schedule some time for students to work completely independently. Working completely independently is an important life skill so during this time teachers and/or paraeducators are

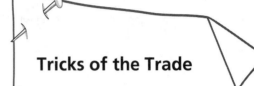

Tricks of the Trade

File folder games are games that can be copied, colored, and pasted in a file folder then laminated. The games are completed using Velcro or a wipe-off marker so that they can be used again and again. File folder games review various basic academic concepts such as matching, sight words, and basic math skills and are a great independent work time option that can provide practice for a variety of already mastered or nearly mastered skills. Free file folder games can be found at filefolderfun.com.

present to officially supervise the students working independently, but these adults are assigned to work with other students and do not assist the independent workers.

Students will need to be directly taught what to do for "learning free time" that still reinforces academic skills if they get stuck and the teacher is not available, and highly reinforced for displaying these skills. Some activities appropriate for learning free time are listed in Table 8.3.

Table 8.3 Options for Students Working Independently During Learning Free Time

Academic games on the computer

Silent reading

Partner reading

Playing a quiet math game with someone who is also finished

Studying spelling words using the dry erase board, chalkboard, stamps, a magnetic drawing board, or magnetic letters

Writing a letter to or making a card for someone

Looking at an atlas or globe

Studying math facts with flash cards

File folder games (see Tricks of the Trade)

Maintaining Academic Engagement

Certainly in our classrooms, we spent time dealing with interfering behaviors. However, we focused just as heavily on the behaviors that are conducive to learning and are often overlooked because they are not disruptive. Students should be reinforced for learning behaviors such as participating in class discussions, completing assignments, and putting forth their best effort.

Failure Is Not an Option

One strategy for maintaining academic engagement, especially at the elementary level, is to remove failure as an option. Many students are content with a low grade as long as they have done the task and can move on to something else. We strongly believe that allowing students to complete academic tasks incorrectly without requiring them to correct it and learn from their

> Many students are content with a low grade as long as they have done the task and can move on to something else.

mistakes simply gives them permission and practice doing things incorrectly and allows them to escape and avoid work, which reinforces their behavior.

We always required that our students correct their work and gave them half-credit rather than none at all. This meant that we had to stay on top of our daily grading, often doing it immediately in order to provide instant feedback and students had to miss free-time activities or stay after school as a logical undesirable consequence (more on that in Chapter Thirteen) in order to correct their work. This practice serves multiple purposes. First, it ensures that the academic tasks that students are given are truly at the appropriate instructional level. If not, it is the teacher who gets "punished" by having to spend the time helping students make lots of corrections. Second, it holds educators accountable for teaching rather than simply providing academic content and letting students slip through grades without mastering it.

Honor Roll

One of the ways that we reinforced learning behavior was by having a special reinforcer weekly for students on the "honor roll." In order to get this recognition, students needed to complete their work on time and with a score of 85 percent or higher the first time. Students received an honor roll sticker on the packet of assignments we sent home on Fridays and had their name posted in a prominent location and announced over the school intercom. Once they experienced a few weeks of academic success, our students and parents really bought into the "failure is not an option" philosophy and honor roll recognition. Many of our students had finely tuned escape and avoidance behaviors and had never completed enough work to experience academic success in previous settings. Students started actually enjoying school and learning, and behavior problems caused by inappropriate academic instruction and low expectations greatly decreased. Success truly does breed success.

Key Points to Remember

- Students are less likely to act out if they are engaged in quality academic instruction.

- Teaching students coping skills and learning strategies to deal with the academic requirements of school and giving them an authentic context in which to practice and generalize them is crucial.

- Meeting the learning needs of all students through differentiated instruction is a preventive strategy that allows all students to be engaged in academic learning at their level.

- Providing choices within an academic task can help a student resistant to learning to engage in the activity.

- Many students with challenging behaviors do not like to write. You can prevent problems during writing tasks by providing alternatives, making writing tasks more reinforcing, and providing structure and assisted practice.

- The consistency and routine of a well-planned daily schedule where students are academically engaged allows little opportunity for downtime when students are more likely to exhibit problem behaviors.

- Maintenance of academic engagement can be achieved through requiring students to correct work and reinforcing successful performance on academic tasks.

Discussion Questions and Activities

1. Think about an assignment you recently assigned your class. Briefly describe it, and list some way you could embed choices into this task.

2. What are some ways technology can be embedded into a writing assignment to make it more engaging for students who have difficulty writing or just don't like to write?

3. List some activities your students could do during learning free time in your classroom.

Part Four

Reinforcing Desired Behavior

Instruction

Prevention

Reinforcement

Chapter 9

Reinforcing Desired Behavior: The Basics

Up to this point, we have focused on instruction and prevention strategies that address the two key concepts of functional behavior assessment that occur before problem behavior: setting events and triggering antecedents. In this part, we turn to the third key concept of functional behavioral assessment: maintaining consequences, or what happens after behavior that serves as the payoff or reinforces it. Reinforcement is something that the individual values or desires; it happens after a behavior and results in an increase or maintenance of the behavior. There is much confusion surrounding reinforcement in the educational setting, and we start out by clearing up this confusion.

Reinforcement Versus Rewards

As educators, when we hear the word *reinforcement*, we typically think of things like token systems, working for edibles, desired activities such as computer time, or other systems that follow Premack's principle of first doing something less desirable to earn the privilege of doing something more desirable. Although these are good examples of simple reinforcement systems, they lead to the misunderstanding that reinforcement equals rewards. We hear

117

many educators say, "I don't believe in rewards. Students shouldn't be rewarded for just doing what is expected." In fact, reinforcement and rewards are not the same thing.

Many years of research in behavior science tell us that behavior, including problem behavior, does not increase or stay steady unless something is reinforcing it.[1] A complete understanding of reinforcement, which is required to master its use in managing student behavior, rests on two

> In fact, reinforcement and rewards are not the same thing.

basics: (1) there is no such thing as a universal reinforcer because individuals are reinforced by different things at different times and what may be desirable to some may not be desirable to all and (2) whether something is a reinforcer is determined by its effect on behavior, and not the intent of the educator.

Teachers often unintentionally reinforce students. Table 9.1 provides two examples that illustrate this concept.

Focus on Common Unintentional Reinforcers: Attention and Escape

Many things that educators do daily to attempt to discourage problem behavior from happening actually reinforce the problem behavior and have the opposite effect. We will say this many times in slightly different ways in different chapters. Recall that in Chapter Two, we identified the two most common reinforcers of behavior as attention and escape. So if problem behavior is continuing in your classroom, consider whether

> Many things that educators do daily to attempt to discourage problem behavior from happening actually reinforces the problem behavior and has the opposite effect.

you are inadvertently reinforcing it by giving the student attention or a reaction or allowing

Table 9.1 What's the Reinforcer?

Example 1	Every day that Justin finishes his math assignment on time, Ms. Sittner allows him to play a math game with a friend. If Justin enjoys playing the math game with a friend, he is likely to continue finishing his math assignment on time. What's the reinforcer? Did Ms. Sittner intend for it to be reinforcing?
Example 2	Mr. Brandon sends Scott to the principal's office because of repeatedly talking disrespectfully in class. The principal is not available, so Scott sits in the office area and watches other students walk by in the hall and talks to the secretary in addition to avoiding his work. The next day in his class, Scott talks disrespectfully again. What's the reinforcer? Did Mr. Brandon intend for it to be reinforcing?

him or her to escape an aversive situation or task. Changing behavior to respond to these situations more effectively is the first step to successful behavior management and the first tier of matching reinforcement to the function of the behavior.

Reinforcement Versus Bribery

Another common protest we often hear from educators is, "I don't believe in bribing kids to behave." We definitely agree. However, it is possible to reinforce students without bribing them. The key is to be preventive and proactive rather than reactive. If you set up a system where students get something desirable after they exhibit appropriate behavior, you are providing reinforcement. If you wait until the student is misbehaving and then tell her she can get something desirable by stopping the inappropriate behavior, you are bribing her, and this is a dangerous practice indeed.

We have known students who have figured out that educators and parents need them to behave in a certain way in school in order for the learning environment to remain safe and productive. Therefore, they are constantly negotiating deals: "What will you give me to behave?" This is extortion, plain and simple, and it gives students with chronic behavior problems a great deal of power and control over others—the possible function of the inappropriate (and in the future illegal) behavior. Again, be proactive and intervene early. Don't wait until students act out before engaging in behavior management, or you are asking for trouble.

> Don't wait until students act out before engaging in behavior management, or you are asking for trouble.

Many educators will adamantly insist that students should not be rewarded for doing what is expected of them. At the primary level of positive behavior supports when intervening with the typical student population (those without serious behavior problems), we tend to agree with that to a certain extent. However, unless you are the meanest teacher in the world, in your classroom you are probably giving things away for "free" that students commonly desire, and you could structure them to make them contingent on demonstrating appropriate behavior. For example, having free time, sitting where they choose, playing educational games, recess, and access to technology are all things that most students typically find reinforcing and exist in most classrooms as a part of daily routines. It is important to remember that we are trying to teach students the behavior and social skills they will need to be successful later in life and that we all work for something and are reinforced daily by a variety of things.

> We are trying to teach students the behavior and social skills they will need to be successful later in life and that we all work for something and are reinforced daily by a variety of things.

We adults do things that we don't always want to do or that are difficult for us. Sometimes we do these things simply because they are the right thing to do or they are good for us, but not always. We do many things solely for the paycheck or for the paycheck in combination with altruistic, internal reinforcement. We may do things for less monetary gain if we get more free time or flextime or gain attention or prestige. We also often do things for those we have positive relationships with that we wouldn't do for others.

Remember that students are little adults, and the positive reinforcement systems that we create for them should mirror real life. Setting up reinforcement systems that mirror adult systems ensures that we are truly teaching students skills that will help them be successful in the adult world.

How to Determine What Is Reinforcing for Students

Reinforcement is very student specific. What is reinforcing to one individual may not be to another. Individual students often are reinforced by very unique and unusual things according to their interests and strengths. For example, we once had a student who loved to take apart vacuum cleaners as a reinforcer and another who found looking up the Latin names for various plants reinforcing. There are many ways to determine what is reinforcing for individual students or groups of students. Next we will discuss several of our favorites, including interviews and surveys, observations, and reinforcement journals.

Interviews and Surveys

How do you determine what is reinforcing to students? The first place to start is to ask them. You can do this in an interview or conversational format or in a more formalized manner through reinforcement surveys.[2] Often students don't know what they are reinforced by or have never really thought about self-reinforcement, and it helps them to see what other students have tried. Reinforcement surveys provide this, in addition to suggesting many creative options that students and educators may have never thought of. Various sources offer premade reinforcement surveys. One of our favorites is Intervention Central's On-line Reinforcer Survey Generator (www.jimwrightonline.com/php/jackpot/jackpot.php). Along with many other valuable and free tools for educators, this Web site has a link for customizing a reinforcement survey for individual students categorized by common functions of problem behavior (adult attention, peer attention, escape, tangible items) and include both academic and nonacademic items.

Don't overlook the power of asking parents for reinforcer ideas by also interviewing them or having them complete surveys. Parents know their children well and often come up with ideas that educators would never have the opportunity to observe or think of asking students about.

Observations

Another way to determine what is reinforcing to students is simply to observe what activities they choose when they have free access to do whatever they want or what they do a lot of in general both at school and at home.

Reinforcement Journals

We tell our students to always be thinking of new things that they would like to work for and add them to their reinforcement journals wth teacher approval. This can take the form of a simple spiral notebook that individual students use to brainstorm possible reinforcers in and add to on an ongoing basis.

Kaye Says . . .

I used the reinforcement journal technique for a student who was constantly making multiple deals with different adults throughout his elementary school. The minute he entered the building in the morning, he would start asking, "If I have a good day today, will you give me [a can of pop, a piece of candy, or something else]?" And he would regularly hit up the attendance secretary, the health aide, the custodian, and others for these. He was a charming student, and the well-meaning adults he targeted, who wanted to help, often enthusiastically agreed to his deals, having no clue what he was actually doing. When his multiple daily deal makings were discovered, we remedied this practice by having the adults respond that of course they wanted to help him have a good day and that he should add whatever it was he wanted to his reinforcement journal and talk to his teacher about what he wanted to choose to work on for that day.

Reinforcement Menus

Reinforcement interviews, surveys, observations, and reinforcement journals can help create individualized reinforcement menus that give students variety and help the intended reinforcers maintain their effectiveness. Teachers have a tendency to choose one or two reinforcers and have the students work for them every time. The problem with this is that students tend to start to satiate on reinforcers if they experience them too often, making them less effective. If they get the same thing all the time, they will tire of it.

Reinforcement menus are effective tools for many reasons. Through their use, students have some ownership of the reinforcers. Through surveys or interviews, you have already given them some voice about what items will be on the menu. By allowing them to choose an item from the menu when they earn the reinforcer, you have added another aspect of choice (which we discussed as a preventative strategy in Chapter Eight), and the student can choose what is reinforcing to him or her at a particular moment.

Another reason menus are powerful is that they teach students the self-management skill of self-reinforcement. If we can teach students to self-reinforce effectively, no longer will delivery of reinforcement rely on an outside party because students will have the tools they need to motivate themselves. Our goal is to make them independent.

Reinforcement menus can be individually designed according to the strengths and interests as well as academic and social needs of each particular student.

Jodie Says...

When I have a report to write or had chapters in this book to complete, I set aside time to do this work and decided how much I needed to get done in the time frame. I find that I am much more productive if I choose something I like to do when I get done, like watching a favorite television program or calling a friend. Successful adults self-reinforce in similar ways all the time.

Jodie Says...

One of the sixth-grade students I recently worked with was very athletic. His menu included helping the physical education teacher and basketball time with a friend on the playground. He also enjoyed helping younger children, so reading to younger students during their free-read time was also a reinforcement menu option. This not only tapped into an interest of his, but also provided practice on the academic skill of reading. In addition, his volunteering improved his reputation with teachers at school because he was often somewhat abrasive and disrespectful.

Seeing him help younger students allowed his peers and school staff to observe a softer side of him and changed some perceptions and beliefs about him. This young man not surprisingly loved video games, as most other boys his age do, and had a social skills deficit in the area of making friends and getting attention properly. One of the reinforcers on his menu was time on the computer playing games with a friend of his choosing. Once he earned the reinforcer, we worked with him on how to invite a friend and were able to watch him interact in a social situation with a peer.

> This reinforcer gave him friendship-making skills and us the opportunity to focus our individual social skills instruction on the interaction skills he needed to work on.

A list of some of our favorite individual, group, and home reinforcers and some suggestions for simple tracking systems are provided in Table 9.2.

Reinforcement Schedules: Determining How Much and How Often

One of the keys of developing a successful reinforcement system is determining what level of reinforcement to provide and how frequently to provide it. This is often referred to as the *schedule of reinforcement* and is a dynamic process that is always being adjusted based on the needs of individual students. As a general rule, if the skill is difficult, reinforcement needs to be more frequent, more predictable, and at a higher level. As the skill gets easier, reinforcement can be slowly faded, becoming less frequent, less predictable, and at a lower level. Many factors bear on skill difficulty: (1) the novelty of the skill, (2) the environment in which it is being performed, (3) what other supports are in place, (4) how long the inappropriate behavior was in place, and (5) opportunities for practice. A visual of the concept of schedules of reinforcement and factors involved with skill difficulty is provided in Table 9.3.

Kaye Says...

When I do presentations on behavior management for educators, I often ask how many of them would hypothetically like to go for a mile run during their lunch break; usually one or two people at most raise their hand. Obviously, running a mile is not a preferred activity for a majority of adults. I then successively offer increased rates of reinforcement and support by offering them $100, $1,000, the choice of walking if they wanted, taking the rest of the afternoon to finish, and so on. More and more people start raising their hand as I add new items. Eventually I am able to offer some combination of reinforcement and support to get every person to agree to participate.

Table 9.2 Reinforcement Menu Favorites

Quick: Takes less than thirty seconds	Telling the class a joke
	Sharing a high-five with a peer or adult who is present
	A pat on the back from a peer or adult who is present
	A round of applause from the class
	A sticker to put on his or her shirt or special book (students usually really like scratch-and-sniff stickers)
	Stamp on hand or in a special book
	A ''brag walk'': the student shows or tells a chosen adult how well he or she is doing
Small and quick: Good for the middle or end of the day and takes less than fifteen minutes	Extra recess time
	Playing a game with a chosen peer or adult
	Eating lunch with a chosen peer or adult in a special location
	Making a positive phone call, e-mail, or note to a parent or adult relative or friend
	Line leader
	Class behavior monitor (see Chapter Ten)
	A visit to the computer lab or media center
	Talk or read over the school loudspeaker
	Read to younger students
	Helper for the teacher or other adult at school (the physical education teacher or the principal, for example)
	Free or half-off assignment (to use immediately or as a coupon for the future)
	An extra reinforcer for the entire class (see classwide reinforcers later in this table)
	Sit in a preferred place to work (beanbag chair, teacher's desk, near a friend)
	Draw on dry erase, chalk, or SMART Board
	Special snack

Table 9.2 (*continued*)

Larger and longer: Good for the end of the week or for the long term	Lunch with or school visit by parent or adult relative or friend
	Choice of something from a treasure box of small items (pencils, pens, bookmarks, and small toys, for example)
	An inexpensive gift certificate donated by a community partner (such as a restaurant or movie theater)
	Bring a preferred activity from home (magazine, listen to headphones/iPod) to use for one day during free time
Smaller Classwide: Good for the end of the day	Extra recess or free time
	Choice of seating arrangement for the next day
	Special snack
	Classwide game
	Pair or small group game time (Uno, Mad Libs, board games)
	Extra teacher read-aloud time
	Extra time in the computer lab or media center
Classwide and larger: Good for the end of the week or working for the long term	Class party (piñata, movie, ice cream sundaes, academic theme tied to social studies)
	Wear costumes, silly outfits, or hats to school the next day
	Special guest speaker or visitors (the students could vote on this person)
	Class pet
At home and smaller: Good for the end of the day	Choice of what to have for the evening meal or a restaurant to go to
	Ice cream outing
	Play game or other special activity with chosen adult or entire family
	Choose television program or movie to watch
	Bedtime ten minutes later than usual
	Special snack
At home and larger: Good for the end of the week or working for long term	Special weekend outing with a chosen adult or the entire family
	Progress toward buying something special

(*continued*)

Table 9.2 (*continued*)

Simple tracking systems	Stars or tokens: Earn so many, and get a reinforcer.
	Dot-to-dot: Earn connections toward a reinforcer.
	Paperclip chains: Reach a certain length, and earn a reinforcer.
	Spell it out: Earn letters to spell the reinforcer.
	Puzzle pieces: Cut a picture of the reinforcer into a puzzle and earn a piece at a time.

Table 9.3 Schedules of Reinforcement

New skill	Familiar skill
New environment	Familiar environment
Low level of support	High level of support
Not in place very long	In place a long time
Few practice opportunities or haven't practiced for a while	Lots of practice opportunities

More frequent / More predictable / Higher levels ⟷ Less frequent / Less predictable / Lower levels

An analogy to illustrate the importance of an appropriate reinforcement schedule goes back to a previous example of adults who are learning a new language. A beginning French speaker may be fairly successful in a low-stress environment with lots of support, such as at home speaking to a familiar individual with the reference book handy. This same individual may find that he or she cannot remember a word of French when in Paris at a busy intersection in an emergency situation and speaking to a native. Learning certain behavior skills is a similarly daunting task for many students, and just because they seemingly mastered a skill one day in a specific situation does not mean that they can do so fluently in all environments and situations. Reinforcement and support may need to increase at any time depending on a variety of variables.

Differential Reinforcement of Zero Rates of Behavior

Educators typically like to operate on a schedule of differential reinforcement of zero rates of behavior (DRO). That is, we reinforce students when they do not exhibit the problem behavior at all during a set period of time. The common problem with this is that it often sets students up for failure because not exhibiting the behavior at all is too difficult for them. Think of a student who talks constantly due to poor impulse control. To expect her to go from high rates of talking out to nothing in order to receive reinforcement is unrealistic. Another schedule of reinforcement may be more effective.

Differential Reinforcement of Lower Rates of Behavior

In a differential reinforcement of lower rates of behavior (DRL) schedule of reinforcement, the student is reinforced for exhibiting progressively lower rates of the undesired behavior. A good example from our experience was a student who exhibited a great deal of aggression. We used a DRL for both frequency of aggressive episodes and the amount of time it took him to calm himself once agitated. At the end of each episode, we graphed the time it took him to calm down, and he received high rates of praise and progress toward a special reinforcer if he calmed down more quickly than the previous episode, even if it was just by a minute. At the end of the day, we graphed the number of aggressive episodes he had that day; he immediately received high rates of praise and progress toward a special reinforcer if he had fewer episodes than the day before.

> In a differential reinforcement of lower rates of behavior schedule of reinforcement, the student is reinforced for exhibiting progressively lower rates of the undesired behavior.

It seemed very odd to those witnessing the aggression that the first response after the aggressive episode was praise and tangible positive reinforcement, and we were often told, "You just rewarded him for being aggressive." Our response was, "No. He was reinforced for exhibiting less aggression than yesterday." Over time this approach was highly successful. We had him in our program for four years, and he went from being a highly aggressive second grader who could not recognize letters or numbers (academic tasks of any kind were common triggering antecedents) to exhibiting one act of aggression in all of fifth grade. Moreover, he passed all district and state assessments and was included in the general education classroom for a majority of his day.

DRL can be a powerful tool over time. As Plato wrote, "Never discourage anyone . . . who continually makes progress, no matter how slow." If you have a student who is seemingly stuck, and you are out of options, consider using a DRL schedule of reinforcement, meeting him where he is and highly reinforcing slight improvements in his behavior performance. It may feel unnatural at first and you may feel as if you are rewarding his misbehavior, but this often can be a highly effective intervention if you stick with it.

Differential Reinforcement of Incompatible Behavior

In a differential reinforcement of incompatible behavior (DRI) schedule, students are reinforced for behavior that is incompatible with the undesired behavior; that is, they cannot do both at the same time. This is particularly appropriate for extinguishing extreme attention-seeking behaviors that you do not want to acknowledge at all in order to avoid providing any reinforcement inadvertently through attention. The key to DRI is making sure that the inappropriate behavior is completely ignored by everyone in the environment and that the incompatible behavior is frequently reinforced at a very high level. This includes teaching peers to ignore and highly reinforce them for doing so (see Chapter Four). Very subtle facial expressions and body language can be interpreted as attention by many students with chronic behavior problems, making the task of complete ignoring very difficult. It is something that must be taught and practiced.

> In a differential reinforcement of incompatible behavior schedule, students are reinforced for behavior that is incompatible with the undesired behavior; that is, they cannot do both at the same time.

Jodie Says . . .

A good example of the successful use of DRI is a student I had who picked his nose for peer attention. I taught his peers and others in the environment to completely ignore him when he was engaged in this less-than-appealing activity and highly reinforced him for having his hands at his sides or in his lap because he could not have his hands in his lap or sides and in his nose at the same time. Eventually this behavior died out because he was given no attention for engaging in the behavior and high levels of reinforcement for incompatible behavior.

Other Issues Surrounding Reinforcement

A few topics are particularly important for the design of a reinforcement system. These include setting appropriate criteria, pairing educators and schools with reinforcers, deprivation, and teaching peers to reinforce appropriately.

Setting Appropriate Criteria

Differential reinforcement of lower rates of behavior leads us directly into a discussion about setting appropriate goals or criteria for earning reinforcement. Often criteria for earning reinforcement for students with chronic behavior problems are set at unrealistic levels, and the students we are targeting don't buy into the system because they never experience success. We can't tell you how many times we have had educators describe an excellent reinforcement system and when asked when the last time the student earned a reinforcer, they respond, "They've never earned it." and wonder why the system is not working. Another common mistake with setting success criteria is that educators inadvertently set it at a higher level than they expect typical students to perform. Overall, students demonstrate general positive classroom behaviors such as staying on task and raising their hand before talking out about 80 to 85 percent of the time. It is unreasonable to expect students with disabilities to achieve at a higher level than their nondisabled peers. Many times, educators or parents try to change a behavior in students with chronic behavior problems that actually is at a similar level to their peers. Consider taking some peer comparative data if you think this may be the case. Reproducible 5 is a peer comparison data sheet provided for this purpose.

Pairing Educators and School with Reinforcers

Often students with challenging behavior come to view their schools and educators as aversive because they have been paired with the punishing effects of various variables that exist in the school environment. It is important to combat this view by pairing ourselves with variables that have reinforcing effects. Giving students lot of positive attention and engaging in reinforcing activities with students will help with this.

Kaye Says . . .

I worked with a preschool student who absolutely hated school. He came in every day and tried to do anything possible to avoid teachers or anything they directed him to do. I suggested that they let him do only highly preferred activities for awhile and join him in his play. Several teachers questioned this, saying, "Well, he's going to have to learn to follow teacher directions." My response was, "He's *three*. We have plenty of time for that. First, it needs to be established that school, learning, and teachers can be fun."

Deprivation

If something is to have a reinforcing effect, students need to be denied access to it except during the scheduled reinforcement time or they will satiate on it and it will lose its effectiveness. For example, a student who is working for a specific food treat or computer time as a reinforcer should be denied that treat or computer access until reinforcement time. The use of reinforcement menus will help with this common problem because the student can simply choose something else on the list that still has reinforcing value.

Teaching Peers to Reinforce Appropriately

Although you as the adult may be able to change your behavior to minimize the reinforcing effects of attention, it is important that you also train peers to minimize the attention they give to problem behavior and maximize the attention they give to replacement behavior. Research calls this "entrapment," or recruiting natural communities of reinforcement,[3] and shows that when the peer group participates in the reinforcement, the effects are more powerful.[4] We have successfully taught peer groups to ignore even the most disruptive behavior and have personally seen the powerful reinforcing qualities of peer attention and acceptance. We have witnessed a student screaming obscenities and all the other students diligently working as if nothing was happening, and the next day, that same student is invited to play with the same peers during free time after he had made better choices.

Key Points to Remember

- Reinforcement is not the same as reward. If behavior is increasing or remaining steady, it is being reinforced (commonly by getting attention or escaping an undesired task), even if it has not been the educator's intent to reward it.

- The incidence of a behavior does not increase or remain steady unless something is reinforcing it.

- Many things that educators do on a daily basis to discourage problem behavior from happening actually reinforce the problem behavior and have the opposite effect.

- Even as adults, we behave in certain ways to obtain reinforcement. Setting up reinforcement systems that mirror adult systems ensures that we are teaching students skills that will help them be successful in the adult world.

- We can find out what is reinforcing to a student through reinforcement surveys, observation, interviews, and reinforcement journals.

- Reinforcement menus are powerful because they use student input, allow choices, prevent satiation, promote self-reinforcement, and can be designed to address a student's individual strengths and interests.

- One of the keys to developing a successful reinforcement system is determining what level of reinforcement to provide and how frequently to provide it.

- Criteria for reinforcement need to be set at realistic levels that take into consideration the level of the behavior the student is currently performing and the level of the same behavior of his or her peers.

- Teachers can build positive relationships with students by pairing themselves with reinforcement.

- If something is to have a reinforcing effect, students need to be denied access to it except during the scheduled reinforcement time or they will become satiated with it and it will lose its effectiveness.

- Peer attention can be a powerful reinforcer. Train peers to minimize the attention they give to problem behavior and maximize the attention they give to appropriate behavior.

Discussion Questions and Activities

1. John is a sixth-grade student who struggles at school. He does not like to read and resists assignments. John was aggressive around two times a month at the beginning of the year. It is now January, and he is aggressive around seven times a month. Typically the school relies on the district code of conduct to determine consequences. The consequence for aggression is typically out-of-school suspension. Why is John's aggressive behavior increasing? What could be a reinforcement plan for decreasing John's aggressive behavior?

2. This chapter described DRO, DRL, and DRI rates of reinforcement. Identify which schedule of reinforcement is being used in the following scenarios:

   a. Sun refuses to work. She typically engages in refusal about seven times a day. The teacher designs a reinforcement plan that says Sun can earn fifteen minutes on the computer if she refuses to work three or fewer times a day.

   b. Jared uses profane language on average nine times a day. His teacher designs a schedule of reinforcement where he can earn free time at the end of the day if he uses appropriate language all day (no swear words).

   c. Mehmet puts his hands on others in group circle time. He engages in this behavior on average eighteen times a day. The teacher has taught him to sit "like a pretzel" with his hands in his lap in group time; he also has a visual prompt of sitting properly taped on the floor in front of his space on the floor. Mehmet earns a token each time he sits properly in group time. When he earns five tokens, he gets to play a game with a friend.

3. Teaching peers to reinforce appropriate behavior is a powerful behavior management tool. Describe a plan where students ignore Eduardo, who frequently makes noises in class. How could you teach students to ignore this behavior? How would you reinforce peers for ignoring? How would you reinforce Eduardo for remaining quiet in class?

Chapter 10

Group Reinforcement Systems

School and classwide reinforcement systems often take the form of group-oriented contingencies: an entire class is reinforced based on the behavior of one student, a number of students, or the entire class.[1] There are three types of group-oriented contingencies: independent, dependent, and interdependent.[2] Interdependent and independent group-oriented contingencies are discussed in this chapter and dependent group-oriented contingencies in the next chapter on individual reinforcement systems.

Interdependent Group-Oriented Contingencies

In interdependent group-oriented contingences, the reinforcement of the group is based on the behavior of the group as a whole. The positive aspect of this is that peer pressure, which occurs naturally in the classroom, is used to encourage positive behavior. However, it can be negative if peers continually blame one student for not earning the reinforcement or a saboteur emerges who intentionally tries to keep the group from earning the reinforcement.

We have found that using interdependent group-oriented contingencies is usually highly effective and mirrors structures that exist in many corporations, businesses, and other organizations, so using them will help develop life skills that will serve students well in their adult life. Students learn to work together, monitor each other, and productively handle conflicts and problems to the benefit of the group.

> We have found that using interdependent group-oriented contingencies is usually highly effective and mirrors structures that exist in many corporations, businesses, and other organizations.

Student Teams

Dividing a class into teams is a common and simple way of forming an interdependent group-oriented contingency. Teams are given names often based on academic content being covered (colors, shapes, continents, Native American tribes, and so on). The number of teams can vary, and the name variations are unlimited. Points are awarded to teams based on various positive behaviors exhibited—for example, the first team to line up, the first team showing the teacher they are ready for math, the first team where everyone is demonstrating appropriate listening skills. Then either the teams can work to simply "win" or the winning team can earn various reinforcers. The options are truly endless for creative educators.

Kaye Says . . .

I am a big fan of Jeanne Gibbs's "tribes" concept described in her book *TRIBES: A New Way of Learning and Being Together,* and the team interdependent group-oriented contingency approach to classwide behavior management could easily be incorporated into this system. It is important to note that describing the tribes concept is way beyond the scope of this book and we highly recommend exploring it in more depth if you are interested in developing supportive peer teams in your classroom for purposes beyond behavior management. *TRIBES* was chosen by the Collaborative for Academic, Social, and Emotional Learning as one of twenty-two select evidence-based social and emotional learning programs, which is their highest possible rating.[3]

Interdependent Group-Oriented Contingency Games

A classic example of an interdependent group-oriented contingency is the good behavior game. We have seen various variations of this idea in the research literature and used in classrooms. Procedures for setting up a group-oriented contingency good behavior game are outlined in Table 10.1, and various examples follow.

Recommended Resource

TRIBES: A New Way of Learning and Being Together, by Jeanne Gibbs (Windsor, CA: CenterSource Systems, 2001).

Table 10.1 Steps to Creating a Group-Oriented Contingency Game

Step 1: Directly teach the target behaviors and game procedures.	Choose two to three target behaviors that are the most problematic. Students are directly and systematically taught alternative desired behaviors that are defined in positive terms. (See Table 3.1 for lesson plan template.)
Step 2: Set the goals or criteria for success.	The goals or criteria for success are set for either teams or the entire class. They should be easily attainable when beginning the game to encourage student buy-in and increased in difficulty over time.
Step 3: Determine the interval to be used and how it will be cued.	Intervals can be set or random. Cuing tones such as beeps or vibrations can be used (see ordering information in Table 7.1) or teachers may cue based on whenever they think about it. If the second choice is used, the teacher needs to remain vigilant about doing this frequently enough for the game to be effective.
Step 4: Assign monitoring responsibilities.	The monitor has the responsibility of determining whether students are successfully exhibiting a desired behavior when cued. The teacher can serve as the monitor, or a student or multiple student monitors can be so designated.
Step 5: Create a group reinforcement menu.	Involve students in brainstorming a group reinforcement menu. (See Table 9.2 for group reinforcement ideas.)
Step 6: Determine fines for procedural violations.	Brainstorm possible problems or conflicts, such as arguing with monitors, and determine if points will be lost for these problems.
Step 7: Determine how the game will be "won."	If the entire class is working together, they "win" when a certain point criterion is reached. If teams are playing against each other, "winners" can be determined when certain point criteria are reached or the game can end after a certain time period and whoever is ahead "wins."

The Good Behavior Game

The original good behavior game divided a class into teams and gave them tally marks on a chalkboard whenever a member of the team broke one of the rules.[4] Any team with fewer than five marks won reinforcers at the end of the day. Although the basic idea has been shown to be effective, many recommend (and we agree) modifying the game procedure so that students are recognized for positive rather than problem behaviors. Maag described a positive version of the game with the teacher posting both appropriate and inappropriate classroom behaviors and a random beep tone cuing the teacher to monitor the class. If only positive behaviors are being exhibited at the time of the beep, the class is given three marbles in a jar. If any students are engaging in negative behaviors at the time of the beep, one marble is taken out of the jar. Reinforcers are earned at the end of the school day, and there is a predetermined number of marbles set for earning various reinforcers from a group menu.[5]

The Red/Green Game

In the red/green game, the teacher makes a large card that is green on one side and red on the other.[6] When the cue is given, the teacher monitors the class to determine if they are exhibiting appropriate behaviors. If they are, they get a green point, and if they are not, they get a red point. At the end of the designated time, if the class has more green points than red points, they earn a group reinforcer.

We recommend using this system if the class has free time at the end of the designated period. Green points minus red points could equal the number of minutes of free time they earn. This uses the common and logical reinforcer of free time and is similar to what may happen to adults in a similar situation (they have to work longer if they waste time during the day, and they get more free time if they stay on task).

The Classwide Peer-Assisted Self-Management (CWPASM) Program

Most interventions used to modify student behavior are traditionally teacher designed and implemented. In peer-mediated interventions, the teacher designs an intervention but trains students to deliver needed social cues and reinforcement to each other. Many peer-mediated interventions use self-monitoring interventions to help students reach the ultimate goal of self-management. Such is the case with the classwide peer-assisted self-management program (CWPASM). In this program, the teacher trains all students in a self and peer monitoring intervention.

Students are asked to choose three students in the class with whom they would like to be partnered, and the teacher assigns pairs based on these preferences. Each partnership is then assigned to one of two teams at the beginning of each day. Each student evaluates and marks both his or her own behavior and partner's behavior on a point card at the end of every marking period. Students earn points for appropriate behavior as well as a bonus point for having matching marks with their partner. Each pair earns points for their team, with daily team winners being announced at the end of each day.[7] An example of a CWPASM program card is shown in Figure 10.1.

> In peer-mediated interventions, the teacher designs an intervention but trains students to deliver needed social cues and reinforcement to each other.

Independent Group-Oriented Contingencies

In an independent group-oriented contingency, each student is responsible only for his or her own behavior and is reinforced for positive choices. No student is penalized for the behavior of anyone else. The only thing that makes this group oriented is that everyone

Student name: Jason									Partner name: Scott	
Date: 12/11/04									Team: Blue	
	Follow directions		In seat		On task		Courteous		Partner match (bonus points)	
	Me	Partner	Me	Partner	Me	Partner	Me	Partner		
Period 1										
Period 2										
Period 3										
Period 4										
Period 5										
Period 6										
Period 7										
Period 8										
My column totals		+		+		+		+		
								My total		

Figure 10.1 Classwide Peer-Assisted Self-Management Program Monitoring Card

How to Reach and Teach Children with Challenging Behavior

participating has access to the reinforcers on the same terms. The teacher could choose to have all of the students in the class participate or just the students who need assistance with improving their behavior.

Lottery Systems

Lottery systems are sometimes referred to as "catch them being good" and are easy to develop and manage. Students are given lottery tickets when they are randomly "caught" exhibiting positive behaviors. They write their name on the ticket, and turn it in to be part of a lottery drawing for various reinforcers at the end of the day or week. Adults and peers can do the "catching," but adults make the final decision on whether the ticket is given.

Lottery systems can also be used for teachers who are "caught" by their peers or administrators using positive behavior supports in their classrooms with teacher reinforcement lotteries including such benefits as longer lunches, special parking spaces for a designated period of time, and gift certificates to local merchants, who are usually enthusiastic about supporting public education in their communities and benefit from the positive publicity.

Token Economies

Token economies are popular independent group-oriented contingencies that mirror our real-life system of money, exchanging tokens that in and of themselves are valueless for individualized reinforcers. Token economies can be set up as a reinforcement system for groups of students or individual students. (We discuss examples of token economies for individual students in the next chapter.)

The most popular form of token economies for groups of students are tickets, or "classroom cash," that students exchange on a regular basis to buy things from a classroom "store" or reinforcement menu, with each menu item being assigned a certain value. There are limitless ways that teachers can set up token economies. Sticking with our philosophy of mirroring real life, we highly recommend creating an economic simulation system because it provides multiple opportunities to embed life lessons in financial management, math, and citizenship.[8] In an economic simulation, pretend currency and a mini-economy are created in the classroom that can range from simple to complex. Just like adults, students receive a paycheck for exhibiting positive, responsible behavior, which they can use to make purchases from a class "store." There are a variety of creative ways to teach economic lessons in addition to managing behavior through this type of token economy—for example:

- Establishing "savings accounts" and "checking accounts" for students

- Establishing "credit cards" for students that charge interest

- Charging students "rent" for desks and charging for supplies

- Having students "purchase" privileges typically given away for free

- Paying extra for special projects, extra effort, or extra-credit assignments

- Establishing charitable foundations to which students can contribute

- Assigning students classroom jobs for which they are paid

The Importance of Tier 1 Reinforcement

Building positive behavior support from the ground up with all students not only benefits everyone but also provides more powerful upper tiers of intervention. In addition, providing group reinforcement systems decreases the feeling educators often express that "it wouldn't be fair to my other students. Why do only the troublemakers get rewarded?" and the probability of hearing the common, "Why do they get that, and I don't?" from other students when students with challenging behavior are put on individual reinforcement systems. If all students feel that their positive choices are recognized, appreciated, and encouraged, they will not feel cheated when students who truly need extra support get it.

> Providing group reinforcement systems decreases the feeling educators often express that "it wouldn't be fair to my other students. Why do only the troublemakers get rewarded?"

We have found throughout years of experience in both general and special education that providing reinforcement systems as motivation for all students greatly reduces the feeling that some students are getting an unfair advantage and results in improved student behavior overall. And that leaves time and energy resources to be devoted to the tougher cases.

Key Points to Remember

- There are three types of group-oriented contingencies: independent, dependent, and interdependent.

- In interdependent group-oriented contingencies, students learn to work together, monitor each other, and productively handle conflicts and problems to the benefit of the group. Examples of this contingency are the good student game, the red/green game, and the classwide peer-assisted self-management program.

- Lottery systems and token economies are types of independent group-oriented contingencies where each student is responsible only for his or her own behavior and everyone earns reinforcement on the same terms.

- Token economies can be set up as an economic simulation system, providing multiple opportunities to embed life lessons in financial management, math, and citizenship.

- Building reinforcement systems from the ground up with all students not only benefits everyone but also provides more powerful upper tiers of intervention and helps decrease the feelings that only students with chronic behavior get reinforced for making positive behavior choices.

Discussion Questions and Activities

1. Compare and contrast the three interdependent group-oriented contingency games: the good student game, the red/green game, and the classwide peer-assisted self-management program. What do you like about each of the games? Is there anything you do not like about them?

2. Let's say you are setting up a token economy in your classroom. Create a list of desired behaviors you would like to reinforce with tokens. Do you consider any of the behaviors you listed more valuable than others? Assign token values to each desired behavior you listed.

Chapter 11

Individual Reinforcement Systems

I n this chapter we discuss reinforcements systems that are designed with the unique strengths and interests of individual students in mind, along with the possible unique functions of each student's problem behavior(s). Included are target behavior sheets, point and level systems, token boards, contracts, punch cards, and positive attention trackers.

Target Behavior Sheets

We start this chapter on individualized reinforcement systems with target behavior sheets for two reasons: they are the most common tool we recommend to help manage the problem behavior of individual students, and they are often used as a tool within other interventions such as level systems and contracts, which are discussed later in this chapter. Target behavior sheets come in many different formats, and identify behaviors to be targeted and a schedule for how often these behaviors are monitored (see Tables 11.1 and 11.2).

Putting the behaviors and monitoring schedule in writing raises the student's level of awareness of the behaviors to work on. Target behavior sheets are also a good source of functional behavioral assessment data that can be used to identify setting events and triggering antecedents, such as patterns surrounding time of day, academic subjects, and the presence of particular adults or peers. In addition, these sheets can provide time interval data used to monitor progress or lack of progress over time, a topic we discuss more fully in Chapter Fourteen.

Use Positive Language

The target skills listed on the target behavior sheet should be the desired replacement or target behavior, so it needs to be stated in terms of what you want the student to do rather than what you don't want him to do. For example, instead of "no yelling," state the target behavior as, "Use an inside voice." The target behavior sheet should remind the student of positive rather than negative choices.

Limit the Number of Skills

Often when we ask teachers to identify a target behavior for a particular student, they say, "Everything! The student behaves terribly!" and proceed to give a lengthy list of behaviors that the student needs to improve.

It is simply not realistic for any individual to work on changing more than one or two behaviors at a time. Other behaviors that are fairly well developed but are being maintained may be added, but we recommend putting no more than four or five behaviors on a target behavior sheet. Prioritize the behaviors that are safety issues or interfere with the student's learning or the learning of others the most. Once the more serious behaviors improve, the focus can shift to the less intrusive behaviors. To decide which behaviors to prioritize, follow these guidelines:

- Examine the behavioral data. Which behaviors are the most frequent? Which behaviors have resulted in suspensions or other school disciplinary actions?

- Think about what bugs you the most. Chances are, this is the behavior that is the most problematic.

- Ask students and their parents what behaviors should be worked on. Many times parents have suggestions about the behaviors they would like their child to improve, and students themselves may have ideas about what they want to change. This also gives an idea if the student has any self-awareness about what problem behaviors she has or if she is even aware that she has any problem behaviors at all. Usually we ask the student, "How do you think you are doing at school?" "What behaviors do you think are causing you the most problems?" or "What are you doing that is getting you in the most trouble at school?" Even primary-aged children can be brutally honest about their behaviors, assuming a sense of partnership with the teacher has been established.

Table 11.1 Basic Target Behavior Sheet: Front Page

Name: Date:					
Target Skills/ Schedule	Stay on Task	Follow Directions	Use a Polite Voice	Bonus Points	Turnaround Points
8:30–9:00					
9:00–9:30					
9:30–10:00					
10:00–10:30					
10:30–11:00					
11:00–11:30					
11:30–12:00					
12:00–12:30					
12:30–1:00					

How to Reach and Teach Children with Challenging Behavior

Table 11.2 Basic Target Behavior Sheet: Back Page

Time	Comments
Parent Signature:	

Individualize the Target Skills

Targeted skills should be taken directly from the student's individual education plan or student assistance plan if applicable. If you are working in a classroom or school where all students have behavior challenges, make sure target behavior sheets are individualized based on specific student needs. Too many times we see programs where every target behavior sheet looks exactly the same. Not all students have the same goals or need to work on the same skills. The "individualized" in "individualized education plan" is important to remember.

Be Specific

Students and educators marking the target behavior sheet should be completely clear about exactly what behavior earns or does not earn a point. Operationalize the behavior so that it passes the "stranger test": any stranger walking into a room would be able to reliably determine if the student is or is not demonstrating the target behavior.[1] For example, "Follow adult directions the first time" is more specific than "Let the adult be in

> Students and educators marking the target behavior sheet should be completely clear about exactly what behavior earns or not does not earn a point.

charge," and, "Use a polite voice tone" is more specific than "Treat others with respect." If there is a need to be more general in describing behaviors, make sure that a more specific definition is provided somewhere (we suggest the back of the card) for reference. When the sheet is specific, every adult in every environment (lunch, music, recess aides, and so on) can be consistent when marking the target behavior sheet, which reduces arguments and misunderstandings between the adults and the student.

Along these same lines, we also recommend providing specific directions regarding how to mark everything on the target behavior sheet for paraprofessionals and other teachers who may be involved. An example is provided in Figure 11.1.

> ### Kaye Says . . .
>
> I did my dissertation research in another teacher's classroom where a kindergarten student was receiving points for appropriate behavior. When I asked the child what specific behaviors he could earn points for, he replied "not being a fool" and "being good," but he had absolutely no idea what specific behaviors constituted "not being a fool" and "being good." Directly teaching him specific positive behaviors that passed the stranger test made a big difference in his behavior.

Options deal with removals for misbehavior. #1 is marked here if a student was removed from a group but remained in class (sent to seat/work area). #2 is marked if he was sent to think time area. Staff should mark their initials so we know who to talk to if follow up is needed. Reasons for removal should be marked on the back of the card.

Turnaround points (marked with a +). A turnaround point is given when a student has been redirected and stopped an inappropriate choice, gone to his or her seat or work area and handled it, and was able to come back to class. Turnaround points can also be given for a proper think time and cooperative problem solving. It is counted as a regular point when we count point totals, so it acts as an incentive to make up for points not earned. Also should be noted on back of card.

Bonus points can be given (marked with a slash) if the student chooses good behavior with no reminders, is especially kind, etc. Note reason for bonus point on back of card.

+ marks an earned point. / in corner marks a point he chose not to earn.

Name:
Dates:

Options: #1: Option in class
#2: Think time area

Behaviors/Schedule	Target skill Appropriate word choices	Target skill Hands and feet to self	Follow directions	Stay on task	Treat others nicely	Option/Teacher initials	Bonus points	Turnaround points
8:30–9:00 Social skills								+
9:00–9:30 Math						#1 JT #2 JT	1	
9:30–10:00 Writing								
10:05–10:30 Recess/Snack								
10:30–10:50 Spelling/Journal								
10:50–11:15 Reading								
11:15–11:40 Math seat work/Cursive		+	+	/				
11:45–12:20 Lunch/Recess	+				+			
12:20–1:00 Class read-aloud								

Appropriate word choices: Student earns this point if teacher does not hear OR have reports of profane language.
Hands/Feet to self: Student earns this point if teacher does not witness or have reports of student's hands or feet on others or others' property without permission at any time during the class period.
Follow directions: Student earns this point if he is able to comply with teacher directions with one or fewer redirection or reminder from staff in a given class period.
Stay on task: Student earns this point if he pays attention to teacher and/or works on assigned activity with one or fewer reminder in a given class period.
Treat others nicely: Student earns this point if he is commonly courteous to students and staff with one or fewer redirection.

Figure 11.1 Target Behavior Sheet Directions

Embed Visual Supports and Special Interests

The target behavior sheet may be more effective if you embed visual supports in it. In this way, the sheet acts as a visual reminder of the target behaviors and serves as a visual schedule for the student. Students can personalize the target behavior sheet by adding pictures of things they are interested in such as a picture of a favorite cartoon or movie character, which has the benefit of making the sheet more motivating and reinforcing for the student.

Partner with the Student to Help Develop

Target behavior sheets should be created with the student's input to increase their buy-in and make using it more motivating. Often students have specific ideas about how they want their target behavior sheet to look, what skills they want to work on, and what special interests and visuals they want embedded in it.

Set Realistic Criteria

It may not be appropriate to set criteria for all target behaviors at 80 to 90 percent, which is what we often see. If the student is currently performing the behavior 45 percent of the time, a 30 to 45 percent increase would not be a realistic expectation. We want students to experience success with the target behavior sheet from the start so that they will buy in to the monitoring process and partner with us in changing their behavior. When they rarely or never experience success, they often give up and refuse to participate.

One effective way to determine realistic criteria is to create a baseline target behavior sheet and fill it out based on what you observe in the classroom for a couple of weeks without the student's knowledge. This will provide an accurate picture of the student's behavior prior to intervention. Once baseline percentages are established, realistic goals and criteria for reinforcements can be determined. We recommend setting success criteria at ten to fifteen percentage points over baseline.

Let Students Keep Their Sheet with Them (If They Wish)

Students should have the option of carrying the target behavior sheet with them throughout the day. They can put it in a folder or three-ring binder, or copy the sheet onto sturdy paper or cardstock. We have found that middle and high school students usually do not want to carry their sheet with them because it calls attention to the fact that they have behavior challenges. In these cases, we have used electronic target behavior sheets that were are put on a shared drive that could be accessed by every teacher the student had throughout the day. It is assumed all points are earned unless a teacher made a specific comment. Students meet with their case manager in the morning, halfway through the day and at the end of the day to review their target behavior sheet, practice replacement behavior, and problem-solve if needed.

Review Regularly with the Student

Many teachers fill out the target behavior sheet at the end of the set time interval without discussing it with the student, or they wait until the end of the day to fill out the entire target behavior sheet. When this happens, students start to view the sheet as something the teacher controls or something that is done "to" them.

Target behavior sheets provide a structure for incidental teaching opportunities with the goal of developing personal responsibility and problem-solving skills if the educator engages the student in the process. After each scheduled time interval, staff should have a conversation with the student about whether points were earned for exhibiting each targeted behavior. This is an opportunity to point out any patterns in behavior that occur throughout the day and assist the student in making a plan for how to improve the behavior. A brief social skills lesson could occur during this time using a social story, role play, or other instructional strategy. If there is a discrepancy between the perspective of the teacher and student, it should be discussed and resolved immediately rather than waiting until the end of the day when memories of the events are not as clear.

Use Turnaround Points

A few years into our careers teaching students with chronic behavior challenges, we noticed that too often when a way to track these students' behavior was created, they became perfectionists and would get very upset if they failed to earn a point. They developed the attitude, "Now that I've blown it, I might as well keep going!" writing the day off and continuing the negative pattern of behavior.

To remedy this problem, we added a component to our target behavior sheets called turnaround points. We discussed with our students that it was okay to make a mistake. The life skill we were trying to help them develop was to recognize when they made a mistake and "turn it around." If they failed to earn a point, we told them that if they worked really hard on exhibiting that skill during the next monitoring period, they would earn a turnaround point. Turnaround points cancelled out points lost when determining reinforcement but indicated that they had some difficulty with that skill. Turnaround points provide a sometimes much-needed incentive to get back on the right track and were a breakthrough in our behavior management system.

Use Bonus Points

Bonus points are extra points that any adult in the school can give a student without affecting the data collection system. These points are not figured in when determining reinforcement but contribute to earning an additional reinforcer. In our program, this additional reinforcer took the form of a class party. We had a large poster with a picture of the party theme (ice cream sundaes, pumpkin carving, pizza, and so on), covered it with small circles the size of color coding labels that can be found at any office supply store, and hung it in the hallway. A student who received a bonus point put his or her initials on a color coding label and covered a dot. When the poster was covered, the students had earned the party (although we fixed the number of points needed so the parties happened about once a month). Before the party, each student shared a positive skill he or she had exhibited to contribute to earning the class party, and we practiced various social skills during the event. Bonus point parties provided positive peer pressure, public positive recognition for exhibiting prosocial behavior, and a common goal for students to work toward together.

Allow Students to Self-Monitor When Ready

When students have consistently demonstrated the target behaviors and disagreements with teachers on how their sheet should be marked are minimal, they are ready to start to self-monitor, moving toward the ultimate goal of self-management. This can easily be done by adding a "teacher agreement" column to the target behavior sheet, dividing each cell in half, with the student marking one half and the teacher the other, or having the teacher indicate agreement by circling or highlighting the student's mark. Students fill out their own sheets, and if the teacher agrees with the student, he or she marks the target behavior sheet accordingly. If there is disagreement, no punishment is given; the teacher simply explains why he or she disagrees and marks the card accordingly. If this happens repeatedly, the student is not ready to self-monitor, and the teacher again takes on this responsibility.

Bonus points can be used for extra reinforcement when students are honest when they make a mistake. We have found that when students are not penalized for mistakes, they are extremely honest when allowed to self-monitor and view the practice as a reinforcer in and of itself, because it allows them to have some control. In our program, we made the sheets of students who were self-monitoring a different color so others in the program could easily see that they had earned this privilege, adding prestige—another aspect of reinforcement. Most of our students loved to self-monitor, and many times keeping this privilege was a strong enough motivator to be honest.

Communicate to Parents What Constitutes a Successful Day

Target behavior sheets can be a valuable communication tool. It is easy for communication to break down between paraprofessionals, educators in the general education classroom, and special education staff, and target behavior sheets provide a consistent communication tool. We typically recommend sending copies of student target behavior sheets home to parents daily as they appreciate ongoing communication and feedback regarding their child's behavior at school. If this is done, it is imperative to communicate what a successful day is with the parents. Many times when parents have a concrete way to track their child's behavior progress at school, they try to support the

> Target behavior sheets can be a valuable communication tool.

school's efforts by giving reinforcement or undesirable consequences at home. Although their intentions are good, this often backfires. For example, the parent may tell their child, "If you have perfect target behavior sheets all week, we will buy you a video game on Friday." Then when the student makes a mistake, this serves as a trigger for a meltdown because the student has lost the home reinforcer. It is not realistic to expect perfection. We always tell students that if parents and teachers were on target behavior sheets, they would not earn all of their points all of the time. We have even put ourselves on target behavior sheets to demonstrate this concept and model the skill of how to handle making a mistake. Express your appreciation for the parental support, and then help parents understand what a successful level of performance is and what appropriate home reinforcement would look like. Discourage parents from buying their children reinforcers, and instead suggest developing a home menu of things they may already be giving away for free or that will provide positive attention and time together, such as choosing what they have for dinner, shooting hoops with a parent, or playing a family game. (See the reinforcement menu favorites in Table 9.2.) Table 11.3 provides a checklist to help you successfully design and use a target behavior sheet.

Table 11.3 Target Behavior Sheet Checklist

☐ The number of target behaviors for the student to work on is realistic.

☐ Target behaviors are stated in terms of what I want the student to do.

☐ Target behaviors are specific: the student is clear about what it means to exhibit the skill and not exhibit the skill.

☐ The student helped me create the target behavior sheet.

☐ The student and I agreed on a realistic goal or criterion to earn a reinforcer.

☐ The student has a system for keeping the target behavior sheet with him or her.

☐ We have scheduled a regular time to go over the target behavior sheet together multiple times during the school day.

☐ Turnaround points are included on the target behavior sheet, and the student clearly understands what they mean and how to earn them.

☐ If the target behavior sheet is being sent home, adults at home understand the student's goal and have an appropriate plan for home reinforcement.

☐ A time has been scheduled for reinforcement, and a list of appropriate reinforcers has been generated.

Dependent Group-Oriented Contingency

We discussed interdependent and independent group-oriented contingencies in the previous chapter. The third type of group-oriented contingency is a dependent group-oriented contingency where the entire group earns a reinforcer based on one student's behavior. This is especially helpful if the function of the targeted student's behavior is attention because he or she becomes the hero for the group and the others will naturally root the student on and give praise and attention. The downside is that the student may be blamed if the reinforcer is not earned, so the possibility of that reaction will need to be taken into consideration.

Kaye Says . . .

I used a dependent group-oriented contingency for a particular student who tended to get very silly, and when he did, he had great difficulty calming down. The other students thought he was funny, so they often encouraged him by making silly noises or faces at him. The class desperately wanted a guinea pig for the classroom, so I made getting the pet contingent on the silly student staying serious for a certain number of days and gave his peers direct instruction on how to encourage him to do this. I used a chart similar to the one shown in Figure 11.2 to track progress toward their goal.

Level Systems

Point and level systems are designed to be an organizational framework for managing student behavior where students earn more privileges and responsibilities as they demonstrate more control over their behavior. Point and level systems mirror real life due to the fact that in our society, privileges are given or removed based on our behavior. Take speeding, for example. If an adult is caught speeding, he or she might first receive a warning. If this person continues speeding and is caught again, he or she may be fined. If the speeding continues, this person may lose his or her license, and therefore the privilege of driving, but have the opportunity to earn it back for good behavior.

Point and level systems work in a similar way, with clearly defined behavioral expectations linked to rewards, privileges, and consequences. There are specific criteria for advancement to the next level, where the student enjoys more freedom and privileges. The intention is that students who proceed through the levels are better able to self-manage and capable of handling more responsibility, and therefore enjoy greater independence.

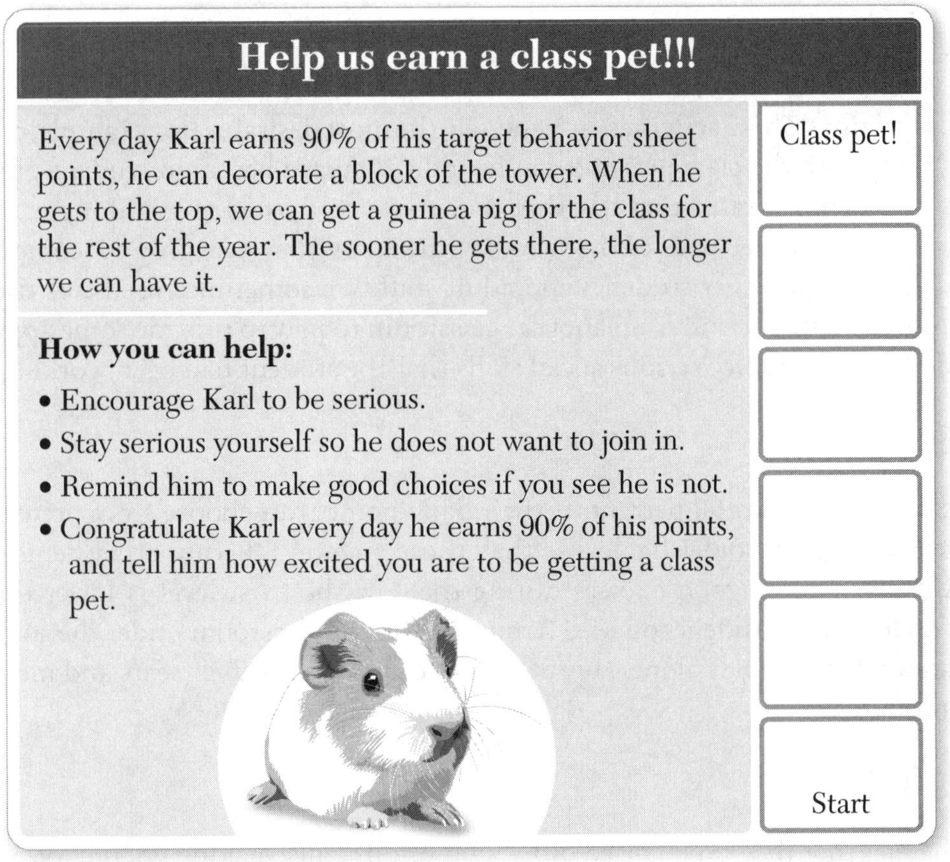

Help us earn a class pet!!!

Every day Karl earns 90% of his target behavior sheet points, he can decorate a block of the tower. When he gets to the top, we can get a guinea pig for the class for the rest of the year. The sooner he gets there, the longer we can have it.

How you can help:

- Encourage Karl to be serious.
- Stay serious yourself so he does not want to join in.
- Remind him to make good choices if you see he is not.
- Congratulate Karl every day he earns 90% of his points, and tell him how excited you are to be getting a class pet.

Class pet!

Start

Figure 11.2 Dependent Group-Oriented Contingency Example: Help Us Earn a Class Pet

There are many examples of point and level systems that have been used to manage challenging student behavior in a variety of settings.[2] We describe in detail several examples of systems that we have used with individual or small groups of students.

Structured Behavioral Skills Program: Daily Level System

We developed this point and level system in the program we taught in together and used it for over fifteen years in various elementary programs for students with behavioral challenges in the public school setting. We know from anecdotal reports that it has been used or adapted in several other school districts at all grade levels, with reported effectiveness.

Students have a daily target behavior sheet, and their performance on the sheet determines how their "reward" or "preferred activity" time is structured for the last twenty minutes of the school day. No student receives an undesirable consequence during reward time. Rather, the activities and privileges they have access to during that time are based on how much they demonstrated that day that they could be trusted to make good choices and get along with others.

Level 1

Students who earn 90 percent of their daily points can choose from activities on level 1 during reward time. These activities are generally the most desirable (for example, computer games, playing with the class pet) and can be individualized based on student preference. Students who demonstrated that day that they could be trusted to get along with others are allowed to go to other areas of the school with supervision (playground, computer lab) and can interact with other students and adult staff. We sometimes used this time as an opportunity to invite a friend from another classroom to play to provide some appropriate peer modeling and practice various social skills that the student had been working on.

Level 2

Students who earn 80 to 90 percent of their daily points can choose from activities that are still reinforcing but somewhat less so than those on level 1. Because they demonstrated some difficulty making good choices during the day, the trust level is lower than with students on level 1, so students on level 2 must stay in the classroom under the supervision of the lead teacher and play alone. However, they can be out of their seats and move about the classroom freely.

Level 3

Due to the fact that they experienced quite a bit of difficulty making good choices during the day, students who earn less than 80 percent of their daily points are allowed to choose only from activities that can be done at their desk where they are in close proximity to the teacher and can be highly supervised. These activities are still reinforcing and are generally things like drawing, reading, or putting together a puzzle.

Climbing the Ladder of Success

We have used this system or variations of it successfully in situations where the student's teachers had difficulty with the idea of providing him with extra reinforcers for behaving appropriately. We got the teachers to agree to using a level system by structuring the reinforcing privileges that the student enjoyed as a natural part of his school day (recess and reduced adult supervision), and making his access to them contingent on appropriate behavioral choices.

In this system, the student's behavior is tracked by a target behavior sheet throughout all environments daily. Once a week, the average daily percentage of points earned is calculated, and determines what level of privileges the student will enjoy for the next week. If the average is over 90 percent, the student moves up a level; if the average is between 80 and 90 percent, the student stays on the same level; and if the average is below 80 percent, the student moves down a level. If any extreme behaviors occur that would be against the law for adults (referred to as red or level 5 behaviors, which we discuss in more detail in Chapter Thirteen), the student immediately is moved to the bottom or red (for *stop!*) level.

Students always have the option of earning something from their daily reinforcement menu at the end of the day, so they never feel that they have nothing to work for regardless of their level. Students can design their own way to visually track their level. We have had students laminate their school picture and attach it to the ladder with Velcro, moving their picture up a ladder with each level being a different color. Examples of visuals that can be used in Climbing the Ladder of Success are provided in Figures 11.3 and 11.4.

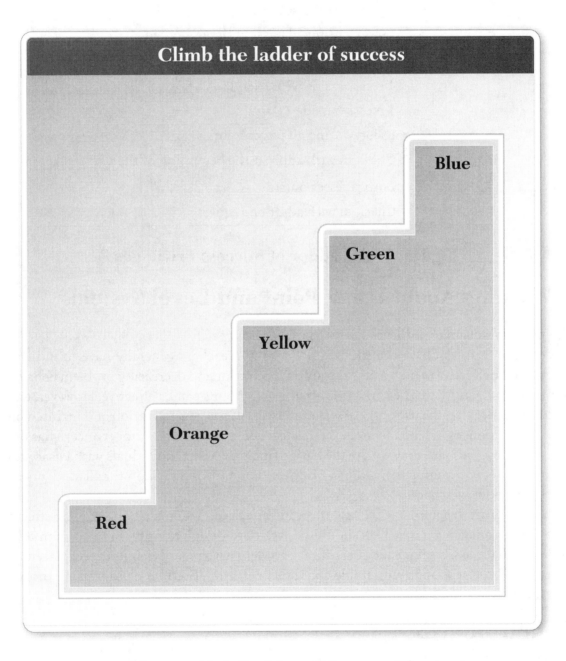

Figure 11.3 Ladder of Success Chart

Red	Red schedule all day (Red schedule will be discussed in detail in Chapter 13)
Orange	2 recesses inside study hall
	Escort during all passing times
	Check in with adult at the beginning, middle, and end of day
Yellow	1 recess inside with friend
	1 recess study hall
	Escort during all passing times
	Check in with adult at the beginning and end of the day
Green	1 recess inside with friend
	1 recess outside
	Escort during all passing times
	Check in with adult at the beginning of the day
Blue	Both recesses outside
	Check in with adult on request

Figure 11.4 Ladder of Success Privileges

A Warning About Using Point and Level Systems

The primary advantage of level systems is that they specify a hierarchy of skills that are needed to be successful in the educational setting. Teachers generally have found these systems to be effective in increasing appropriate behavior and decreasing problem behavior. Our experience supports the conclusion that level systems can be effective. However, there is little evidence that the use of these systems results in the generalization and maintenance of behavior changes independent of external teacher control. In addition, concern has been raised that level systems may violate the basic principles of the Individuals with Disabilities Education Act when implemented in a uniform, standardized fashion for all students in a given classroom or school.

Although we recommend the use of point and level systems as one tool of effective behavioral management, teachers should be careful to design the system to accommodate the individual needs and specific goals of each student with regard to initial level placement, use of reinforcement and undesirable consequences, and criteria for progressing through the system.

Token Boards

Individual token boards are commonly used with very young students or students with limited cognitive abilities (Figure 11.5). Many teachers use poker chips, pennies, or star

Figure 11.5 Individual Token Board

tokens on Velcro that are then attached to a strip that visually shows progress toward a picture of a reinforcer or a general picture that represents their reinforcement menu. Tokens are given at frequent intervals paired with behavior-specific praise, and when all the tokens are earned, the student gets a short break when he or she has access to a reinforcer of his or her choice. This type of system can easily travel with the student to various environments and provides a consistent way of providing reinforcement for all adults who work with him or her.

Contracts

Contracts are an effective way to negotiate with students in a way that mirrors real life. A contract in the adult world is a written agreement between two or more parties that stipulates the responsibilities of each party. Contracting with students

> Contracts are an effective way to negotiate with students in a way that mirrors real life.

is much the same in that it clearly communicates exactly what both the teacher and the student are expected to do. It combines operationally defining and directly teaching the desired target behavior and outlining the consequences (both positive and negative) for choosing or not choosing this behavior.

One way to make contracts more effective is to have the students write their own contract, choosing the behaviors to work on, criteria, and consequences contingent on the stipulations of the contract and then negotiate the fine points with them to develop the final product (Figure 11.6). This is yet another way of embedding choices and giving the student some appropriate control, automatically leading to student buy-in that you may not have gotten if you had outlined the entire contract. Students can work on their self-management skills by helping to choose their criteria for success with teacher guidance, starting by examining their current level of functioning. This can be done by showing them their target behavior sheet graph (which we discuss in detail in Chapter Fifteen) that visually depicts at what percentage they are performing now and asking them what they think would be a reasonable goal.

Contracts should outline both the positive reinforcement students will experience by choosing to perform the goal at the set criteria and undesirable consequences they will experience if they choose not to. This mirrors real life: adult contracts have positive and

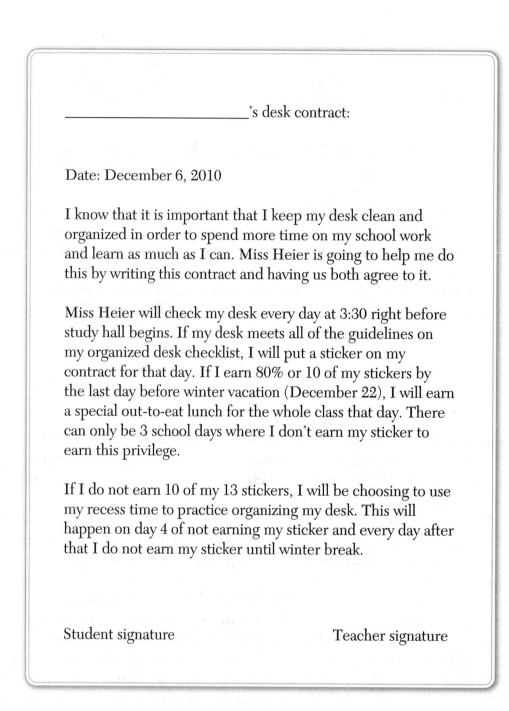

_____'s desk contract:

Date: December 6, 2010

I know that it is important that I keep my desk clean and organized in order to spend more time on my school work and learn as much as I can. Miss Heier is going to help me do this by writing this contract and having us both agree to it.

Miss Heier will check my desk every day at 3:30 right before study hall begins. If my desk meets all of the guidelines on my organized desk checklist, I will put a sticker on my contract for that day. If I earn 80% or 10 of my stickers by the last day before winter vacation (December 22), I will earn a special out-to-eat lunch for the whole class that day. There can only be 3 school days where I don't earn my sticker to earn this privilege.

If I do not earn 10 of my 13 stickers, I will be choosing to use my recess time to practice organizing my desk. This will happen on day 4 of not earning my sticker and every day after that I do not earn my sticker until winter break.

Student signature   Teacher signature

Figure 11.6 Example of a Contract

negative ramifications for abiding or not abiding by the contract. They also leave no room for arguments or power struggles. Letting students know exactly what will happen if they choose the desired behavior or not is another way to communicate that they are charge of the things that happen to them, and consequences, both positive and negative, are not something handed out by teachers to make their life difficult.

The contract itself can act as a visual prompt. Many times we let the student choose a place to post the contract. Some want the contract in a place visible to all, and some like to post it in a private place like inside their desk or in their binder. It is helpful to include a task record on the contract itself by including a mini-calendar on the contract with the days it covers. At the end of the day, the student consults with the teacher and marks whether the criteria were met. Depending on the age and preferences of the student, this can be done with a sticker, smiley face, star, stamp, or a simple check mark. An example of this is provided in Figure 11.7.

Troubleshooting

Make sure you can deliver the reinforcement contracted for at the contracted time and with the contracted people involved. Children with challenging behavior tend to be distrusting already, and breaking a contract you made with them erases any trust you may have worked hard to build. If you contract to have lunch with the student on the day the student earns the contract, and you have a lunch meeting that day or you are home sick, the student may feel as if you have broken the contract. To prevent this, be a little more general in the wording of the contract to provide some flexibility. You may want the contract to state that once the contract is earned, the student will meet with the teacher to schedule lunch together.

My sticker chart

December

Monday	Tuesday	Wednesday	Thursday	Friday
6	7	8	9	10
13	14	15	16	17
20	21	22 Special class lunch out!!!	WINTER BREAK	

Figure 11.7 My Sticker Chart

Punch Cards

Punch cards are especially effective when the function of the behavior is escape or avoidance because it allows the student to minimize the undesired task by actually doing it. For example, a student who hates to do homework (and what student doesn't?) can be allowed to get out of homework on Fridays by completing all homework assignments for Monday through Thursday. Every day the homework is completed, he or she gets a punch on the card to track progress toward the goal (Figure 11.8).

We have also typically used a punch card system for finishing work on time (earning a free assignment coupon) and for silent reading (earning the choice of an alternative activity on the fifth day during the time scheduled for silent reading).

Positive Attention Trackers

A positive attention tracker is a good intervention to use when the function of the student's problem behavior is clearly attention. The student chooses an icon of a favorite character or special interest, and rows of this are put on a target behavior sheet for each time interval (Figure 11.9). The numbers 1, 2, and 3 are also included at the end of the row for each time

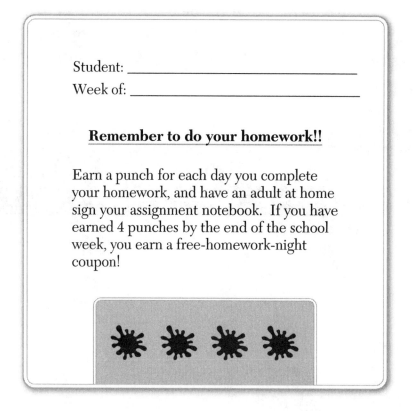

Figure 11.8 Homework Punch Card

How to Reach and Teach Children with Challenging Behavior

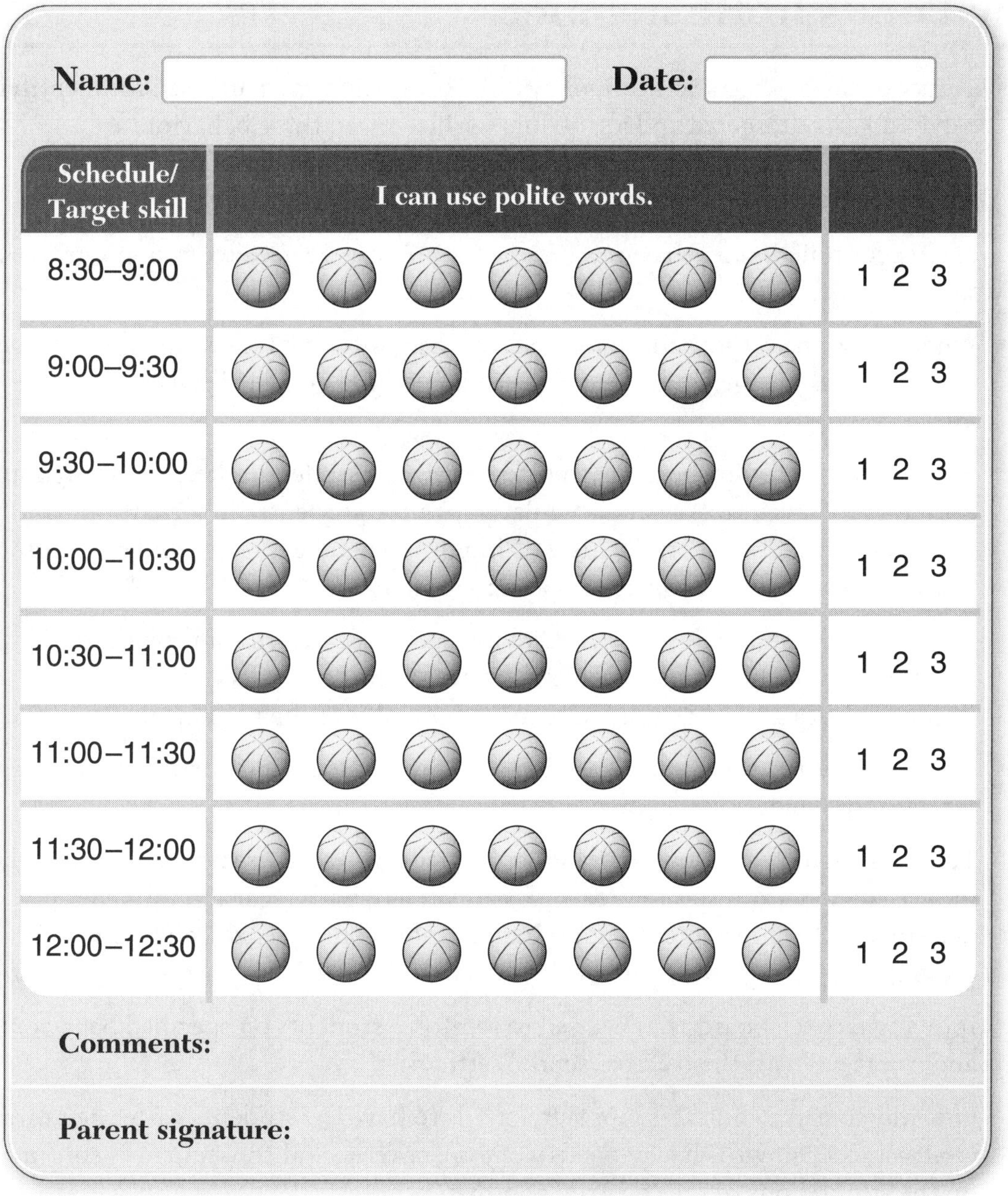

Schedule/ Target skill	I can use polite words.								
8:30–9:00	⬤	⬤	⬤	⬤	⬤	⬤	⬤	1 2 3
9:00–9:30	⬤	⬤	⬤	⬤	⬤	⬤	⬤	1 2 3
9:30–10:00	⬤	⬤	⬤	⬤	⬤	⬤	⬤	1 2 3
10:00–10:30	⬤	⬤	⬤	⬤	⬤	⬤	⬤	1 2 3
10:30–11:00	⬤	⬤	⬤	⬤	⬤	⬤	⬤	1 2 3
11:00–11:30	⬤	⬤	⬤	⬤	⬤	⬤	⬤	1 2 3
11:30–12:00	⬤	⬤	⬤	⬤	⬤	⬤	⬤	1 2 3
12:00–12:30	⬤	⬤	⬤	⬤	⬤	⬤	⬤	1 2 3

Name: _____   Date: _____

Comments:

Parent signature:

Figure 11.9 A Positive Attention Tracker

interval to record the number of redirections given. Every time the teacher or another adult gives the student behavior-specific praise, he or she also circles an icon. When a certain number of icons are circled, the student chooses a reinforcer from his or her menu. This provides a way to check that adults are meeting that four-to-one positive-to-negative ratio in a visual way that also provides additional reinforcement for the student.

Key Points to Remember

- Target behavior sheets come in many different formats and are used for identifying behaviors to be targeted and a schedule for how often these behaviors are monitored.

- Target sheets raise the student's awareness of behaviors targeted, are a good source of data for functional behavior assessments, and can be used to track progress over time.

- When designing target behavior sheets, teachers should let the student participate, use positive language, limit the number of skills, and embed visuals and special interests.

- When target behavior sheets are in place, allow the student to keep it throughout the day if they want to, review it regularly with the student, use turnaround and bonus points, allow the student to self-monitor when he is ready, and communicate to adults at home what constitutes a successful day.

- Point and level systems are designed to be an organizational framework for managing student behavior where students earn more privileges and responsibilities as they demonstrate more control over their behavior.

- Point and level systems mirror real life due to the fact that in our society, privileges are given or removed based on our behavior.

- Teachers should be careful to design point and level systems to accommodate the individual needs and specific goals of each student with regard to initial level placement, use of reinforcement and undesirable consequences, and criteria for progressing through the system.

- Individual token boards can be used to reinforce students on specified behaviors and can travel with them across school settings.

- One way to make contracts more effective is to have the students write their own contract, choosing the behaviors to work on, criteria, and consequences contingent on the stipulations of the contract, and then negotiate the fine points with them to develop the final product.

- When contracting, make sure you can deliver the reinforcement contracted for at the contracted time and with the contracted people involved.

- Punch cards are especially effective when the function of the behavior is escape or avoidance because they allow the student to minimize the undesired task by actually doing it.

- A positive attention tracker is a good intervention to use when the function of the student's problem behavior is clearly attention.

Discussion Questions and Activities

1. Think of a student you teach who has challenging behaviors. Using the guidelines provided in this chapter (use positive language, limit the number of skills, have specific target skill individualized to each student's needs, and let the student give input on what skills to target), make a list of targeted behavioral skills for this student.

2. Setting realistic criteria for reinforcement of desired behaviors is important. If Jamal averages 38 percent on a baseline target behavior sheet monitoring the skill "Complete Your Work on Time," what would be realistic criteria for earning a reinforcer?

3. List the reinforcers available in your classroom. Separate them into three levels based on what the students in your class want the most.

Part Five

Using Undesirable Consequences

Instruction

↓

Prevention

↓

Reinforcement

↓

Undesirable Consequences

Chapter 12

Using Undesirable Consequences: The Basics

Logical undesirable consequences are often confused with punishment. *Punishment* is defined as the "the contingent presentation of a stimulus immediately following a response, which decreases the future rate and/or probability of the response."[1] Of course, teachers want the inappropriate behavior of students to decrease and have historically delivered verbal reprimands, writing sentences, seclusion, corporal punishment, and other similar consequences to attempt to manage behavior, which has led to many ethical and legal considerations. In fact, many individuals who exhibit undesirable behavior have been subjected to consequences that are dehumanizing and unethical. As a result, the term *punishment* has become associated with pain and humiliation. It has become unacceptable to many in the educational field and partially prompted the positive behavioral support movement in the early 1990s.

Problems with Punishment

We briefly discussed in Chapter One several problems with the use of punishment in schools.[2] Because this is such an important topic, we provide a review here.

Punishment Does Not Work in the Long Term

Punishment often appeals to practitioners because they are reinforced by the short-term effect. A typical scenario goes like this: A student is disruptive, the teacher sends him out of class or threatens some sort of punishment (writing sentences, calling parents, or something else), and the student stops the misbehavior. Order is restored in the classroom, at least temporarily, and the teacher can continue teaching. This feels pretty good to the teacher!

The problem is that punishment rarely has long-term effects on the behavior, especially for students with chronic behavior problems. And often when the inappropriate behavior reoccurs, it does so at a higher level. In addition, the student who was sent out of class may have wanted to escape or avoid the assignment being given or the educational environment in general. Removing this student from class got him exactly what he wanted. He will be more likely to perform the disruptive behaviors again because it actually served as a reinforcer rather than a punisher. So while punishment may reduce behavior problems in the moment, it actually makes the problem worse over the long run.

Punishment Does Not Teach the Student What to Do Instead

Another problem with punishment is that it does not teach the student replacement behavior, or what to do instead. The punishment is delivered with the hope that the student will learn from the mistake. However, students who present challenging behavior need to be directly taught what to do. The old-fashioned belief that punishment teaches a lesson is both outdated and inapplicable to students with behavioral problems.

Punishment Encourages Negative Attitudes Toward School and Educators

This population of students has already had numerous negative experiences at school. Traditional school discipline plans almost always include reactive, punishing consequences for negative behaviors. Habitual offenders of the discipline code have continually received punishment and demonstrated little to no positive changes in behavior. A student who is regularly punished often develops a negative attitude toward the punisher and school in general. The student sees the punishment as something done to him by the person in charge, and power and control issues are likely to arise.

Punishment Reduces Motivation to Learn Other Techniques

Punishment is highly effective in controlling the behavior of 80 to 90 percent of the student population, so it is easy to understand why it is so widely used in schools. However, controlling is not the same as teaching, and our ultimate goal is to teach appropriate behavior skills rather than simply control students. Because these short-term controlling effects of punishment have historically been so reinforcing to educators, it is too often the only behavior management technique that teachers know. When teachers rely solely on punishment to manage student behaviors, they do not develop other behavior management techniques that are more effective with all students and lead to those ultimate goals of personal responsibility and life skill development.

Natural and Logical Undesirable Consequences

Talk to most any classroom teacher or individual with hands-on behavioral management experience in the public school setting, and they will agree that not all inappropriate behavior can be decreased to acceptable levels by using proactive strategies and positive contingencies exclusively.

In our experience, no matter how much potential reinforcement is offered, sometimes there is simply nothing more reinforcing to students than the reinforcement they get from exhibiting problem behavior. Despite the implementation of proactive and positive strategies, some students will continue to exhibit problematic behavior, and a consistent, systematic response to this behavior is critical to effective behavior management. It

> The most effective behavioral management plan provides a balance of proactive strategies, positive contingencies, and natural and logical undesirable consequences.

can also be argued that the use of only positive contingencies does not mirror real life and therefore does not promote the generalization of appropriate behavior into nonschool environments. The most effective behavioral management plan provides a balance of proactive strategies, positive contingencies, and natural and logical undesirable consequences that teach students to take responsibility for their behavioral choices and mirror situations that they will face as adults.

Natural Undesirable Consequences

Natural undesirable consequences are unplanned or uncontrolled outcomes that happen as a result of behavior.[3] For example, if a student cuts in front of another student in line, the natural undesirable consequence may be that the other child won't play with her at recess. A teacher did not plan or control this consequence. However, teach-

> Natural undesirable consequences are unplanned or uncontrolled outcomes that happen as a result of behavior.

ers should discuss and help students predict natural undesirable consequences of their behavior to assist them in making the connection between their choices and what happens to them.

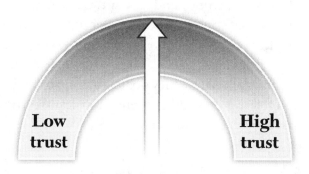

Figure 12.1 Trust Meter

Some examples of other common natural undesirable consequences that can be discussed with students are embarrassment, lack of attention, loss of prestige or respect, and loss of trust. We often used a "trust meter" with our students to provide a visual for the natural undesirable consequence of loss of trust (Figure 12.1). During direct social skills instruction, we discussed the concept and brainstormed behaviors that built trust and behaviors that broke down trust. We pointed out that trust takes a long time to build but a very short amount of time to break and that high levels of trust often result in more privileges. During problem solving or at the end of the day when we reviewed their target behavior sheet, we asked them to self-evaluate whether trust between us was built up or broken down that day and had the students visually move their trust meter to reflect this.

Jodie Says . . .

I had one student who was very into being popular with her peers and came to school every day dressed very fashionably. She started a game at recess called, "Whose outfit is the prettiest, and whose is the ugliest?" basically fishing for wardrobe compliments from the other little girls. I asked her if she was a nice or a mean girl, and she exclaimed, absolutely horrified, "I am a nice girl! Everyone loves me!" I pointed out that telling other girls their outfits were ugly was something a mean girl would do. After that, not only did the game stop, but from then on, pointing out when things she did might be considered mean by others went a long way toward modifying her behavior.

Logical Undesirable Consequences

Logical undesirable consequences do not naturally occur as a result of behavior but are intentionally planned and applied by educators and are similar to what would happen to an adult in a similar situation.[4] As adults, we encounter logical undesirable consequences all the time. If we assault someone, we may experience a loss of freedom in the form of jail time. We are not safe to be around others, so we are monitored. Another good example is the loss of the privilege of driving. If we choose to practice unsafe driving habits such as habitual speeding, reckless driving, or driving under the influence, we take the chance of losing the privilege of driving or having it restricted.

> Logical undesirable consequences do not naturally occur as a result of behavior, but are intentionally planned and applied by educators and are similar to what would happen to an adult in a similar situation.

The Three R's of Logical Consequences

We know whether the consequences we plan are logical when they are consistent with the three R's: related, reasonable, and respectful.[5]

Related

Related means that the consequence is clearly connected to the student's behavior and its function. This requires the teacher getting to know his or her students well and becoming proficient at the process of both formal and informal functional behavioral assessment. The function of the same behavior may be different for each student, or even for the same student at different times. Therefore, it is crucial that teachers take this into consideration and do not use one consequence, such as the very popular and well-known undesirable consequence of time-out, for all inappropriate behavior. An example of the unrelated use of time-out would be imposing it on a student for calling another student a name. A related consequence may be to have the student spend some of her free time discussing the natural consequences of the action with the teacher (such as hurting that person's feeling or possibly getting called a name back) and writing the offended student an apology. In order to be related, the consequence must have a teaching focus and mirror real-life consequences that would happen to adult in a similar situation.

> In order to be related, the consequence must have a teaching focus and mirror real-life consequences that would happen to adult in a similar situation.

Reasonable

Reasonable refers to not giving consequences for a student's inappropriate behavior that are too severe or too far in the future. As an educator applying logical consequences, you do not want to underpenalize or overpenalize. The "punishment" should fit the "crime." It is not reasonable to require that a student lose all his recesses for the week for being silly in class or lose next month's field trip for getting in a minor fight on the playground. A more reasonable consequence may be to stay in for one recess to practice appropriate classroom or recess behavior.

> As an educator applying logical consequences, you do not want to underpenalize or overpenalize.

The "punishment" should fit the "crime." We like to envision behaviors and consequences on a five-point scale, with 1 being a minor infraction (usually the result of forgetting or being impulsive like talking out) and 5 being behaviors that would be against the law if an adult did something similar (such as physical aggression). The books *The Incredible 5 Point Scale* and *A 5 Is Against the Law! Social Boundaries: Straight Up! An Honest Guide for Teens and Young Adults,* both by Kari Dunn Buron, are helpful for teaching this concept and also provide helpful visuals.

> **Recommended Resources**
>
> *A 5 Is Against the Law* (Shawnee Mission, KS: Autism Asperger Publishing Company) and, with M. Curtis, *The Incredible 5 Point Scale* (Shawnee Mission, KS: Autism Asperger Publishing Company), both by Kari Dunn Buron.

One of the most common mistakes educators make is to give a consequence that is at a higher level than the behavior infraction, such as losing recess for impulsively talking out or giving a consequence that is at a lower level than the behavior infraction, such as giving a short time-out for physical aggression and then going on with the school day as if nothing had happened. In order to truly mirror real life and teach students the real-life adult consequences of their behavior choices, matching the level of undesirable consequence to the level of the behavioral infraction is absolutely crucial.

> Matching the level of undesirable consequence to the level of the behavioral infraction is absolutely crucial.

Respectful

Consequences need to be delivered with empathy in a calm, respectful tone of voice. Many times educators give a related, reasonable undesirable consequence but then communicate it to the student in a lecturing, negative way. It is crucial

> Consequences need to be delivered with empathy in a calm, respectful tone of voice.

not to take the student's behavior personally and stay calm and in control of our behavior to the greatest extent possible. Otherwise the student will focus more on the feelings of the adult, his conflict with you, and perhaps his own feelings of anger resulting from being talked to disrespectfully and not reflecting on his choices. Our attitudes and behavior are part of the interaction and can greatly contribute to the escalation or deescalation of the student's behavior. Pay close attention to messages sent not only by the words you choose but also by your tone, volume, facial expression, and body language. Students who are not treated respectfully often become aggressive, passive, resentful, or uncooperative (or some combination of these) and may try to get revenge against you. Avoid these power struggles at all costs. Your role is to provide students with all the information needed and the structure in which they experience the natural and logical consequences of their choices (both desirable and undesirable) and learns life lessons throughout the process.

The second part of being respectful is to deliver undesirable logical consequence with as much privacy as possible by taking the student aside or walking to where he or she is and having a quiet conversation. Would you rather have your boss confront you about a problem with your performance in a private area or in front of your coworkers? We need to give students the same amount of respect that we all want.

Punishment Versus Logical Consequences

The key difference between logical consequences and punishment goes back to the three R's: related, respectful, and reasonable. While the actual consequence may be the same in both situations, the way that the teacher presents it to the student and its relation to the inappropriate behavior is what determines whether it is considered punishment or a logical consequence.

Logical consequences outline the student's choices and their consequences calmly and factually, providing the structure for the student to make an informed decision. The adult's attitude should be of not personally being affected one way or another but hoping the student makes a positive choice for his or her own sake. A teacher who is angry, frustrated, or has the feeling of trying to win when giving an undesirable consequence is using punishment. Table 12.1 illustrates the difference between a punishment and a logical consequence, and Table 12.2 gives a checklist for delivering logical consequences.

Recommended Resource

The Love and Logic Series of resources and trainings does an excellent job of teaching parents and teachers how to differentiate between punishment and logical undesirable consequences on a daily basis. More information can be found at www.loveandlogic.com.

Table 12.1 The Difference Between Punishment and a Logical Consequence

Consequence	Punishment	Logical Consequence
Removal from the group or time-out	"Go to time-out until you can behave in group appropriately!"	"When you act silly in group, it distracts me from teaching and others from learning. Would you like to stay with the group or go to the think time area where it is okay to make silly noises? It's your decision."
Stay in for recess	"If you don't stop goofing around and get your math done, no recess for you!"	"This is the time I have scheduled to do math. It is very important that you get it done so you can learn as much as you can. Recess is the scheduled time to talk to your friends. You can choose to talk now, but the only other time to finish math is at recess. It's your decision."

Table 12.2 Checklist for Providing Logical Consequences

☐ Was similar to what would happen to an adult in real life.

☐ Did not unintentionally reinforce problem behavior.

☐ Had a teaching focus.

☐ "Fit the crime"—wasn't too severe or too mild.

☐ Was given in a calm, respectful way.

☐ Was given as privately as possible.

Key Points to Remember

- Punishment rarely has long-term effects on the behavior, especially for students with chronic behavior problems.

- Punishment does not teach students replacement behavior, that is, what they should do instead.

- Frequent use of punishment often results in the student having a negative attitude toward educators and school in general.

- The most effective behavioral management plan provides a balance of proactive strategies, positive contingencies, and natural and logical undesirable consequences that teach students to take responsibility for their behavioral choices and mirror real-life situations that they will face as adults.

- Teachers should discuss and help students predict natural undesirable consequences of their behavior to assist them in making the connection between their choices and what happens to them.

- Logical undesirable consequences are planned by educators and should be related, reasonable, and respectful.

- The way that a teacher presents a consequence to the student and its relation to the inappropriate behavior is what determines whether it is considered punishment or a logical undesirable consequence.

Discussion Questions and Activities

1. Explain the problems with punishment and the difference between punishment and logical undesirable consequences.

2. What are some natural undesirable consequences that are a result of the following behaviors:
   a. Conner calls a peer names because he won't share with him at recess.
   b. Grant picks his nose at the lunch table.
   c. Priya cheats on her spelling test.

3. Come up with a logical undesirable consequence for the following behaviors that is related, reasonable, and respectful. Write out what you would say to the student in each situation.
   a. Amit refuses to complete his assignment in math class.
   b. Jordan hits a classmate at recess following a disagreement.
   c. Maria runs out of the school when told to go to the principal's office after she yells at her teacher and uses profane words.

Chapter 13

Common Logical Undesirable Consequences

Before you read this chapter, we want to be very clear that undesirable consequences should be used only in combination with direct instruction of replacement behaviors, multiple prevention strategies, and high levels of positive reinforcement for exhibiting these replacement behaviors. Moreover, they should be used only when these positive behavior supports have been ineffective or inadequate in managing problem behavior!

Using only undesirable consequences without positive and proactive behavior supports is ineffective, and at times illegal, because the Individuals with Disabilities Education Act requires that positive behavior supports be considered for students receiving special education services who exhibit behaviors that interfere with learning. Many times we find that when we start talking about undesirable consequences with teachers, they go to these interventions first rather than last because they are most similar to the punitive interventions they are comfortable with. Always tell your students that you are willing to do whatever it takes to support them and will provide them with all kinds of positives if they are working with you and truly trying to learn appropriate behavior skills. If they are not trying, then you care about them too much to let them become their own worst enemy and will provide undesirable consequences to help teach them the skills they need to be successful in life. Their choices determine your choices.

Common Undesirable Consequences Continuum

In this section, we discuss the logical undesirable consequences that we have commonly used, starting with the low end of the continuum for minor offenses (level 1) and moving toward the higher end of the continuum for offenses that would mean big trouble for adults (level 5).

Three Strikes

Giving a predetermined number of warnings or redirects provides consistent structure for both the student and the educator. Many students need to know exactly where the limit is or they will continually feel the need to test it.

> Many students need to know exactly where the limit is or they will continually feel the need to test it.

Unfortunately educators tend to give more warnings and redirects when they are in a good mood and considerably fewer when they are in a bad mood. How many of you have let inappropriate behaviors go by one day and the next day respond to the first occurrence of problem behavior with, "That's it! I've had enough!" and give students an undesirable consequence that they didn't necessarily see coming.

Table 13.1 Undesirable Consequences Continuum

Reminder	Response cost or fine	Red schedule
Three strikes	Wasted time	In-school suspension
	Behavior tutoring	
	Think time	
Minor offenses that may be due to impulsivity, forgetfulness, or lack of attention	Continuing minor offenses or more serious offenses (refusal, disrespect)	Offenses that are against the law for an adult

Teaching students that they will get a certain number of warnings or redirects and consistently following through helps students accurately predict the consequences and therefore make fully informed choices. We feel a reasonable number of warnings or redirects to start with is three. If possible, we recommend doing this visually with no verbal interaction by crossing out numbers on a target behavior sheet, taking previously given tokens, or holding up fingers. This minimizes attention and opportunities for power struggles while still providing a consistent message.

After the third warning or redirect, there needs to be a higher level of an undesirable consequence. Typically in these cases, the student either truly does not know how to perform the desired behavior and needs additional instruction and practice or has moved from simply forgetting or acting impulsively to willfully exhibiting problem behavior.

Response Cost or Fines

Response cost is simply losing or having limited access to privileges or reinforcers.[1] This naturally happens in many of the positive reinforcement systems described in Chapters Ten and Eleven. When a daily level system similar to the one described in Chapter Eleven is used, a repeated behavior problem would automatically result in limited access to reinforcers during preferred activity time. In the case of a penny or token board, a student would not earn all her tokens, thus having to delay her access to reinforcement until she "tries again" and exhibits the appropriate behavior. In systems where a student proceeds through levels over more long-term performance, dropping a level may also be a form of a response cost consequence. In the economic simulation type of token system, students may be given fines for certain behaviors.

Wasted Time

Wasted time is based on the idea that the teacher and students in the classroom are learning partners, both with important jobs to do. The primary reason for attending school is to do these jobs, and anything that interferes with anyone doing his or her best work is not accepted.

This concept is discussed with the students at the beginning of the school year and reviewed often, stressing that each person (including the teacher) is responsible for making choices that ensure everyone is successful. A student who is making a choice that interferes with anyone's job in the classroom is choosing to waste time. The teacher gives the student the choice to either stop the behavior that is interfering with the learning environment or continue. If the choice is to continue, the student will have to make up the wasted time up and work on these learning activities during a more preferred activity, usually free time, recess, or after school. For example, the teacher might say, "You can either start working quietly on your assignment in the next minute, or I will start keeping track of your wasted time."

It is important to back off and give the student a little bit of space and time to comply with the direction. We also recommend telling students that their choice will be communicated by their actions rather than requiring that the student make a verbal choice. We find this removes the power struggle and gives students a way to save face while still following the teacher's direction. However, if the student's actions show that she chooses to continue the inappropriate behavior, her teacher keeps track of this wasted time. A basic stopwatch works well for this purpose.

Troubleshooting

When we recommend the wasted time strategy, educators always ask, "What if they waste hours of time?" In fact, this is a common problem and a good example of a behavior burst that you need to wait out as the student tests to see if you will truly follow through with what you say. Before implementing wasted time, we are always prepared to have two staff members stay after school as long as necessary (or at least for enough of a period of time to make the point) and have arrangements made with the student's parents for transportation. If the student decides to test you and experiences the undesirable consequence of making up the time (usually it just takes once), not only does the student learn that you will truly follow through, but other students who are watching and listening also learn the lesson. Once we established this strategy in our program, we almost never had the situation actually happen because the students truly believed that we would indeed follow through. We often heard, "Dude, don't try it. She will actually do it!"

Behavior Tutoring

Behavior tutoring is based on the idea that the teacher directly teaches and has students practice the behaviors that they are expected to exhibit in the classroom. After this instruction has taken place, a student who exhibits an inappropriate behavior is given a chance to demonstrate the appropriate behavior to show that he has indeed mastered it. If he does not, the teacher assumes that he has forgotten the desired behavioral skill or did not learn it initially and needs practice.

A behavior tutoring session is then scheduled during a more preferred activity, typically during free time or recess, or after school. For example, if a student is not walking down the hall appropriately, the teacher might say, "I know we learned as a class how to walk down the hall appropriately at the beginning of the school year. Have you forgotten how to do that?" If the student replies that she has not forgotten, she is asked to please demonstrate the appropriate hall walking behavior. If she does not, the teacher may respond, "Your actions tell me that you have forgotten. Let's schedule a time to practice. What works best for you: recess or after school?"

Think Time

The think time strategy, designed by Nelson and Carr,[2] is based on a combination of precision requests,[3] time-out from reinforcement,[4] and giving students feedback and assisting them in planning for similar situations in the future.[5] We use an intervention that is very similar to this one when a student is disturbing the learning of other students. This strategy is intended to break the chain of inappropriate behavior early, minimizing the time spent in a negative behavior pattern, and allow other students making good choices to continue with their learning uninterrupted.

During think time, the student takes a short break away from the stimulus and distraction of other students to think about his or her choices and their possible consequences. The student goes to the designated think time area—which could be any area slightly away from the other students designated by the teacher, such as a desk or study carrel—or is given a choice of several areas. The think time area may possibly be out of the view of the other students if peer attention is a partial function of the problem behavior. The teacher problem-solves with the student after a few minutes if the student is demonstrating by his or her actions that he or she is ready to engage in the problem-solving process.

The Importance of Problem Solving

A major problem with any undesirable logical consequence that temporarily removes a student from the learning environment is that when it is implemented, educators often just apply the consequence without a teaching component, simply allowing the student to return to the group after a certain period of time. This intervention is actually an incidental teaching opportunity to focus on the direct instruction of replacement behavior. Forgetting or neglecting to include the crucial component of problem solving with the student results in an intervention with a more punitive rather than a teaching focus. "You did something wrong; therefore, you have to go away" is the underlying message. A teaching approach would be to assist the student in identifying the undesirable behavior she chose and its effect on her and others, in addition to making a more appropriate plan for future similar situations. This can be done verbally, using visuals, or through writing. The key is that the student can answer questions that are similar to the following:

- What did you do that was a problem?

- Why was it a problem?

- What are some things you could do differently in similar situations in the future?

- How will you fix the problem (for example, apologize, clean up a mess, or make up missed work)?

- What do you think would happen to an adult in a similar situation?

Some students have great difficulty answering these questions, specifically the first one: What did you do that was a problem? It is crucial that the educator identify whether this is because the student can't identify the inappropriate behavior (in which case, she needs to be directly taught what behavior was a problem and given the rationale of why it was a problem) or if she is simply having trouble admitting to and taking ownership of her behavior (in which case, she needs to be waited out). As any educator can attest to, students (and many adults) can go to great lengths not to take personal responsibility for their choices. Until the student is able to have an honest conversation about the poor choices she made, it is impossible to assist her in seeing the connection between the undesirable consequences she experienced and her behavior.

Troubleshooting

If you are certain that a student does know what inappropriate choice he made but is unable to own his behavior by identifying this choice, simply say, "I can see you are not ready to problem-solve. That's okay. I know this is hard. We can try again in a few minutes." Continue checking with the student until he is able to identify his behavior choices. If this goes on for an extended period of time, you could choose to implement the wasted time intervention to motivate the student to engage in the process. If he truly knows what behavior was inappropriate, it is important not to identify it for the student; simply giving a one-sided lecture is not engaging him in problem solving. His participation in this process is crucial, so the initial identification of what happened and why it was a problem needs to come from him.

We want to help these students solve their own problems, not solve them for the students.

Consequence Maps

It is important that students are fully informed of the possible positive and negative consequences of their choices. They need all the information up front in order to make an informed decision. Consequence maps are a way to visually show students the connections between their choices and the consequences that may or will follow.

Consequence maps can be premade and laminated, drawn on a blank frame like the one shown in Figure 13.1 or drawn on the spot. Consequence maps can also be used as an excellent graphic organization for any type of problem solving by adding as many rows as there are possible solutions or options. When using a consequence map, the teacher sits down with a student and helps her identify a situation where she has been having difficulty—for example, "The teacher gives me an assignment I don't like." The teacher and student

> It is important that students are fully informed of the possible positive and negative consequences of their choices. They need all the information up front in order to make an informed decision.

then map out the positive choice, the negative choice, and the natural and logical consequences that are likely to follow each. The positive choice should always be stressed and put on the top row of the map. We also recommend starting with the natural consequences ("I will be proud of myself," "I will get better grades") so that the internal reinforcement that we want to develop will be stressed. The student identifies which consequences she prefers and therefore the choice she needs to make to experience that consequence. (Reproducible 6 provides a template for the map.) An example basic consequence map is shown in Figure 13.2.

Consequence mapping can be used with all age and ability levels and with individual or groups of students. It can take the form of a simple if-then chart for preschoolers using visuals. (A blank if-then chart is shown in Figure 13.3, and Reproducible 7 provides a template.) The positive choice can be mounted on one side of poster board on a green background to indicate a good or "go" choice and the not-so-positive choice can be

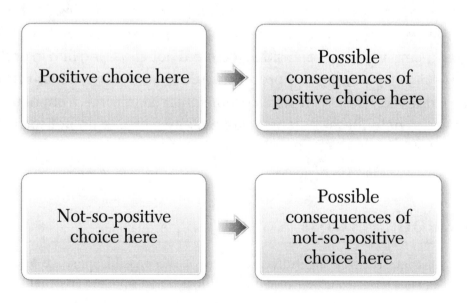

Figure 13.1 Consequence Map

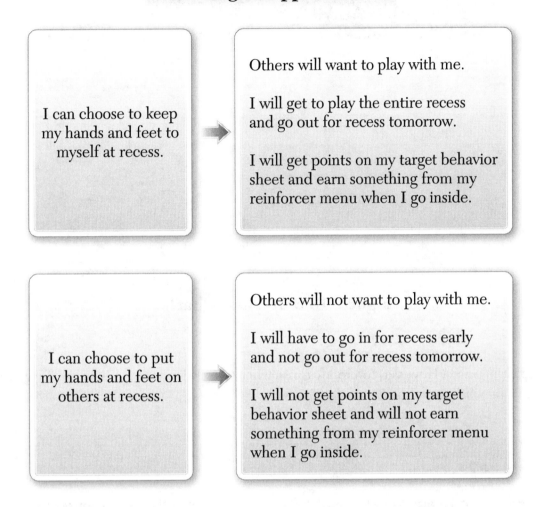

What might happen if . . . ?

I can choose to keep my hands and feet to myself at recess.

→ Others will want to play with me.

I will get to play the entire recess and go out for recess tomorrow.

I will get points on my target behavior sheet and earn something from my reinforcer menu when I go inside.

I can choose to put my hands and feet on others at recess.

→ Others will not want to play with me.

I will have to go in for recess early and not go out for recess tomorrow.

I will not get points on my target behavior sheet and will not earn something from my reinforcer menu when I go inside.

Figure 13.2 Example Consequence Map

mounted on the other side on a red background to indicate a poor or "stop" choice. Teachers can then flip the chart to whichever side is needed to remind students of the consequences of their choices.

Consequence maps can also take the form of a more complex chart for older students that connects their choices with not only the possible consequences but also the perceptions of those around them. An example of this type of consequence map is shown in Figure 13.4.

Alternatives to Out-of-School Suspension

Out-of-school suspensions are a commonly used intervention in response to severe inappropriate behavior in schools. Many times, suspensions are written into the district discipline codes and therefore are frequently used in response to aggression, disruption, disrespect,

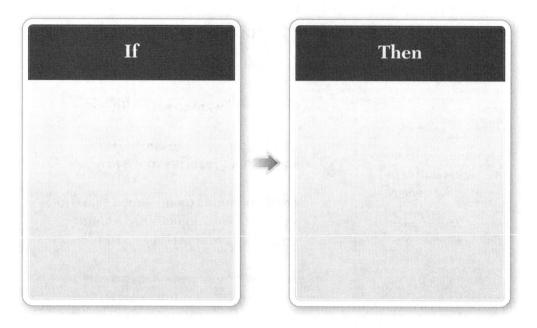

If	Then

Figure 13.3 If-Then Chart

and repeat offenses. However, too many times when we send students home, we are giving them exactly what they want.

Kaye Says...

I experienced a good example of giving students exactly what they wanted when we sent them home in the early years of our program for students with behavioral challenges. Tom was a fifth-grade student who had struggled in school for many years. He had significant learning disabilities, and school was hard for him. On top of learning difficulties, he also had increasingly aggressive behaviors in school, which resulted in his placement in our program. In his previous schools, Tom was suspended when he became aggressive.

On one of the first days in our program, Tom was given a task that was difficult for him. He resisted and quickly became agitated, escalating to the point of punching the teacher. Once Tom had been removed to a safe area, the teacher went in to problem-solve with him about the incident.

After this happened several times, he asked "What do you have to do to get suspended around here?" It was obvious to me that Tom had used aggression as an avoidance technique to escape school, which was very difficult for him. To send him home would have provided Tom with the out he was looking for, reinforcing his choice of aggressive behaviors at school. This would only increase the likelihood that the aggression would recur and possibly intensify. A better option for Tom and many other students like him would be to provide a true time-out from reinforcement through alternatives to out-of-school suspension.

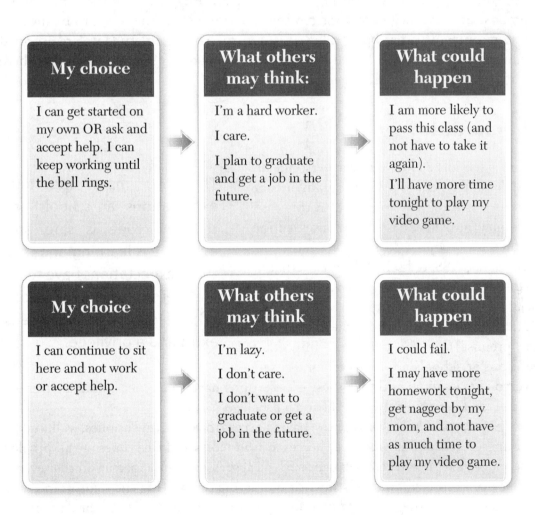

Figure 13.4 Consequence Map of Others' Perceptions

Source: Created by Kelly Lee, autism specialist.

In-School Suspension

Most educators are familiar with in-school suspension (ISS) programs. However, just keeping students at school in what is referred to as an ISS program will not be effective if it is not designed and implemented appropriately. It is not uncommon for students to enjoy ISS because they get a quiet place to work, one-on-one assistance, and adult attention. If this is the case, those components need to be embedded in their typical school day and minimized to the greatest extent possible in ISS.

A crucial component of an effective ISS program is the behavior of the adult supervisor. It is important for the supervisor to be consistent and respectful while limiting engaging and potentially reinforcing attention and interaction. The effectiveness of ISS is also highly dependent on how reinforcing the regular education environment is compared to the ISS environment. Students have to want to get back to the typical education environment and demonstrate that they have mastered the behavioral skills they need to be successful in that environment before being allowed to return. Too often students are assigned a certain number of days in ISS and are not required to make any behavioral progress before returning to the regular classroom environment.

Red Schedule

Many times schools do not have the personnel or space to develop an effective ISS program outside the typical classroom environment. In this case, teachers may implement a similar intervention within their classroom in the form of what we call *red schedule*. Like ISS, red schedule, an alternative to out-of-school suspension for severe behavior, provides the student with supervised behavioral skill learning opportunities. Red schedule is based on the premise that the two most important expectations at schools are that everyone is safe and everyone is learning and that these expectations have to be met before anything else can take place. Everything else is extra and a privilege.

> The two most important expectations at schools are that everyone is safe and everyone is learning and that these expectations have to be met before anything else can take place. Everything else is extra and a privilege.

Sitting by and talking to classmates, having access to your own supplies, walking down the hall unescorted, and having free choices during recess and free times are all privileges. If a student engages in a severe behavior such as aggression, the expectation that everyone is safe has not been met, and the student's typical life of enjoying the reinforcement that accompanies these privileges would literally stop (thus the word *red*) until he demonstrates that he has mastered and is ready to exhibit the two most important expectations. Thus, this student would be put on a red schedule.

During red schedule, the student sits in a defined area where he can still hear and see instruction as needed and remains there for the day unless escorted by an adult. We often used a study carrel with the student's area defined by tape surrounding it on the floor and a colorful, portable screen that could be used to block him from the reinforcing view of other students nearby if needed. Students are of course taken on bathroom and drink breaks, but they are escorted and closely supervised during those times to the greatest extent possible while still maintaining their dignity and privacy. Students participate in all typical activities but do so alone in the defined area. For example, during the student's physical education time, alternate exercise activities are done as recommended by the physical education teacher. All choices are made by the teacher, including what materials are used to complete assignments and the order in which assignments are given. Students interact only with adults (and possibly only one adult), and access to special activities such as parties, special assemblies, and recess is temporarily suspended or greatly restricted.

Students earn a defined percentage of daily points on their target behavior sheet to earn the privilege of returning to "green schedule" when their normal school routine and activities resume. The amount of time spent on red schedule is determined by the severity of the inappropriate behavior and the developmental level of the student. We recommend teaching students about red schedule using a social story and have provided possible text content including type of each sentence according to Carol Gray's guidelines in Table 13.2 (also see our discussion in Chapter Five) and written directions and cues while on red schedule in Table 13.3.

Troubleshooting

If red schedule or in-school suspension does not work fairly quickly, something about it is reinforcing the student. Does he enjoy the personal attention from the one adult providing the supervision? Is he getting more help on his work than normal? Does he enjoy working in a quiet environment? Is he escaping peer interactions that he finds stressful?

If this is the case, you need to build those things into the student's regular day or minimize them to the greatest extent possible during red schedule or other in-school suspension. In our experience, these interventions work because there is minimal reinforcement present. The student is pretty much bored to tears. But this is not a punishment, and although the supervising adult should interact minimally with the student, he or she should not do so in an angry or lecturing manner.

Table 13.2 Red Schedule Social Story Text

Text	Type of Sentence
Almost every day, we go to school to learn and see our friends and teachers.	Descriptive
Students get to do lots of fun things at school, like have recess, eat lunch in the lunchroom with their friends, and learn with their friends.	Descriptive
At school, the most important thing is that everyone stays safe. This means that everyone keeps their bodies to themselves.	Affirmative Descriptive
Sometimes things happen at school that I don't like, and I start to feel upset. It is okay to feel upset. I can still stay safe when I feel this way if I make good choices to help me calm down and feel better.	Perspective Affirmative Directive
Some good choices I can make to help me calm down and feel better are: 　1. I can use my words to tell an adult how I feel. 　2. I can ask for a break. 　3. I can take deep breaths. 　4. I can think about things that I like to do and that make me happy.	Directive
It is okay to feel upset at school. It is NOT okay to hit, kick, scratch, or bite when I feel this way. These things are NOT safe. They may hurt other people's feelings or scare or bother them. These are called level 5 behaviors and are against the law for adults.	Affirmative Descriptive Affirmative Perspective Descriptive
If I choose to do a level 5 behavior at school, my teacher will tell me that I am on RED schedule. This means I will need to sit by myself away from my friends and practice staying safe. An adult will help me. My teacher is not angry with me but wants me to learn how to stay safe at school.	Descriptive Descriptive Cooperative Perspective
When I can show by my behavior choices that I know how to stay safe, I will be able to return to my normal GREEN schedule. On green schedule, I will be able to do fun things with my friends and other teachers.	Directive Descriptive
When I stay safe at school, I can stay with my friends and teachers and do fun things. My parents and teachers are very happy and proud of me when I stay safe at school. I am proud of myself when I stay safe at school.	Directive Perspective Perspective

Table 13.3 Red Schedule Directions

The two most important things at school are to be safe and to learn. Everything else is a privilege. Your behavior shows that you cannot make positive choices to stay safe and learn on your own, so temporarily Ms. Tuttle will make many of your choices for you. No one is angry with you. Your parents and Ms. Tuttle just want to make sure that you and everyone else can stay safe and learn at school, and so you will spend the morning practicing making good choices. If you show that you can be trusted to make good choices by earning 90 percent of your points this morning, you will be back on your regular green schedule this afternoon.

For the morning:

You must stay in the taped area unless you have permission to leave it from Ms. Tuttle.

You may talk only to Ms. Tuttle.

You must raise your hand and wait patiently for Ms. Tuttle if you need help or have a question.

You will be given the supplies you need and will not have access to your own supplies.

You will not attend lunch in the cafeteria. You will eat in the red schedule area and do a quiet activity there when you are finished.

Ms. Tuttle will choose an adult to go with you to recess, where you will play in an area by yourself with a choice of two activities.

If you need to leave the room for any reason such as going to the bathroom or nurse's office, you will be escorted by Ms. Tuttle in the hallway.

Advantages of Alternatives to Out-of-School Suspension

We find alternatives to suspension that truly provide time-out from reinforcement, such as ISS and red schedule, to be effective for many reasons. These interventions eliminate the probability that the student will be unsupervised during the day and able to engage in reinforcing activities or cause trouble in the community. Parents generally tend to be more supportive because they are often frustrated by frequent out-of-school suspensions that create problems for them in terms of finding child care and going to work. ISS and red schedule are similar to real-life consequences students may encounter in the future. If adults are repeatedly aggressive in society, their participation in it will be restricted and monitored, and ISS and red schedule mirror that reality.

Students need to learn that severe inappropriate and unsafe behavior is serious and be taught replacement behaviors while the penalty is still minor and reversible.

ISS and red schedule help students learn the connection between their severe problem behavior and the natural and logical consequences of the loss of trust and privileges. Students are still required to complete their work and engage in the learning process, and they are not allowed to escape and avoid any school activity, making time spent in ISS or on red schedule a valuable learning experience.

> Students need to learn that severe inappropriate and unsafe behavior is serious and be taught replacement behaviors while the penalty is still minor and reversible.

In Tom's case, red schedule eradicated his aggressive behaviors at school. He was able to stay at school and learn. Because he was at school more, he made amazing academic progress. Experiencing success helped him to feel better about school and made him want to be there. The positive effects trickled down as success breeds success. We have seen many other students experience this same kind of success because of the effective use of alternatives to out-of-school suspension.

Key Points to Remember

- Undesirable consequences should be used only in combination with direct instruction of replacement behaviors, multiple prevention strategies, and high levels of positive reinforcement for exhibiting these replacement behaviors.

- Undesirable consequences should be used only when these positive behavior supports have been ineffective or inadequate in managing problem behavior.

- Teaching students that they will get a certain number of warnings or redirects and consistently following through help students accurately predict consequences and therefore make fully informed choices.

- Wasted time is a logical consequence based on the premise that if a student is not doing her job, her behavior is getting in the way of the teacher's doing his job. The student is wasting time that she will have to make up during the school day instead of engaging in more preferred activities like recess, free time, and after-school programs.

- Once a behavioral skill has been directly taught and practiced, teachers may use extra practice through behavior tutoring as a logical consequence. The teacher can assume a child has forgotten the skill and schedule a time during recess, free time, or after school to remediate and practice the skill.

- Think time involves breaking the chain of problem behavior early by having the student take a short break away from the stimulus and the distraction of other students. It is based on a combination of precision requests, time-out from reinforcement and giving students feedback and assisting them in planning for similar situations in the future.

- Problem solving should be used following any removal from the class. It is a teaching opportunity where the student and teacher can review choices made, connect behavior with consequences, and review previously taught replacement skills.

- Out-of-school suspension is ineffective for students with challenging behavior who may be looking for ways to escape the academic or social demands of school. A structured in-school suspension or red schedule are two alternatives to out-of-school suspension.

Discussion Questions and Activities

1. Wasted time is a logical consequence that has been effective with many students with challenging behavior. What are some arguments you would foresee coming from teachers when this intervention is recommended? What would your justification be?

2. Using the examples of consequence mapping given in this chapter, create a consequence map for "throwing things when you are mad."

3. Formulate a persuasive script outlining reasons that alternatives to suspension should be used with an aggressive student you teach.

Part Six

Putting It All Together

Chapter 14

Conducting Effective and Efficient Functional Behavioral Assessments

Now that your behavior intervention toolbox is well stocked, how do you determine which behavior interventions to use when? This is the primary purpose of functional behavioral assessment: to help in the design of behavior intervention plans that match the function of the behavior and are efficient and effective. We have discussed multiple examples of brief and informal functional behavioral assessment in this book that lead to effective responses from educators and result in the successful modification of behavior without any paperwork. Table 14.1 gives some examples of interventions previously discussed in this book that may "match" common functions of the behavior.

There are times when using a more formalized process and written format is helpful and sometimes this is required by law. Remember that the goal is to work smarter, not harder. Do not let yourself become intimidated by this process or make it overly complicated. Most of the time, functional behavioral assessments in the educational environment can be fairly simple and straightforward. Functional behavior assessments are

Table 14.1 Matching Intervention to Function

Function	Possible Interventions Based on Function
Attention	Social story about how to get attention appropriately
	Behavior-specific praise
	Positive attention tracker
	Reinforcement items that give attention (play game with a preferred adult, get round of applause from the class)
	Group-oriented contingency—earn something for the class
	Planned ignoring by adults and peers
Escape or avoidance of task	Social story on how to take short, appropriate breaks
	Task assessment to determine whether the task is too difficult or overwhelming
	Break tasks into chunks with small reinforcer after each chunk
	Punch cards—use getting out of part of the task as reinforcer
	Wasted time—not allowing the student to escape the task through problem behavior
Impulsivity or hyperactivity	Social story about how to calm your thinking or body
	Chart moves self-monitoring system
Communicate feelings	Social story about how to communicate feelings appropriately
	Regular check-in with an adult with whom the student has built a positive relationship

conducted *before* designing a behavior intervention plan, so that the information collected during this process can be used to make the plan more effective. For this reason, we are covering the two processes in two separate chapters. In this chapter, we will discuss the first three steps of the functional behavioral assessment process, which ends in the development of a hypothesis about why the problem behavior is occurring. Chapter Fifteen will then focus on using this information to design the behavior intervention plan. The final steps are determining whether the hypothesis was correct and the behavior plan resulted in improved behavior, then monitoring the behavior plan over time to ensure this improvement is maintained.

Step One: Operationally Define the Problem and Replacement Behaviors

To start the functional behavioral assessment process, all team members must know exactly what the problem behavior being targeted is. The definition of the problem behavior must pass the stranger test, meaning that if a stranger who has never met the student walked into the classroom, he or she would be able to accurately identify if the problem behavior was occurring. For example, the definition, "Johnny does not allow adults to be in charge," does not pass the stranger test because it is not clear exactly what behavior determines this. Is Johnny saying no when asked to do something? Is he arguing when the teacher gives him a direction? "Johnny speaks out without permission" is a better example of a behavior that is defined following the stranger test.

Step Two: Collect Information

For a functional behavioral assessment, you want information for three purposes. The first is to find out the student's strengths and interests in order to build on them when designing the behavior intervention plan. The second is to accurately identify setting events, triggering antecedents, and maintaining consequences. And the third is to get an accurate baseline of the frequency, duration, and intensity of the problem behavior, which serves as a starting point for determining if progress is being made after implementing the behavior plan.

We know that a lot of people see gathering data as a pain. However, we believe that many times this is because they haven't been taught to take data in a way that makes sense to and is useful for them. We used to feel the same way about data, and now that we understand, we find data a bit addictive. Data that are collected appropriately will make your life much easier. So let's address this challenge. The most common questions that we get asked are, "How much information is needed?" and "How exactly do I collect the data?"

How Much Information Is Needed?

In our experience, educators frequently collect a lot of information that they ultimately do not use. It is important to be thoughtful about the data that are truly needed to obtain a factual, accurate picture of the problem behavior and what is contributing to its occurrence and maintenance, while using the least amount of valuable educator time.

More Is Not Always Better

In a functional behavioral assessment, the objective is "to collect the *smallest amount* of useful information that results in summary statements to which key individuals can agree and have high confidence about their accuracy."[1] In the world of behavior intervention, time is of the essence because the longer a student practices an inappropriate behavior, the harder it is to change that behavior. As soon as enough data are collected for key individuals to agree on a hypothesized function, a plan that matches this hypothesis needs to be designed, implemented with fidelity, and monitored for effectiveness. Functional behavioral assessment is an ongoing process, and the plan will need to be tweaked and changed over time. Don't spend a great deal of time collecting a lot of data or worrying about conducting a flawless functional behavioral assessment. There is no such thing, and you will lose valuable intervention time in the process.

> In a functional behavioral assessment the objective is "to collect the smallest amount of useful information that results in summary statements to which key individuals can agree and have high confidence about their accuracy."

Just the Facts, Please!

Many teachers think that if they write everything down, certainly they will have all the necessary data. The fact is that many times, this results in a lot of unnecessary information that is not useful, and it leads to frustration on the part of the individual who took the considerable time to do that work. In addition, this type of information has the tendency to take the form of anecdotal notes that really function as a "gripe dairy" and include the opinions of the person recording the information. Make sure that you are sticking to the facts of the situation and not opinions that are often skewed by individual emotions that often accompany working with students that exhibit challenging behavior.

What About Adequate Baseline Data?

In a functional behavioral assessment, baseline data are always preferred. However, they are not necessarily required before designing a behavior intervention plan. In cases of extreme and dangerous behavior such as aggression, it is our strong opinion that the team should convene immediately and design a behavior intervention plan based on the limited information they do have and start a data collection system at that time for progress monitoring purposes. The quickest way to alienate and frustrate implementing team members is to require that extended baseline data be collected before assistance with designing a behavior intervention plan is offered. This is the real world, not a formal research experiment for publication in a peer-reviewed journal.

Think Math for Baseline Data

When collecting baseline data for the purposes of progress monitoring (which we discuss in more detail in the next chapter), it is important that the data can be graphed over time, so think in terms of hard numbers.

How Do I Collect the Data?

There is no specific recipe or magical form for collecting data that works in every situation. We have provided forms in the case studies in the next chapter that can provide some models. However, every situation is different, and you must be able to problem-solve and design your own data sheets.

> There is no specific recipe or magical form for collecting data that works in every situation.

The quick reference guide in Table 8.1 for making tables in Microsoft Word can be helpful in making individualized data sheets. Data can come from indirect sources or direct sources.

Indirect Data Sources

Indirect data sources are those that provide information on behavior that has happened in the past (even the very recent past) rather than observing the behavior as it happens. These types of data are helpful for providing information on student strengths and interests, setting events, triggering antecedents, and maintaining consequences but not for collecting baseline or ongoing levels of problem or replacement behavior.

We start collecting indirect data by having informal discussions with individuals who are involved in the student's life, such as teachers, other school personnel, parents, and the students themselves. The place to start in figuring out why a student is doing something is to ask the student. It may be as simple as that. There are formal questionnaires that have been created to guide this process, but we find the most effective way is to simply ask the individual to start telling us about himself or herself or the student having the problems. Many times if individuals are told that we are starting a "functional behavioral assessment," they become intimidated, freeze up, and insist there are no patterns or triggers, but if we start with, "Tell me about school," or "What is Johnny's day typically like?" patterns often emerge. Another common way of obtaining indirect data is reviewing the student's educational record, including discipline files, grades, and past assessment results if applicable.

Kaye Says...

I often use a note template (see Reproducible 8) or divide my notebook paper into four columns—labeled Strengths and Interests, Setting Events, Triggering Antecedents, and Maintaining Consequences—and start jotting down notes in the appropriate categories as they talk to get the process started. "We always know Monday and days after breaks are

(continued)

going to be hard" (possible setting event: after extended time away from school), "He likes to entertain the other students—total class clown" (possible maintaining consequence: peer attention), "Fire drills always set her off" (possible triggering antecedent: loud noises).

Direct Data Sources

Direct data are recorded in real time. In other words, someone is observing the student and recording the behavior as it is happening or as soon as possible after it happens. Direct data can be collected by anyone in the environment—the teacher, a paraprofessional, or an outside observer such as a behavior specialist or school psychologist. The most important thing is to use a data collection system that is simple, clearly understood by the collector, and lends itself to developing a progress monitoring system over time.

ABCF Charts

ABCF stands for antecedent, behavior, consequence, and function. These charts are a good way to collect both baseline levels of problem behavior and information on possible setting events, triggering antecedents, and maintaining consequences (see Table 14.2).

We like to do an informal interview with the student's educational team first and get some of their initial hypotheses and then create an individual ABCF chart for the student

Table 14.2 ABCF Chart

Date and Time	Possible Setting Events	Triggering Antecedent (What Happened Just Before Behavior)	Behavior Observed	Consequence (What Happened Immediately After)	Hypothesized Function	Notes

with check boxes for the top three in each category. This makes data collection extremely quick and easy in addition to determining if the hypotheses are correct or if there are other contributing factors they are overlooking that need to be added. Using check boxes also ensures that the data are simply a factual record of the variables in the environment and not the opinions of the recorder because it provides structured and limited language. Table 14.3 shows an example of an ABCF chart with check boxes.

Other Direct Data Sources for Monitoring Progress

Common ways to collect ongoing data for monitoring progress, when they are appropriate to use, and helpful data collection tools are identified in Table 14.4. For the candy technique mentioned in Table 14.4, see Table 14.5.

Step Three: Develop Hypotheses About Why the Problem Behavior Is Occurring

The next step is to examine the data you have collected and ask yourself the following questions:

- What patterns emerge?
- What conditions are occurring in the environment: time of day, day of the week, people in the environment, tasks that the student is being asked to do, and so on.
- What happens immediately before? What happens immediately after?

These are the potential setting events, triggering antecedents, and maintaining consequences and should lead directly to your hypothesized function by addressing questions such as the following:

- Is the child looking for attention?
- Is he or she trying to escape an undesired task or environment?
- Is he or she simply communicating feelings?

We have talked about all of these functions in depth and strategies for intervening throughout this book. Reproducible 9 provides a template for summarizing this information.

The last three steps of the formal functional behavioral assessment process are to design the behavior intervention plan based on the hypothesized function, test and confirm the functional behavioral assessment hypotheses, and monitor whether the plan is working, making adjustments if needed. These steps are the focus of the next chapter.

Table 14.3 ABCF Chart with Check Boxes

Date/ Time	Possible Setting Events	Antecedent (What Happened Just Before Behavior)	Behavior Observed	Consequence (What Happened Immediately After)	Hypothesized Function	Notes
	☐ Doesn't feel well ☐ No medication ☐ Bad weather ☐ Difficult morning at home ☐ Other (specify)	☐ Nonpreferred task ☐ Change in routine ☐ Preferred activity stopped ☐ Other (specify)	☐ Vocalization ☐ Aggression ☐ Other (specify)	☐ Attention given ☐ Break given/removed demand ☐ Other (specify)	☐ Escape demand ☐ Communicate feelings ☐ Get attention ☐ Other (specify)	
	☐ Doesn't feel well ☐ No medication ☐ Bad weather ☐ Difficult morning at home ☐ Other (specify)	☐ Nonpreferred task ☐ Change in routine ☐ Preferred activity stopped ☐ Other (specify)	☐ Vocalization ☐ Aggression ☐ Other (specify)	☐ Attention given ☐ Break given/removed demand ☐ Other (specify)	☐ Escape demand ☐ Communicate feelings ☐ Get attention ☐ Other (specify)	
	☐ Doesn't feel well ☐ No medication ☐ Bad weather ☐ Difficult morning at home ☐ Other (specify)	☐ Nonpreferred task ☐ Change in routine ☐ Preferred activity stopped ☐ Other (specify)	☐ Vocalization ☐ Aggression ☐ Other (specify)	☐ Attention given ☐ Break given/removed demand ☐ Other (specify)	☐ Escape demand ☐ Communicate feelings ☐ Get attention ☐ Other (specify)	

Table 14.4 Types of Direct Data

Type of Data	Description	When Appropriate	Collection Tools	Example
Frequency	How many times did the behavior occur in a set period?	Has clear beginning and end Happens frequently enough that progress can be seen over a four-week period Does not happen so frequently that the data collector will have difficulty recording every occurrence of the behavior	Golf counter Tally marks Candy technique	Tadahisa talked out without raising his hand 20 times during a 30-minute lesson.
Duration	How long does the behavior last?	Has clear beginning and end Does not happen frequently, but when it does happen, it lasts for an extended period of time or in clusters (like tantruming)	Stopwatch	Suzy exhibited tantruming behavior (hitting, kicking, and screaming) for 10 minutes.
Time interval	Does the behavior occur within a set interval?	Behavior may not have a clear beginning or end Provides an estimate when it is not possible or desirable to record all occurrences	Target behavior sheet	Viviana had difficulty following directions during 40% of time intervals recorded. (Time interval length approximately 30 minutes)
Momentary time sampling	Does the behavior occur at the exact end of a set interval?		Cuing system	Tommy was off task for 50% of the 10 time samples recorded. (Time interval length 1 minute)

Table 14.5 The Candy Frequency Count Strategy

Fill a small cup with enough M&Ms or Skittles to go beyond the high range of predicted occurrences of the student's behavior. For example, if a student talks out between approximately ten and twenty times each morning, put twenty-five pieces of candy in a cup. Eat a piece of candy every time the student talks out; then count the number left at the end of the morning and record that number. If there were five left, for example, the frequency count would be twenty.

Troubleshooting

We are often asked by educators, "What if no patterns emerge?" We have been doing functional behavioral assessments for a long time, and we have found that there are always patterns, but it may take more complex data collection and analysis to detect them. If no patterns emerge, enlist the help of other professionals—possibly a school psychologist or behavioral specialist.

Key Points to Remember

- The first step to a functional behavioral assessment is to define what the problem target behavior is so that it is clear to all team members.

- For a functional behavioral assessment, collect information to (1) find out the student's strengths and interests in order to build on them; (2) accurately identify setting events, triggering antecedents, and maintaining consequences; and ideally, (3) get an accurate baseline of the frequency, duration, and intensity of the behavior. This serves as a starting point for determining if progress is being made after implementing the behavior plan.

- Baseline data collection is intended to give an accurate picture of where the student is functioning prior to intervention and should be done in a timely manner so the behavior plan can begin.

- It is important to determine what types of data are truly needed and will lead to a factual, accurate picture of the problem behavior and what is contributing to its occurrence and maintenance.

- It is important for baseline data for the purposes of progress monitoring to be graphed over time, so think in terms of hard numbers.

- There is no universal way to collect data, although some published forms may be helpful. Educators must design data sheets that are individualized for each student's situation.

- The last step of a functional behavioral assessment covered in this chapter is for the team to formulate a hypothesis based on the data compiled about why the problem behavior is occurring. This information is used to design an effective and efficient behavior intervention plan.

Discussion Questions and Activities

1. Operationally define the following behaviors so they pass the stranger test.
   a. Disruptive in class
   b. Treats others rudely
   c. Avoids work

2. Determine the type of data (frequency, duration, time interval, momentary time sampling) that would best match the following behaviors:
   a. Sleeping in class
   b. Making noises in class
   c. Talking
   d. Off task

Chapter 15

Designing and Implementing Effective and Efficient Behavior Intervention Plans

Y ou now are familiar with the student's strengths and interests and have a good hypothesis about which setting events, triggering antecedents, and maintaining consequences are contributing to the problem behavior or why it is occurring. You are now ready for the final three steps of the process: designing a behavior intervention plan based on this information, testing and confirming the functional behavioral assessment hypothesis by determining whether the behavior improved, and monitoring the behavior plan over time and adjusting it as needed.

Step 4: Design a Behavior Intervention Plan Based on the Functional Behavioral Assessment

A behavior intervention plan has these essential components:

- A definition of the acceptable or desired replacement behavior that serves the same or similar function as the problem behavior and other important target behaviors—that is, what you want the student to do instead

- A plan for directly teaching these behaviors

- Prevention strategies that remove or modify the influence of each identified setting event and triggering antecedent or provide additional support

- Planned, systematic reinforcement for the student when he or she exhibits the desired behaviors

- Logical undesirable consequences for the student if he or she continues to exhibit the problem behavior

All of these components should sound familiar: they provided the framework for and are focused on in detail in the previous chapters. Now the goal is to organize them into a written, usable framework. Reproducible 10 provides a template for creating behavior intervention plans.

Step Five: Monitor and Adjust the Behavior Intervention Plan as Needed

This step involves collecting data on levels of the problem and/or replacement behavior over time and comparing them to baseline levels in order to confirm the hypothesis about the function(s) the problem behavior is serving. This process of confirming the hypothesis is much more complex in school settings than in clinical settings, because variables are constantly changing and therefore problem behaviors and their functions can also change. Too often, an Individual Education Plan (IEP) team meets once a year, develops the behavior intervention plan, and then does not review it again until the next IEP cycle twelve months later. In order to test and confirm the hypothesis, the following two questions must be answered on a regular basis. (1) Was the plan implemented as written? (In clinical settings, this is referred to as *fidelity*.) (2) Did the plan result in an improvement in behavior (testing and confirming the initial hypothesis), and did this improvement continue over time (progress monitoring)?

Was the Plan Implemented as Written?

We recommend that all behavior intervention plans include a simple checklist of essential components to determine at approximately what level of fidelity it is being implemented. Many times such plans are well designed but fail to improve behavior because they are not adequately implemented. Potentially effective plans can be prematurely abandoned when this happens, resulting in the loss of a great deal of valuable time spent creating multiple plans when the true issue is lack of fidelity during implementation.

If the plan is overly detailed, it is impossible to follow with 100 percent fidelity, which means it is out of compliance with the Individuals with Disabilities Education Act (IDEA) and will likely cause frustration for implementing team members. Consider this example: "Johnny will check in every morning with Mrs. Jones at 9:00 and have access to his individualized reinforcement menu every two hours based on exhibiting his replacement behavior." This statement is pretty much impossible to implement as written all the time. What if Mrs. Jones is sick? What if there is a fire drill at 9:00 and check-in doesn't happen until 9:15? There must be enough flexibility so that teams can realistically stick to the plan while still being able to adjust it based on unforeseeable changes in routine. A more workable plan would be: "Johnny will check in every morning with an available adult and have regular access to his individualized reinforcement menu throughout the school day based on exhibiting his replacement behavior."

> If the plan is overly detailed, it is impossible to follow with 100 percent fidelity, which means it is out of compliance with the Individuals with Disabilities Education Act and will likely cause frustration for implementing team members.

If the team needs an extremely detailed document to make sure everyone is on the same page and provide accountability, write a teacher- and paraprofessional-friendly implementation plan and summarize it in the official and legally binding behavior intervention plan.

Kaye Says . . .

In one of the school districts I work with, we include a prominent statement at the top of this implementation plan so there is no confusion: "This document is a flexible working document and is NOT an official part of the IEP. This plan is summarized in the behavior intervention plan in the IEP." I explain to parents that this is to reduce the number of meetings they are required by law to attend (and therefore time they are away from work or other responsibilities), not to try to find loopholes in the behavior intervention plan. I also provide parents a way to directly contact me or the case manager with any concerns they may have. I have yet to meet a parent who didn't embrace this system once it was thoroughly explained.

Did Behavior Improve, and Was This Improvement Maintained over Time?

Coming to an IEP meeting with everything marked "teacher judgment" simply does not work in this era of accountability. Decisions not based on objective data are often emotional and unreliable. We call this a "cardiac assessment": "I feel in my heart that he or she is doing better [or not doing better]." We would not make decisions about our health without objective data such as monitoring vital signs. In addition, it is impossible to make an objective and accurate judgment about whether the plan is working if ongoing, consistent data are not available. Moreover, you will save considerable time when you have objective data that show whether or not progress is being made, and you won't lose time in confusion and debate.

If the behavior goal is an IEP goal that is intended to be met in one year's time, the team should use a decision rule to determine if adequate progress is being made. For example, if the student's behavioral goal is, "Seth will demonstrate on-task behavior and earn 85 percent of his daily points as documented on his daily point card and graph" and the baseline data said the student was on task 71 percent of the time, the teacher would need to establish a graph with a goal line that starts at 71 percent and ends at 85 percent. The goal line would map out how much progress Seth would need to make in the year in order to meet the goal. The team could decide that intervention would be changed if Seth's growth plot showed that he was not on track to meet the set goal.

> If the behavior goal is an IEP goal that is intended to be met in one year's time, the team should use a decision rule to determine if adequate progress is being made.

Our preferred method of collecting progress monitoring data is to use target behavior sheets because they collect data daily, are often part of a student's plan, and can easily be graphed. Every student in our program had data taken on target behaviors from the day they stepped foot in our program so we had data to evaluate progress sometimes over several years. Figure 15.1 shows what these data, collected using daily target behavior sheets, might look like for an individual student. The line graph shows overall behavior, and the bar graph is broken down by individual target skills.

Progress monitoring data can be collected in a variety of ways (see Table 14.3), but they must be collected consistently using the same format in order for the data to be compared over time. Although data can be compared through graphing by hand, we highly recommend electronic graphing. Because the graphs can easily be printed, faxed, or e-mailed, this is especially helpful for reporting progress on IEP behavior goals to parents and sharing information on a student's behavior at school with doctors who are making medication adjustments. Paraprofessionals can enter the data, and even students can work on their self-management and technology skills by entering their own data. Table 15.1 provides a quick reference for graphing data using Microsoft Excel. We also recommend Goal Tracker, a software program developed specifically for special education service providers. More information and a free trial can be found at www.goal-tracker.com.

The next chapter contains several examples of functional behavioral assessments and behavior intervention plans, including forms and visuals needed for plan implementation, fidelity checklists, individualized data collection forms, and graphing systems for progress monitoring.

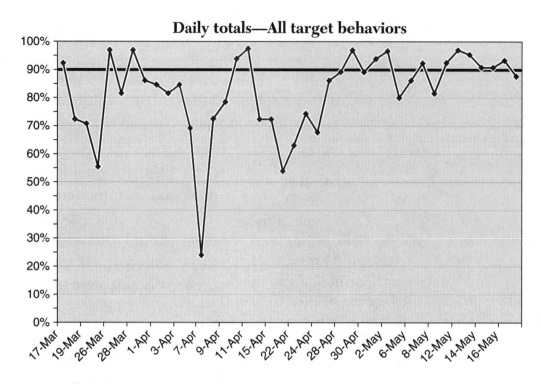

Daily totals—All target behaviors

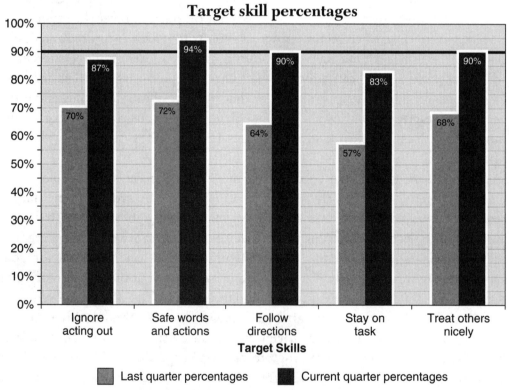

Target skill percentages

Last quarter percentages   Current quarter percentages

Figure 15.1 Target Behavior Sheet Graphs

**Table 15.1 Quick Reference Sheet for Graphing Data
with Microsoft Excel**

Enter date in column A.

Enter data for that date in column B.

Click on Column A, Row 1, and drag to highlight all data.

Click Insert-Chart-Line-Next.

Add titles for chart, category X (date), and value Y (typically frequency, minutes, or percentage)

Click Next-As new sheet-Add chart title (example: Joe's Talk-Outs).

Click Finish, and the graph will appear.

To view the original data, click Sheet 1 at the bottom. To view graphs, click on the name you gave the chart at the bottom.

Key Points to Remember

- A behavior plan has five essential components: (1) a specific definition of the acceptable or desired replacement behavior, (2) a plan for directly teaching this replacement behavior, (3) prevention strategies, (4) planned, systematic reinforcement for exhibiting replacement behavior, and (5) logical undesirable consequences if the student continues to exhibit the problem behavior.

- The hypothesis about the function(s) of the problem behavior is confirmed by answering two questions:

    Was the plan implemented as written?

    Did behavior improve, and was this improvement maintained over time?

- Educators should rely on data taken consistently over time and a decision rule when determining if interventions are working or not working.

- Electronically graphing data collected with daily target behavior sheets is an easy, consistent way to monitor progress over time.

Discussion Question

1. You are on an IEP team that has developed a behavior plan for one of your students. The classroom teacher called a meeting because the plan is not working. In your review, you find that some components of the plan are not being implemented. How would you bring this up tactfully for team discussion?

Chapter 16

Example Success Stories

The example success stories in this chapter are of hypothetical students who have characteristics and exhibit behaviors similar to those of some of the students we have worked with over the years. These stories provide some models of the concepts and strategies that we have set out in this book and how they can be combined to design a comprehensive behavior intervention plan based on a functional behavioral assessment process that is educator and school friendly. Each example presents the functional behavioral assessment and behavior intervention plan, a list and examples of support materials needed, a fidelity checklist, a data collection form, and an example of what the data graph might look like.

Example 1: Joey

Functional Behavioral Assessment Worksheet

Background information Include any information helpful in designing the behavior plan that does not fit into another category	Joey is a five-year-old kindergarten student diagnosed with attention deficit hyperactivity disorder. He lives with his biological parents and has a close relationship with his maternal uncle and grandparents who live on a farm. Joey attends a general education kindergarten class with twenty-four students and one teacher.
Strengths and interests To be used throughout the behavior intervention plan for reinforcers, interest-based curriculum, and so on	Joey does not exhibit any academic learning problems. He loves to play with blocks and computer games and watch Disney videos. He talks a lot about visiting the farm where his uncle and grandparents live. Joey wants to make friends at school.
Problem behaviors Operationally define to pass the stranger test and provide baseline if possible	Joey exhibits minor aggression toward peers and adults (grabs, shoves, hits). This aggression has never continued past one contact or become truly dangerous. Joey exhibited aggressive behavior eight times during a three-day period. He exhibits tantrum behavior (crying, kicking his feet on the floor). Joey has had six tantrums, lasting an average of ten minutes, during a three-day period.

Setting events and triggering antecedents
 	
You know it's going to be a bad day . . .
 	
The straw that broke the camel's back
	Joey's problem behaviors occur more frequently
	
	    After breaks such as weekends or vacations from school
	
	    When the activity is unstructured, such as center time
	
	    When he wants something someone else has or is doing

Maintaining consequences What is the naturally occurring payoff?	Joey has typically gained access to desired items and activities at home after exhibiting problem behavior, as his mother reports she typically "gives up to avoid conflict."

Hypothesized functions	Joey exhibits the problem behaviors to
	
	    Gain access to a desired object or activities
	
	    Communicate negative feelings such as impatience or frustration with peers

Behavior Intervention Plan Worksheet

Target and replacement behaviors	Joey will use his words to indicate what he wants, doesn't want, and feels. Joey will keep all parts of his body to himself.
Direct instruction of replacement behavior: Include what, who, when, and how	The teacher will check-in with Joey as soon as possible in the morning and at least three times throughout the school day, reviewing his target and replacement behaviors, why they are important, and the consequences of his possible choices by reading a social story, role playing, or using a consequence map. Joey will keep a visual reminder of his target and replacement behaviors with him on his token chart.

Prevention strategies: Remove or modify the influence of each identified setting event or triggering antecedent or provide additional support
 	
    After a break from school
 	
    In an unstructured activity
 	
    When given a direction
 	
    When he wants something someone else has or is doing
	The principal will check-in with Joey on Mondays and the first day back after breaks.
	
	More structure will be provided during center time by limiting activities and peers, and the teacher will stay in close proximity.
	
	During other unstructured activities such as recess and physical education, Joey will be paired with a preferred peer who has strong social skills who will remind him to use his replacement behavior.
	
	A brief check-in to provide precorrection will occur again before times during the day when Joey often has difficulty.

Remove or reduce naturally occurring maintaining consequences	Staff will not give in to avoid conflict but will wait out Joey's problem behavior, ignoring it as much as possible.
Positive reinforcement system	Joey will earn Disney or farm animal tokens intermittently throughout the day paired with behavior specific praise. When he earns five icons (which will be timed to correspond with natural breaks), he will choose an activity from his reinforcement menu for five minutes.

Positive reinforcement system (*continued*)	Joey will take an "I was safe" note home at the end of every day when he exhibits no aggression, even if he tantrums.
Natural or logical undesirable consequences	Joey's peers and adults in his environment will be taught to kindly and calmly tell him they don't like it when he touches them or disrupts their classroom with his choices. When early signs of agitation are noticed, an adult will show Joey a yellow card to "stop and think" and encourage him to move to the designated classroom think time area. If Joey moves when asked, he will receive a token paired with behavior-specific praise. If Joey refuses to move, peers will be moved out of his reach and view. He will spend the next recess practicing how to move to the think time area. The teacher will problem-solve with Joey when he demonstrates by his nonverbal communication that he is completely calm and ready to partner in problem solving.
Progress monitoring plan	Frequency of aggressions and duration of tantruming behavior will be taken daily and graphed every three days to compare to baseline. Joey's team will meet again at the end of the first quarter during parent-teacher conferences to review his progress. If Joey's aggression increases dramatically before then, the team will reconvene as soon as possible.

Joey's Safe Note for Home

Joey's Target Token Board (Front)

Joey's Target Token Board (Back)

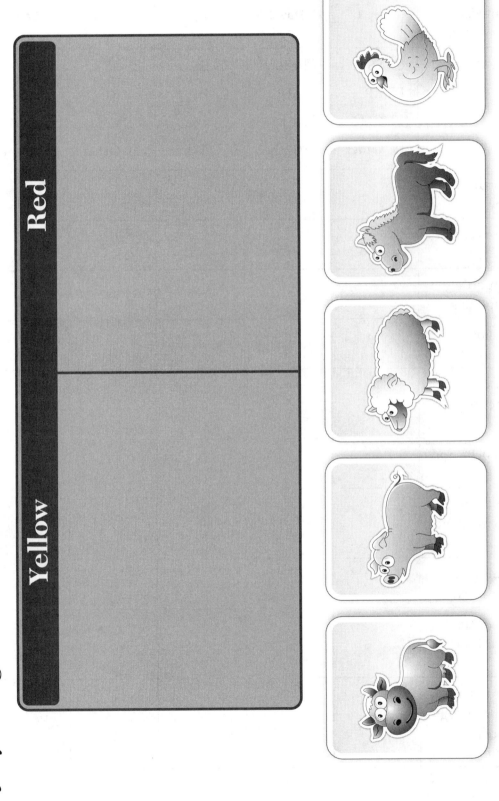

Yellow	Red

All squares are laminated and attached to the token board with sticky fabric so the color cards can be pulled off and shown to Joey as needed and the icons can be pulled off and adhered to the token board on the front as he earns tokens for using his words and keeping his body to himself.

Joey's Fidelity Checklist

Important Plan Components/Day	Day 1	Day 2	Day 3	Day 4	Day 5
Morning triage	☐ SS ☐ RP ☐ CM ☐ Other	☐ SS ☐ RP ☐ CM ☐ Other	☐ SS ☐ RP ☐ CM ☐ Other	☐ SS ☐ RP ☐ CM ☐ Other	☐ SS ☐ RP ☐ CM ☐ Other
Token board kept with Joey					
Structured centers time					
Peer support during specials					
Peer support during recess					
Number of precorrection check-ins					
Problem behavior ignored					
Number of times reinforcement was earned					
Safe note taken home if earned					
Number of times yellow card was shown					
Praise or tokens given for moving to safe area if applicable					

How to Reach and Teach Children with Challenging Behavior

Joey's Data Sheet

Date	Frequency Count: Make a tally mark every time Joey is aggressive toward peers or adults by grabbing, shoving or hitting, or throwing. If other acts of aggression occur, please specify.	Total Acts of Aggression	Duration: Use a stopwatch to measure how many minutes Joey's tantrum behavior lasts, including crying and kicking his feet. If other tantruming behaviors occur, please specify.

Joey's Data Graphs

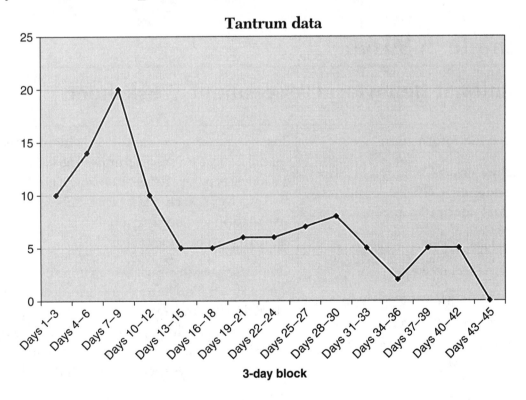

Tantrum data

3-day block

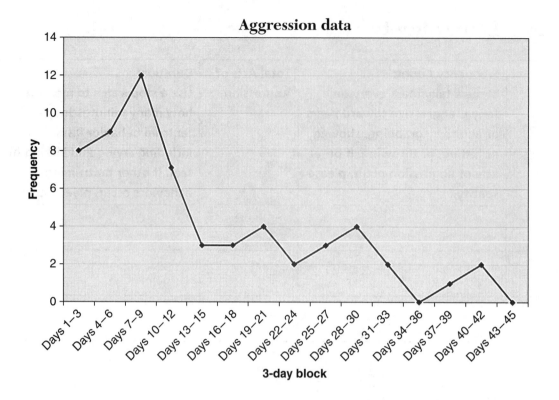

Aggression data

Example 2: Susan

Functional Behavioral Assessment Worksheet

Background information Include any information helpful in designing the behavior plan that does not fit into another category	Susan is a fourth-grade student who receives special education services under the learning disability category for written language. She also receives speech services for language and articulation and occupational therapy services for help with her fine motor skills.
Strengths and interests Use throughout the behavior intervention plan for reinforcers, interest-based curriculum, and so on	On past IQ testing, Susan scored in the average range. Susan likes hands-on learning activities, educational games (especially on the computer), and art. She also likes preteen magazines and other "girly" things like clothes and costume jewelry. She enjoys socializing with the other girls in her class.

How to Reach and Teach Children with Challenging Behavior

Problem behaviors Operationally define to pass the stranger test, and provide baseline if possible	Susan has a difficult time completing her assignments to the best of her ability and within the allotted time. The first three weeks of school she had fifteen late assignments—five each week. Susan often whines or makes crying noises during class. Baseline data were not collected; her general education teacher estimates that this happens about ten to fifteen times a day.

Setting events and triggering antecedents
 	
    You know it's going to be a bad day...
 	
    The straw that broke the camel's back
	Susan's problem behaviors occur more frequently
	
	    When the task involves writing
	
	    When the task has multiple steps
	
	    When the task is difficult for her
	
	    When the task is not of high interest to her
	
	    In a large group environment

Maintaining consequences What is the naturally occurring payoff?	Susan often temporarily escapes or avoids activities that are undesirable or difficult by not putting forth her best effort, so she finishes quickly or does not stay on task. Staff and peers often give Susan attention (both positive by sympathizing or negative by expressing their annoyance) when she whines or cries.

Hypothesized functions	Susan engages in the problem behaviors to
	
	    Escape and avoid written, difficult, or lengthy tasks
	
	    Communicate frustration with or boredom or disinterest in an assignment
	
	    Get attention from others

Behavior Intervention Plan Worksheet

Target and replacement behaviors	Susan will take appropriate, temporary short breaks when needed during work time. Susan will stay on task. Susan will use her words to calmly ask for help from a peer or adult when she does not understand something.
Direct instruction of replacement behavior: Include what, who, when, and how	Susan will be directly taught her target or replacement behaviors through one-on-one social skills lessons during her time in the learning center. Susan will read her "What Might Happen If?" visual with an adult prior to work times that are predicted to be difficult for her to stay on task to remind her of the connection between staying on task and natural and logical consequences.
Prevention strategies: Remove or modify the influence of each identified setting event or triggering antecedent or provide additional support	Susan will be allowed to take one five-minute break for approximately every thirty-minute working period. Every effort will be made to build Susan's assignments around her interests, such as fashion and friendships. Susan will be given a choice of various writing utensils when possible, such as glittery pens and markers, to increase her motivation to complete the assignment. Susan will be paired with a peer tutor during assignments that she is expected to complete in the large group environment, and the peer will be taught to chunk the assignment, set a time goal, and check with Susan after every chunk, in addition to giving her positive attention and encouragement for completing each chunk.

Remove or reduce naturally occurring maintaining consequences	Every effort will be made by staff and peers to ignore Susan's whining and crying.
	Susan will be required to correct all assignments that are incorrect or not completed neatly. During occupational therapy she will make a sloppy, an everyday and a best handwriting sample for self-monitoring of writing quality.
Positive reinforcement system	Susan will self-monitor and be regularly reinforced for using her target or replacement behaviors with the use of a target behavior sheet. Susan's day will be broken into three sections (see target behavior sheet), and she will have a progress check at the end of each section. If her work is completed up to that point, she can choose from the appropriate section of her reward menu (see the target behavior sheet and reward menu for details).
	Susan will take her target behavior sheet home daily and share it with her parents for additional review and practice of her target and replacement behaviors and reinforcement. The parents will sign the sheet, and Susan will take it back to school the following day. This is Susan's responsibility. If she brings her signed target behavior sheet back the following day, she can start her morning by choosing from her progress check reward menu.
Natural and logical undesirable consequences	If Susan does not earn the designated number of target behavior sheet points, she will not be able to choose off her reward menu.
	If this continues, Susan will naturally not earn as high of grades in her classes. This connection will be reviewed regularly with Susan during her direct instruction time using her consequence map.
	On Thursdays, Susan will stay after school to complete any unfinished assignments for the week.

(continued)

Progress monitoring plan	Copies of Susan's target behavior sheets will be kept for time interval data. During the last triage of the day, Susan will figure and record her daily percentage and enter it on her electronic graph.
	The number of incomplete assignments for the week will be recorded on Thursday before Susan starts her after-school session.
	The team will meet at the end of the quarter to review Susan's progress. Susan's parents will track her grades online and will call the school to schedule a meeting if they have concerns before that time.

Susan's Self-Monitoring Target Behavior Sheet

Date _____

Schedule and Target Behaviors	Morning Routine/ Progress Check	Math	Snack/ Restroom	Special Class	Recess/ Progress Check	Grammar	Strategies/ Spelling/ Study Hall	Lunch/ Recess/ Progress Check	Social Studies/ Science	Communi-cation Arts	End-of-Day/ Routine Read Aloud/ Progress Check
I can stay on task with no more than one redirect.	Progress check for signed card				Progress check 10:30			Progress check 1:00			
I can ask for help when I need it.											

I will mark each time period and my teacher will circle it if she agrees.

I must earn twelve (miss no more than two) total points to circle a star at the end of the day.

Teacher Comments: _____

_____

_____

Parent Signature/Comments: _____

_____

_____

Susan's Reinforcement Menu

If I have all my work done at my progress check, I can choose ONE progress check reward from this menu:

Progress check rewards

- I can spend ten minutes doing a preferred activity of my choice with a friend (look at magazine, drawing, computer game, play a quick game, talk to a friend).
- The class will give me a round of applause.
- I can show my target behavior sheet to the principal.
- I can e-mail my mom and dad that I am making great choices at school.
- Other (I can add anything I can think of at any time as long as I okay it with my teacher).

If I earn twelve (miss no more than two) of my daily points, I can circle a star at the end of the day.

When I have circled five stars, I can choose a five star reward from the following menu:

Five star rewards

- ★ I can do a preferred activity of my choice (see above) with a friend for an extra twenty minutes.
- ★ I can eat lunch with an adult of my choice.
- ★ I can take a five-stars note home to my parents.
- ★ Other (I can add anything I can think of at any time as long as I okay it with my parents or teacher, or both).

How to Reach and Teach Children with Challenging Behavior

Susan's Consequence Map

What might happen if . . . ?

| I can choose to stay on task and ask for help appropriately. | → | I will get my work done on time, learn as much as I can, and get better grades.

I will feel proud of myself, and my teachers, friends, and parents will be proud of me.

I will have more time after school to do what I like to do. |

| I can choose to not stay on task and cry and whine when I need help. | → | I will not get my work done on time, won't learn as much as I can, and will get poor grades.

I will feel frustrated, and my teachers and parents will feel frustrated also.

I will have to stay after school on Thursdays to finish or redo my work. |

Susan's Target Skill Progress Computation Sheet

Directions:
1. Calculate your daily percentage for each of your target skills.
2. Enter your daily percentages in the appropriate columns of this worksheet.
3. Choose a friend to show you how to enter your daily percentages into your computerized progress graph.
4. Have your teacher check your work.

Date	Stay on Task Daily Percentage	Ask for Help Appropriately Daily Percentage

Susan's Fidelity Checklist

Important Plan Components/Date	Day 1	Day 2	Day 3	Day 4	Day 5
Social skills lesson					
Number of times read *What Will Happen If?* chart					
Number of breaks taken					
Assignments on interests					
Choice of writing utensil					
Peer support during large group					
Problem behavior ignored					
Required to correct incorrect/sloppy assignments					
Self-monitored with target behavior sheet					
Number of times reinforcers earned					
Computed and graphed progress					
Target behavior sheet sent home					

Susan's Data Graphs

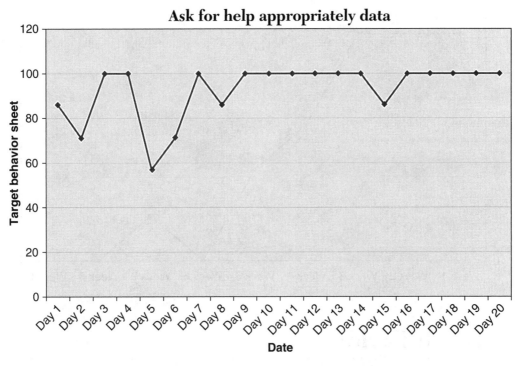

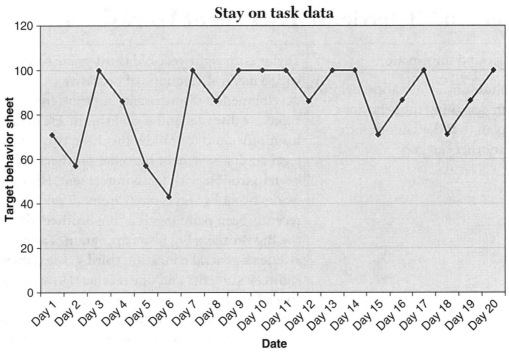

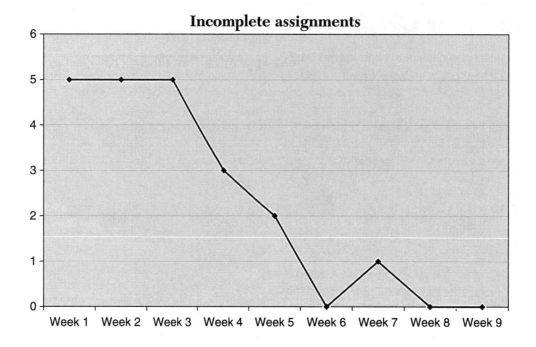

Incomplete assignments

Example 3: Taylor

Functional Behavioral Assessment Worksheet

Background information	Taylor is an eight-year-old third-grade student with a medical diagnosis of pervasive developmental disorder and intermittent explosive disorder and is on lithium. He lives with his mother and four older brothers, two whom are legal adults. Several of his older brothers have been in trouble with law enforcement. His mom works two jobs and is rarely home. Taylor has recently been paired with a "big brother" through the Big Brothers Big Sisters program. Taylor attends a general education third-grade class with eighteen students and one teacher. He receives special education services under the category of "other health impaired" and receives speech and language therapy for sixty minutes weekly for pragmatic language issues. His case manager is the one special education teacher in the elementary building. A paraprofessional is available to support him when needed most of the day.
Include any information helpful in designing the behavior plan that does not fit into another category	

Strengths and interests To be used throughout the behavior intervention plan for reinforcers, interest-based curriculum, and so on	Taylor wants to be with his general education class as much as possible. His intelligence is measured in the high average range. He loves anything related to science fiction, computers, and football.
Problem behaviors Operationally define to pass the stranger test, and provide baseline if possible	Taylor exhibits aggression that at times has endangered other students and adults. He forcibly hits, kicks, scratches, and attempts to bite. He has exhibited aggression that endangered others seven times during a two-week period, leaving marks on a student once and adults three times. (Adults have been hurt when attempting to intervene in order to protect the other student when Taylor is having a conflict with a peer.)

Setting events and triggering antecedents
 	
    You know it's going to be a bad day . . .
 	
    The straw that broke the camel's back
	Taylor's problem behaviors occur more frequently
	
	    After breaks such as weekends or vacations from school
	
	    When there is not an adult within close proximity
	
	    When there is a conflict of some sort with a peer, such as someone "cutting" in line or if someone makes a negative comment toward him, real or perceived.

Maintaining consequences What is the naturally occurring payoff?	Taylor gains a feeling of justification when he hurts someone he perceives is treating him unkindly in some way. In the past, Taylor has been suspended for aggressive behavior and goes home to a largely unsupervised environment where he is allowed to engage in activities that are more reinforcing than school.

Hypothesized functions	Taylor exhibits the problem behaviors
	
	    To express his feelings of anger
	
	    To access a more preferred environment and activities at home

Behavior Intervention Plan Worksheet

Target and replacement behaviors	Taylor will use his words to express his feelings to peers.
	Taylor will ask an adult for help when in a conflict with peers.
	Taylor will keep all parts of his body to himself.
Direct instruction of replacement behavior: Include who, what, and when	The special education teacher will triage with Taylor as soon as possible in the morning, and the paraprofessional will triage with Taylor before unstructured times with peers throughout the day. During triage, Taylor and the adult will "take his emotional temperature" using his visual stoplight, review his target and replacement behaviors, and discuss why they are important and the possible consequences of his choices.
	Taylor will participate in a weekly anger control small group led by the school counselor. The counselor will be provided with a copy of this plan and description of any problematic situation that took place during the previous week to embed into similar role plays and other practice activities, changing the names and other identifying information of the students involved.
	During speech and language therapy, Taylor will receive direct instruction on reading social cues and nonverbal language.

Prevention strategies: Remove or modify the influence of each identified setting event and triggering antecedent or provide additional support
 	
  After breaks such as weekends or vacations from school
 	
  When there is not an adult within close proximity
 	
  When there is a conflict of some sort with a peer
	A paraprofessional will shadow Taylor on days immediately after breaks and on days after an incident has occurred for immediate assistance when there are conflicts with peers and to watch for early signs that Taylor is becoming agitated.

Remove or reduce naturally occurring maintaining consequences	Taylor will not be suspended for aggressive behavior.
Positive reinforcement system	Taylor will receive behavior-specific praise from peers and adults when he exhibits his target behaviors.
	Peers will be taught and encouraged to tell Taylor how much they like being around him when he is not angry.
	Taylor will color one block in on his "tower of success" at the end of every day that he does not exhibit aggression and will be allowed to make a positive call or e-mail to his mom and "big brother." When he colors in all the towers, Taylor's "big brother" has agreed to take him to a high school football game or the new science fiction movie with a friend.
Natural and logical undesirable consequences	Taylor's peers and adults in his environment will be taught to kindly and calmly tell him how they feel when he hurts them after he is completely calm and in a rational state—sometimes the day after an incident if that much time is needed for Taylor to completely calm down.
	If early signs of agitation are noticed, the paraprofessional will show Taylor a yellow card, staying out of his reach, to remind him to "stop and think" and encourage him to move to a private area and take a calm-down break. When in a private area, the paraprofessional will give him as much space as possible while still keeping him within eyesight. Taylor will be allowed to take as much calm-down time as he needs and will return to his class when he tells the paraprofessional he is ready.

(continued)

Natural and logical undesirable consequences (*continued*)	If Taylor is aggressive to the point of endangering himself or others, he will be physically escorted to a private area by adults trained in nonviolent physical crisis intervention, following district crisis policies and procedures. After the incident, he will be on red schedule, minimally for the remainder of the school day, until he demonstrates that he has regained control and can be trusted. (See the red schedule instructions.)
Progress monitoring plan	A frequency of aggressive acts and duration of calm-down breaks in minutes will be taken daily and graphed weekly. Taylor's team will meet again at the end of the first quarter during parent-teacher conferences to review his progress. If Taylor's aggression increases dramatically before then, the team will reconvene as soon as possible.

Taylor's Stoplight

Green light: Go!!!

- I am feeling good!
- I am making good choices!
- I am keeping my body to myself.
- I am letting adults help me.
- I am being a hard worker.
- I get to be with all my friends.
- Good things are happening!

This section would be on a green background and the student will illustrate in a way that is meaningful to him.

Yellow light: Slow down!!!

- I am starting to feel upset.
- I can stop and think.
- I can keep my body to myself.
- I can use my words to tell an adult how I feel and ask for help.
- I can ask for a break.
- I can take deep breaths.
- I can think about things I like about school.
- If I can turn it around, I can stay with my friends, and my teachers will be proud of me!

This section would be on a yellow background and the student will illustrate in a way that is meaningful to him.

Red light: Stop!!!

- I am very upset!
- I am not keeping my body to myself. This may hurt others' feelings or scare or bother them. This is against the law for adults!
- I need to go on red schedule away from my friends and practice keeping my body to myself.
- I can let an adult help me.
- If I can practice keeping my body to myself, I can return to green schedule and be with my friends again.

This section would be on a red background and the student will illustrate in a way that is meaningful to him.

Taylor's Tower of Success

Taylor's tower of success

Congratulations, Taylor!

Decorate a block of the tower every time you have a whole day with safe behavior! Get to the top, and you will get a special surprise!

Taylor's Data Sheet

Date	Acts of Aggression	Date	Acts of Aggression

Taylor's Fidelity Checklist

Important Plan Components/Day	Day 1	Day 2	Day 3	Day 4	Day 5
Morning check-in					
Check-in before unstructured time					
Visual stoplight					
Behavior-specific praise					
Peer feedback					
Stop-and-think card					
Private calm-down area					
Red schedule					

Taylor's Data Graphs

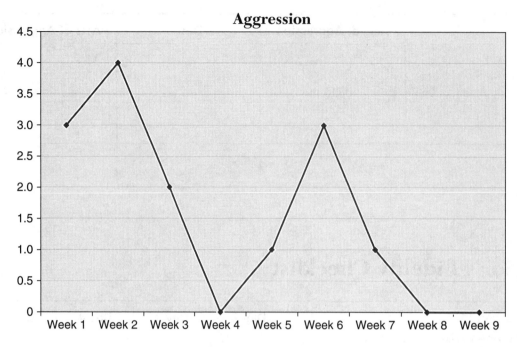

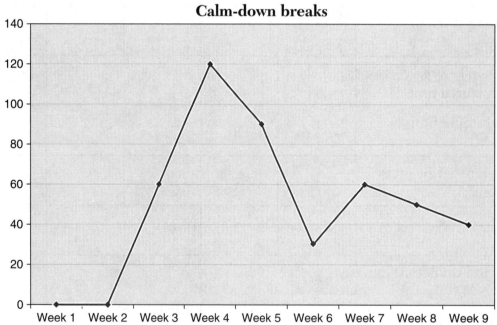

How to Reach and Teach Children with Challenging Behavior

Example 4: Malik

Functional Behavioral Assessment Worksheet

Background information Include any information helpful in designing the behavior plan that does not fit into another category	Malik is a thirteen-year-old seventh-grade student. Malik has no medical diagnoses and takes no medication. He does have significant social skill deficits and has trouble interacting appropriately with his peers. He frequently wears clothes that are considered juvenile (cartoon characters). He attends a middle school alternative program where he is typically in a class of twelve to fifteen students, one teacher, and one paraprofessional. He lives with his mother and father and one older sister. His parents both work outside of the home. He receives special education services under the category of learning disabilities in the areas of reading and writing and receives speech and language therapy for sixty minutes weekly for pragmatic language issues.
Strengths and interests To be used throughout the behavior intervention plan for reinforcers, interest-based curriculum, and so on	Malik is very interested in science and has the ability to retain a lot of factual information on topics of interest such as global warming, biomes, and habitats. He does well in social studies as well. He loves video games and masters them quickly.
Problem behaviors Operationally define to pass the stranger test, and provide baseline if possible	Malik redirects students in his classroom when they are not following the rules or puts peers down. Over a two-week period, Malik's behavior was measured at four random intervals per class period by staff in his classes. Malik made only positive comments to peers 63% of the time. Malik will also cry and walk out of class when upset. In the two-week observation period Malik was observed by staff to see if he was in class during four random interval periods. He was in class or absent from class WITH permission 83% of the time.

(continued)

Setting events and triggering antecedents	Malik's problem behaviors occur more frequently when
You know it's going to be a bad day . . .	He comes in tired and poorly groomed
The straw that broke the camel's back	He finds an assignment is hard and he needs to concentrate
	A peer makes a negative comment (real or perceived) towards him
	He feels like people are not listening to him
Maintaining consequences	Malik feels like he is getting back at other students when he tells them what to do or points out their negative traits publicly in class.
What is the naturally occurring payoff?	Malik escapes the negative peer interactions.
Hypothesized functions	Malik exhibits the problem behaviors to
	Escape negative social situations
	Express feelings of frustration

Behavior Intervention Plan Worksheet

Target and replacement behaviors	Malik will
	Use his words to express his feelings to peers
	Ask an adult for help when in a conflict with peers
	Use a break card when feeling frustrated with a task or peers
Direct instruction of replacement behavior: Include who, what, and when	The special education teacher will check in with Malik as soon as possible in the morning. During check-in, the teacher will inquire how much sleep Malik got and let him use any personal hygiene products he may have not had time to use before school.

Direct instruction of replacement behavior: Include who, what, and when (*continued*)	A paraprofessional will check in before lunch to review peer interaction skills.
	The special education teacher will check out with Malik at the end of the day to review the day and make goals for the next school day. She will review the procedures for using a break signal, role play what to do when a peer says a negative comment to him, and review a consequence map that shows what would happen if he makes a positive choice and if he does not.
	Malik will attend weekly sessions with the school social worker where he will talk about positive ways to handle frustrations and teasing from peers and work on personal hygiene issues.
Prevention strategies: Remove or modify the influence of each identified setting event or triggering antecedent or provide additional support	Teachers and paraprofessionals in each class will have a copy of this plan. They will watch for early signs of frustration and prompt Malik to take a break if he is not using his replacement behaviors.
	Malik will be seated at a table at lunch with positive peer models.
Remove or reduce naturally occurring maintaining consequences	Malik will be encouraged to appropriately escape negative interactions with peers.
Positive reinforcement system	Malik will receive behavior-specific praise from peers and adults when he exhibits his target behaviors.
	Malik will self-monitor his behavior on a target behavior sheet broken down by periods of the day. He will be prompted to self-monitor by a vibrating timer that cues him in random intervals four times in a forty-five-minute class period. He will write a plus if he had performed his target and replacement behaviors in that interval and a zero if he does not.

(continued)

Positive reinforcement system (*continued*)	During the check-out time period of the day, Malik will input his own behavioral data on his electronic graphing system. If his behavior has been at or above the target percentage, Malik will participate in the free time activity of his choice during eighth period privilege time.
Natural and logical undesirable consequences	Malik's peers and adults in his environment will be taught to kindly and calmly tell him how they feel when he delivers a put down or is bossy after he is completely calm and in a rational state.

If early signs of agitation are noticed, the paraprofessional will tap lightly on the corner of his desk. Malik will have been pretaught that this is signal to take a deep breath and stop and think about the situation and decide if he needs a break to regroup. If he chooses a break, the paraprofessional will return him to the classroom once he has said he is ready and completes the problem-solving process with her.

Malik will be responsible for any class work he misses when out of the classroom. He will be given one night to complete the work at home. If he chooses not to do so, he will be enrolled in the after school homework program to complete the work.

If Malik does not earn his target percentage for his target behavior sheet, Malik will participate in a study hall during eighth period privilege time. |
| Progress monitoring plan | During the check-out time period of the day, Malik will input his own behavioral data on his electronic graphing system. His data will be graphed daily and reviewed by Malik and the special education teacher daily during his check-out time. The team will also review Malik's data weekly at the team problem-solving meeting. |

Malik's Data Sheet

Date: _____

Time of Day	Positive Comments to Peers				Stayed in Class or Left with Permission				Break? Y or N	Duration of Break If Used
Period 1										
Period 2										
Period 3										
Period 4 (Lunch)										
Period 5										
Period 6										
Period 7										
Period 8										

Malik's Consequence Map

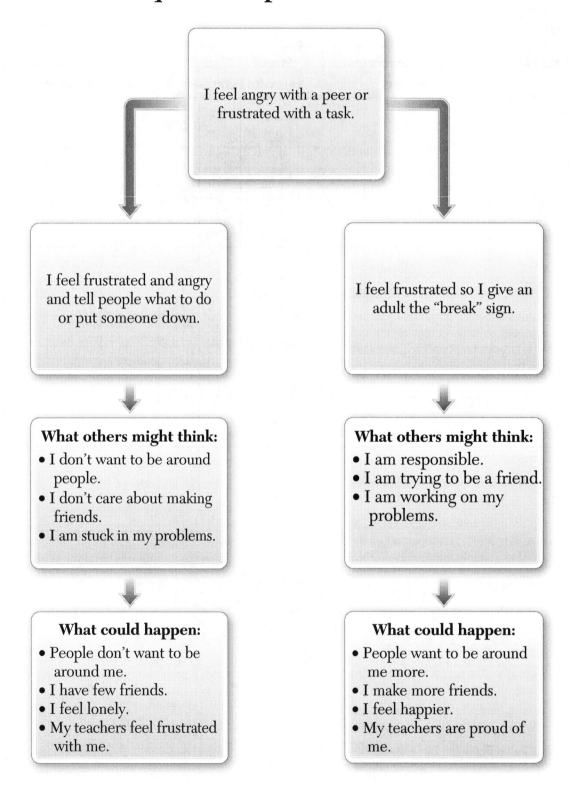

I feel angry with a peer or frustrated with a task.

I feel frustrated and angry and tell people what to do or put someone down.

I feel frustrated so I give an adult the "break" sign.

What others might think:
- I don't want to be around people.
- I don't care about making friends.
- I am stuck in my problems.

What others might think:
- I am responsible.
- I am trying to be a friend.
- I am working on my problems.

What could happen:
- People don't want to be around me.
- I have few friends.
- I feel lonely.
- My teachers feel frustrated with me.

What could happen:
- People want to be around me more.
- I make more friends.
- I feel happier.
- My teachers are proud of me.

How to Reach and Teach Children with Challenging Behavior

Malik's Fidelity Checklist

Important Plan Components/Day	Day 1	Day 2	Day 3	Day 4	Day 5
Morning check-in					
End of the day check-out					
Malik's break signal					
Behavior-specific praise					
Peer feedback					
Stop-and-think signal					
Private calm-down area					
Consequence Map					

Malik's Data Graphs

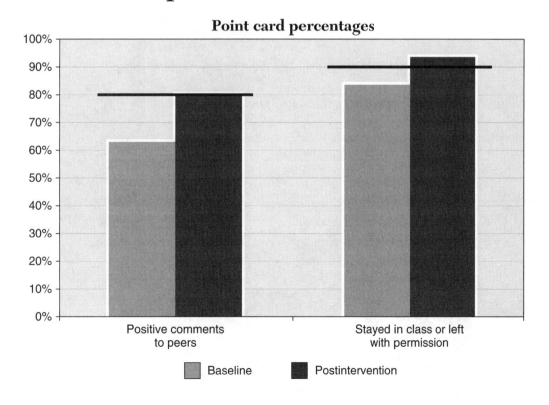

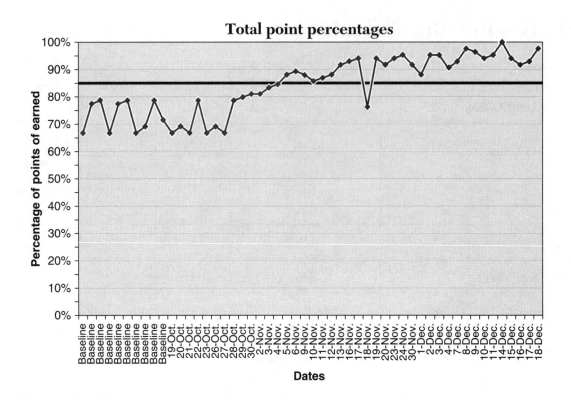

Total point percentages

How to Reach and Teach Children with Challenging Behavior

Part Seven

What About Dangerous Behavior? Managing Crises

Chapter 17

Intervening During the Escalation Cycle

E ven if you conduct the most thorough functional behavioral assessment and flawlessly implement the best-designed behavior intervention plan, no plan is foolproof. There will still be times when an individual student may reach a crisis level and someone will be in danger of getting hurt. This does not mean you failed. Behavior management is tough stuff, and no one has all the answers. We always say that there is no such thing as failure in behavior management, only assessment. So what is best practice in these unforeseen, very difficult situations? The most important thing is to know your student.

Dangerous behavior almost never comes out of nowhere. There are usually signs that trouble is starting to brew long before behavior escalates to an unsafe level, and these signs are very student specific. Different sources call it different names such as the escalation cycle,[1] the rage cycle,[2] or the crisis development model,[3] but the basic concept is the same. The student starts out calm (stage 1),

> There are usually signs that trouble is starting to brew long before behavior escalates to an unsafe level, and these signs are very student specific.

247

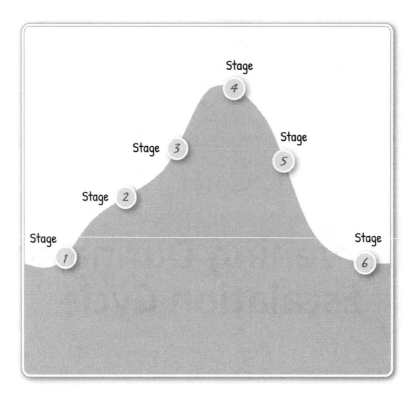

Figure 17.1 Stages of the Escalation Cycle

some combination of setting events and triggering antecedents upsets him (stage 2), he gets increasingly upset (stage 3) and may become dangerous to himself or others (stage 4), and he eventually deescalates (stage 5) and becomes calm again (stage 6). (See Figure 17.1.)

Stage One

If a student has a history of behavior challenges, don't wait until this individual is experiencing problems before intervening. Most intervention should happen at the calm stage, before any problems arise. This should include direct instruction in using calming strategies and helping students understand the natural and logical undesirable consequences if they do become unsafe. Parts Two, Four, and Five of this book provide multiple strategies for intervention at this stage.

Stage Two

To educators it can seem that a student is going through the day in a seemingly fairly calm manner, when something happens that upsets her world. We need to try to identify the antecedents to the crisis (setting events and triggering antecedents) and either remove them or provide additional support to minimize their influence. Once we become familiar with setting events and triggering antecedents that are common to individual students, crisis prevention becomes much easier because we are more likely to be able to accurately predict potential crisis situations and intervene early. Part Three of this book focuses on prevention and provides multiple strategies for intervention at this stage.

Stage Three

Students usually (not always but in our experience almost always) exhibit early signs of agitation, anxiety, and other negative emotions before their behavior escalates to an unsafe level. These early signs and the rate in which students escalate are specific to the individual.

It is crucial that you get to know your students extremely well or if you are just starting to work with them, talk to someone who does so that you become familiar with their unique signals and escalation patterns in order to determine your most effective response. We have had students who would engage in seemingly harmless behaviors such as acting a bit silly, getting a certain look on their face, changing their posture, or simply not following simple directions, when in fact these were early signs of agitation that quickly escalated to dangerous behavior. We call this "going from zero to a hundred." To others it would look as if we were overacting by removing them from the other students and getting them to a private, safe location. However, we had learned their unique individual patterns and found that by intervening at the earliest signs, crisis could often be averted. Some leaders in the field call this intervening when aggression is "low" to prevent it from becoming "high."[4]

> It is crucial that you get to know your students extremely well or, if you are just starting to work with them, talk to someone who does so that you become familiar with their unique signals and escalation patterns in order to determine your most effective response.

Some strategies to try to deescalate the situation at this stage include trying to redirect or distract these students using humor, talking about something they are interested in or are looking forward to, providing a "cool-off" time or area, validating their feelings ("I know this is frustrating. How can I help?"), and providing prompts, reminders, and visuals of replacement behavior that you have taught them during the calm stage. Make sure that you are looking ahead and providing a way for challenging students to have privacy (maybe taking a walk and moving toward a more private area) as well as removing the audience (the audience can often further agitate the individual or reinforce the escalating behavior). In addition, it is crucial that at this stage you are alerting backup assistance to be ready to respond in case your attempts at deescalation are unsuccessful.

If the student continues to escalate, this is not the time to try to establish your authority or worry about what others who may be observing the situation think. In this situation, adults may panic and fall back on traditional management techniques that often cause the behavior to escalate ("Young man, this is not acceptable behavior!"). At this point, it is okay to not know what to do. If the student is in a fairly private area free of potential danger, the best thing to do is to wait it out.

Do not attempt to reason with students, lecture them on their behavior, or threaten consequences because students in this stage often are not rational and simply need to get through the episode. You cannot teach a drowning individual to swim. The time for teaching is during the calm and recovery stages, not when the situation is escalating toward a crisis. Extreme tantrums, cussing, threats, throwing items, destroying things, and kicking walls are all common during this stage. Doing nothing is doing something if no one is truly in danger. Eventually the student will calm down. No human can keep up the physical and emotional energy it takes to remain in this stage forever.

> Doing nothing is doing something if no one is truly in danger. Eventually the student will calm down.

Others who are watching may think that by doing nothing, you are appeasing the student and allowing him to get away with behavior that is clearly well outside what is acceptable in the school setting. The truth is that your options are limited. Do you do something in the moment in order to exert your perceived or hoped-for power and control that will in reality most likely make the situation worse? This is a long-term process, and the student may have undesirable natural and logical consequences when the situation is over and he has become rational again. Getting to the deescalation stage without anyone getting hurt or resorting to emergency controversial interventions such as seclusion and physical restraint (this discussion is coming up in the next chapter) is the top goal.

Stage Four

If you are unable to or unsuccessful in your attempt to intervene early or move the student to the deescalation stage and find yourself in a situation where the student is truly endangering himself or others in the environment, your only goal now is to make sure that everyone remains safe and that the student in crisis is provided as much dignity and privacy as possible. When prevention and interventions are not sufficiently effective and a student is endangering himself or others, two ways to maintain safety are physical restraint and the use of seclusion. These topics are extremely controversial and are discussed in great detail in the next chapter.

Stage Five

During this stage, it is important to be supportive and allow the student time to truly reach recovery, or he may reescalate. Allowing him to get a drink, have a snack, or engage in a preferred calming activity for a short time and giving him encouragement is reinforcing not inappropriate behavior but rather appropriate calming-down behavior. The main goal during this stage is to ensure that the crisis has truly passed and that the student will be able to remain rational and engage in the problem-solving process. A good analogy is if someone ran a red light and was in a car accident that resulted in critical injuries. Would you lecture the driver while he was in the hospital immediately after lifesaving surgery about his poor choice of running the red light? Of course not. The time to address the potentially negative logical consequences of this choice, particularly if others were hurt, is once everyone is calm and stabilized.

Stage Six

During this stage, problem solving and accountability for poor choices take place. Sometimes this does not happen until the next day because the student and others involved in the situation are not truly stabilized until they have had a chance to go home, sleep, and put some time and distance between themselves and the crisis. Deciding to wait to go through this process is a judgment call and is highly dependent on the student's ability to connect choices and their consequences after some time has passed. Nevertheless, this stage is crucial and should not be skipped, so if you do wait until the next day, do not be tempted to just ignore this process.

During this stage, keep the tone positive and praise the student for engaging in and exhibiting appropriate behavior during this process. It is difficult for anyone to talk about his or her mistakes and take personal accountability. Think about how difficult this is even for typical students or adults. This is a time to reestablish communication, rebuild relationships, problem-solve through what happened, and make a plan for what all involved parties could do differently next time. Instructional strategies such as writing social stories, practicing, and role playing are all appropriate during this process.

> During this stage, keep the tone positive and praise the student for engaging in and exhibiting appropriate behavior during the process.

After this process, the student may return to his normal routine—or he may not. We strongly believe that experiencing logical undesirable consequences for aggressive or out-of-control behavior is part of the learning process. This logical undesirable consequence may take the form of a red schedule (discussed in Chapter Thirteen) until complete trust has been reestablished or by having those who were physically or emotionally hurt by the student not interact with him for a certain amount of time, thereby providing the lesson that others do not like to be around those who scare or hurt them. The reasoning for the undesirable consequence should be clearly explained to the student so that it has a teaching rather than a punitive focus. Acting as if nothing happened and going on with a normal day in many cases can send the student the inaccurate and unintended message that there are no real-life consequences for these dangerous behavior choices. Remember that we want to teach life skills by structuring consequences that are related, reasonable, and respectful and mirror real life.

Table 17.1 summarizes the stages of the escalation cycle.

Table 17.1 Aggression Cycle Reference Chart

Stage	Student Behavior	Main Goal	Possible Adult Responses
One	Calm	Remain calm	Relationship building
			Proactive direct instruction of calming-down and coping behavior and consequences of dangerous behavior
			Identifying potential setting events and triggering antecedents
Two	Agitation Anxiety Frustration	Return to calm	Validate feelings ("I know this is hard. I will help you.")
			Remove or minimize trigger
			Provide support
Three	Escalation	Deescalation Move to private location	Remove the audience and potentially unsafe environmental variables
			Escort to private, safe location
			Alert backup support
			Provide distraction (humor, talk about interests or something positive)
			Provide cooling-off time
			Prompt replacement behavior (perhaps using visuals)
			Wait it out; doing nothing is doing something

Table 17.1 (*continued*)

Stage	Student Behavior	Main Goal	Possible Adult Responses
Four	Dangerous	Maintain safety of all with as much dignity as possible for the student who is acting out	Physical restraint or seclusion
Five	Deescalation	Return to complete calm	Allow drink, snack, or preferred calming activity Encouragement
Six	Calm	Problem solving for the future	Praise for engaging in the process Make a plan for the future Direct instruction of calming-down or coping behavior and consequences of dangerous behavior

Key Points to Remember

- Dangerous behavior almost never comes out of nowhere. There are usually signs unique to each student that he or she is escalating to an unsafe level.

- During the first stage in the escalation cycle the student is calm. Direct instruction of calming strategies and interventions should occur at this time to prevent escalation.

- Setting events and triggering antecedents that cause the student to become upset occur in stage 2.

- Students usually exhibit early signs of agitation, anxiety, and other negative emotions during stage 3 before their behavior escalates to an unsafe level. A teacher who knows the student well enough can identify these signs and intervene before his or her behavior reaches a dangerous level.

- Educators need to refrain from threatening consequences or trying to establish their authority when the student is agitated and escalating, as this will make the situation worse.

- In stage 4, the student reaches the peak of their dangerous behavior. Safety of all parties is the only goal at his stage.

- The recovery process begins in stage 5. It is important to reinforce and encourage calming strategies during this time to ensure the crisis has passed.

- The student returns to a calm state in stage 6. It is crucial during this stage for the student to identify the behavior, connect the behavior to the consequences, and make a plan for positive, safe choices in the future.

Discussion Questions and Activities

1. In stage 3 of the escalation cycle, the teacher needs to try to redirect or distract escalating students to prevent them from engaging in dangerous behavior. Brainstorm some ways to distract students. Remember to use humor and student interests. This is not a time to establish your authority. Be creative!

2. Dustin is a student who has engaged in dangerous behavior in your classroom. He has returned to a calm state in stage 6 but is having difficulty owning his behavior, stalling the problem-solving process. Since you know this is a crucial step to working through the crisis, what should your next steps be?

3. Brittany, a student in your class, escalated to a level where she hit a paraprofessional in your class. You feel that using the red schedule intervention is appropriate to ensure she can be safe at school. The principal thinks that Brittany should be suspended, and other school staff and Brittany's parents think that she should be allowed to start fresh with no undesirable consequences. As the case manager, you now have to call a meeting with the parents and administration and explain why you have decided that Brittany will be on red schedule. Script that conversation.

How to Reach and Teach Children with Challenging Behavior

Chapter 18

Physical Restraint and Seclusion

Prevention and early intervention and the use of positive behavioral supports and interventions, including ongoing functional behavioral assessment and individualized behavior intervention plans, are best practice when managing problem behavior and attempting to prevent dangerous situations from developing. However, these practices are not foolproof, and dangerous situations still may occur. It is important to remember that positive behavior support is a process, and it should not (and in cases of students that qualify for special education legally cannot) be abandoned if dangerous situations occur. It takes time for both students and staff to learn new, more effective ways of doing things. However, when prevention and positive interventions are not sufficiently effective and a student is endangering self and others, two ways to maintain safety for the student and others in the immediate environment are physical restraint and seclusion. Both practices are extremely controversial and have the potential to cause physical or psychological harm, and even death, so are to be taken extremely seriously.

This chapter provides a definition of seclusion and restraint, a historical overview of the debate regarding their use and what has led up to the proposed federal legislation regarding regulation of these practices, our perspective concerning the roots of this controversy, and advice for educators who find themselves in dangerous situations with students.

Definitions

Physical restraint is defined as "any method of one or more persons restricting another person's freedom of movement, physical activity or normal access to his or her body. It is a means of controlling that person's movement, reconstituting behavioral control, and establishing and maintaining safety for the out-of-control individual, other individuals, and school staff."[1] This typically does not include devices designed for specific and approved safety purposes such as seat belts in vehicles or physical escorts such as holding a child's hand firmly while crossing a street.

Seclusion is defined as "the involuntary confinement of a child or youth alone in a room or area from which the child or youth is physically prevented from leaving. This includes situations where a door is locked, as well as when the door is blocked by other objects or held closed by staff."[2] This definition does not include rooms used as private places with minimal sensory stimulation and interaction with peers (which can often be agitating) for students to go to voluntarily independently or when prompted at early signs of aggression in order to break the escalation cycle and calm down. We have seen a variety of seclusion rooms in our careers and have heard them referred to as *quiet rooms, safe rooms, cool-down rooms,* and *time-out rooms.*

Historical Overview

The use of seclusion and restraint has been debated in special education since its inception. Over the past decade, the controversy has reached an all-time level of prominence in the national public arena. In 1998, the *Hartford Courant* ran a series of articles on patient injury and death due to medication, restraint, and seclusion combinations, primarily in psychiatric settings.[3] This increased public awareness of the use of these practices sparked a move toward drastic reduction, if not zero tolerance, of seclusion and physical restraint in all settings, including schools. In May 2003 the federal administrator of substance abuse and mental health services issued a national call to reduce and eventually eliminate these practices. In April 2004 the Alliance to Prevent Restraint, Aversive Interventions, and Seclusion was founded. The vision of this organization is that "all children with disabilities should grow up free from the use of aversive interventions, restraints and seclusion (ARS) to respond to or control their behavior and free from the fear that these forms of behavior management will be used on themselves, their siblings or their friends."[4] Many professional groups joined this movement by issuing statements supporting reduction of seclusion and restraint and considering their use acceptable only as a last resort as an emergency intervention to maintain safety. These organizations include the American Psychological Association, American Medical Association, American Academy of Pediatrics, American Academy of Child and Adolescent Psychology, and International Society of Psychiatric Mental Health Nurses. Accompanying this increased awareness of the use of these controversial procedures was an increase in litigation against public school districts across the United States involving restraint and seclusion issues.

In January 2009, the National Disability Rights Network issued *School Is Not Supposed to Hurt: Investigative Report on Abusive Restraint and Seclusion in Schools*, which led to calls for a congressional ban on the use of seclusion and prone restraint in schools and all other restraints except as applied by trained staff where required to prevent immediate physical injury.[5] Congressman George Miller, chair of the U.S. Education and Labor Committee, then asked the U.S. Government Accountability Office (GAO) to investigate recent reports of seclusion and restraint of students in public and private schools. The Education and Labor Committee held a hearing in May 2009, and the GAO issued its report *Seclusion and Restraints: Selected Cases of Death and Abuse at Public and Private Schools and Treatment Centers*.[6] Secretary of Education Arne Duncan responded in July 2009 by writing a letter to chief state school officers in every state encouraging them to review current policies and, if needed, have revised policies in place to start the 2009–2010 school year, publish these guidelines and notify parents as to what the guidelines contain, and use American Recovery and Reinvestment Act funds for training in positive behavior intervention and supports.[7] In December 2009, Congressman Miller introduced the Preventing Harmful Restraint and Seclusion in School Act, with a similar bill from the Senate soon to follow.[8] Federal legislation on this issue was still pending at the time this chapter was written.

Roots of the Problem

It has been a source of great frustration during our careers that this topic seems to have been largely avoided. We have often heard, "Well, if teachers program correctly, that just shouldn't happen." In reality, no teacher is perfect, and regardless of the best intentions and efforts of educators, sometimes dangerous situations do arise. So we are not going to avoid this topic, but rather confront it honestly and head-on in hopes of providing guidance to other teachers who may also be frustrated. This crisis has been many years in the making and has multiple roots.

Current School Culture

Public schools today face pressure to ensure that learning environments are safe places for everyone. Extreme and rare cases, such as the fatal stabbing of a music teacher by a sixteen-year-old special education student in Texas in 2009, can lead to overreaction in terms of zero tolerance policies and being too quick to use or abuse physical restraint or seclusion practices.

Lack of Regulation

At the time of GAO's investigative report on the use of restraint and seclusion in public schools, only twenty-four states had established policies or provided any type of guidelines to school districts, the content was varied, and the policies were not necessarily legally binding in all cases. The use of seclusion and restraint is regulated and controlled in every other setting that serves youth with emotional and behavioral challenges (state hospitals, psychiatric residential treatment facilities, and others). The Individuals with Disabilities Education Act (IDEA) does not mention seclusion and restraint, providing no legal recourse for their misuse or abuse in school settings.

Lack of Training

Teachers of students with emotional and behavioral disorders are consistently among the highest-ranked personnel shortage area, and a disproportionate number of them are uncertified or alternatively certified, resulting in a lack of much-needed specialized training.[9] In fact, approximately 65 percent of teachers of students with emotional and behavioral disorders enter the field without being fully certified,[10] and their burnout is higher than that of any other group of teachers.[11] The result is that the teachers holding these positions have significantly fewer years of teaching experience than other special and general education teachers.

Paraprofessionals who are often assigned to be one-on-one aides to potentially aggressive students are not required to have any specialized training in positive behavior support. Those in leadership positions, such as building and district administrators, often have even less experience and training in working with this population than do special education staff. The bottom line is that the most difficult-to-manage students are being taught in too many cases by the least prepared educators.

> The most difficult-to-manage students are being taught in too many cases by the least prepared educators.

This is a recipe for disaster and not solely the fault or responsibility of the local education agency. State departments of education, institutions of higher education, and government accountability agencies all need to become involved in the solution to this problem. The goal is to ensure that teachers certified to teach this challenging population have had the specialized training needed to be considered minimally qualified, if not highly qualified, as required by No Child Left Behind.

Kaye Says...

At the start of my career I intended to be an elementary teacher, and few of these positions were available. I enjoyed the challenge of teaching students who struggled behaviorally or academically so began taking classes to get a special education endorsement. At the same time, I desperately needed a job, so I started taking substitute positions in special education programs and quickly developed a reputation as someone who was willing to work with students with challenging behavior. I had several long-term substitute jobs working with very challenging and potentially aggressive students with absolutely no training on handling aggressive behavior. Apparently the only qualification needed was the willingness to try.

Lack of Research

Little research has been conducted to determine the efficacy, appropriate applications, or prevalence of either seclusion or restraint in educational settings. This fact is surprising, if not negligent, because the use of these procedures has been debated among special educators for over three decades and in fact has been controversial since the initial development of these procedures in the late eighteenth century for use in psychiatric hospitals in Europe.[12] In addition, the terms *restraint* and *seclusion* are almost always combined in research and policy discussions when they are very different things. Our experience is that the use of one can actually reduce the use of the other, and so their use needs to be researched and discussed separately.

Concern About Increase of More Aversive Options

Many well-meaning and ethical educators are concerned that banning the use of seclusion and restraint in public schools would result in an increase in unintended and possibly more aversive consequences. There could be an increase in more restrictive placements that lack appropriate peer models and access to many aspects of the general education curriculum; the involvement of law enforcement, which often has had little or no training in positive behavior supports and tends to rely heavily on force and punitive methods; and student and staff injuries.

Lack of Options

Public schools are the only entity legally obligated to provide services for students with disabilities who exhibit high levels of aggression. Hospital facilities can discharge them (often citing lack of insurance coverage), parents can (albeit tragically and very reluctantly) make their child a ward of the state, child care facilities can expel them, and private schools that specialize in meeting the complex behavioral and mental health needs of these students can send them back to their school district of residence with little warning. Public school districts are left with the legal responsibility of providing a free and appropriate public education to even the most challenging students. However, currently many times public schools do not have the resources or personnel with the skills needed to meet the needs of students who exhibit dangerous behavior.

What Can Educators Do?

In this time of intense public pressure to reduce and possibly eliminate seclusion and restraint while still maintaining a safe learning environment for staff and students, what can educators do while awaiting additional guidance from leaders in the field and governmental authorities?

Be Informed

Any educator who works with students with chronic behavioral challenges should know and follow their state and district policy and procedures (if they exist) regarding the use of seclusion and restraint. In addition, educators need to be aware of the dangers that exist every time seclusion or restraint is used. Many children have died or been physically or psychologically injured due to the misuse of physical restraint or seclusion.

> Educators need to be aware of the real dangers that exist every time seclusion or restraint is used. Many children have died or been physically or psychologically injured due to the misuse of physical restraint or seclusion.

Provide or Ask for Training

We strongly believe that all teachers, and at the least any teacher certified to teach students at high risk of exhibiting dangerous behavior, should be provided formal crisis prevention and intervention training as part of their requirements for certification. If they do not have this training prior to employment, it is the public school district's responsibility to provide it.

> **Kaye Says . . .**
>
> I am a master associate level trainer for the Crisis Prevention Institute (CPI) and can confidently recommend its program in training teachers in nonviolent crisis prevention and intervention. However, there are many crisis prevention programs available to school districts.

The three crisis intervention programs we are most familiar with are those listed in Table 18.1. Additional information on these and other crisis intervention programs can

Table 18.1 Nonviolent Crisis Prevention and Intervention Programs

Program	Contact Information
Nonviolent crisis intervention	Crisis Prevention Institute
	3315-K North 124th Street
	Brookfield, WI 53005
	800–558–8976
	http://www.crisisprevention.com, info@crisisprevention.com
The Mandt system	David Mandt & Associates
	P.O. Box 831790
	Richardson, TX 75083–1790
	972–495–0755
	http://www.mandtsystem.com/, comment@mandtsystem.com
Therapeutic crisis intervention (TCI)	Residential Child Care Project
	Family Life Development Center
	Beebe Hall
	Cornell University, Ithaca, NY 14853
	607–254–5210
	http://rccp.cornell.edu, eas20@cornell.edu

be found in an article by Mike Couvillon and his colleagues including summaries of their content and Web site and contact information.[13]

If you are a teacher working with students who have a history of or potential for aggression and your district has not provided you with crisis prevention and intervention training, request it in writing, and keep a copy of this request. Too many times teachers of the most behaviorally challenging students are expected to figure things out and fend for themselves. Providing a free and appropriate public education for these students is not solely your responsibility. Be professional yet assertive about what you need to accomplish this challenge. If you are an administrator, invest in crisis prevention and intervention training—ideally for all staff and minimally for those involved with potentially aggressive students—and develop crisis policies and procedures at the building and district levels consistent with those developed by your state.

Commit to Positive Behavior Support in Philosophy and Practice

The positive behavior support movement started in part to develop alternatives to aversive behavior management procedures such as restraint and seclusion. Reading this book and putting the interventions it contains into practice is a start. Read as much and go to as many trainings as you can on positive behavior support, and implement these practices at all three tiers of intervention.

Monitor Use of Restraint and Seclusion

By the time this book is published, your state should have guidelines for monitoring the use of restraint and seclusion. Even if they do not, we believe it is unethical to use physical restraint and/or seclusion without monitoring their use through a data collection system. Lack of a mandate by governing officials does not excuse educators from this responsibility. Examples of physical management (restraint) and safe room (seclusion) logs that we have used are provided in Figures 18.1 and 18.2.

Key Points to Remember

- When prevention and positive interventions are not sufficiently effective and a student is a danger to self or others, two ways to maintain safety are physical restraint and seclusion.

- The use of physical restraint and seclusion in schools is highly controversial and should be used only as a last resort when a student is endangering self or others.

- The use of physical restraint and seclusion has been debated in special education since its inception. In the past decade, the controversy has reached an all-time level of prominence in the national public arena.

- Secretary of Education Arne Duncan wrote a letter to all chief state school officers in July 2009 encouraging them to review current policies and, if needed, have revised policies in place to start the 2009–2010 school year, publish these guidelines, and notify parents as to what the guidelines contain.

- Public schools face pressure to ensure that learning environments are safe places for everyone. The result has been zero tolerance policies and potentially abusive physical restraint and seclusion practices.

Student: _____ **Date:** _____

School/Grade: _____

Date of student's most current behavior intervention plan: _____

Person completing form: _____

A. Setting

☐ Special Ed classroom   ☐ Regular Ed classroom   ☐ Other (please explain)

_____

B. Individuals present during use of physical management

☐ Special Ed teacher   ☐ Regular Ed teacher   ☐ Paraprofessional

☐ Administrator   ☐ Other (please explain)

_____

C. Antecedent (what happened just prior to the use of physical management?)

☐ Redirected   ☐ Transition   ☐ Given task/direction

☐ Issue related to peer(s)   ☐ Change in routine   ☐ Other (please explain)

_____

D. Please explain in detail the specific behavior(s) that resulted in the use of physical management.

_____

E. What was the duration of the physical management?

_____

F. What types of behaviors were exhibited by the student during the use of physical management?

☐ Yelling/screaming   ☐ Physical aggression   ☐ Crying

☐ Still/quiet   ☐ Other (please specify)

_____

G. What preventive measures were attempted prior to the use of physical management?

☐ Redirected/set limits   ☐ Given break   ☐ Offered choices

☐ Respond to student's questions   ☐ Informed of consequences   ☐ Removal of audience

☐ Other (please explain)

_____

H. What type of physical management was used?

☐ Children's control position   ☐ Team control position   ☐ Interim control position

☐ Other (please explain)

_____

I. Were both the student and staff member(s) involved seen by a district nurse/health clerk following the incident?

☐ Yes (please indicate the date/time seen) _____   ☐ No (please explain)

_____

J. Were parents contacted?

☐ Yes (please indicate date contacted) _____   ☐ No

K. Was the district behavior and/or autism specialist contacted, and was postintervention completed?

☐ Yes (please indicate date contacted) _____   ☐ No

Once completed, copies of this documentation should be provided to your building administrator and the district behavior/autism specialist serving your building.

Figure 18.1 Example Physical Management Documentation Form

Safe Room Log for _____   **Month:** _____

	Date	Time In	Time Out	**Reason for Safe Room Use:** A. Aggression B. Student choice C. Other (specify) The following reasons must be based on the student's current functional behavioral assessment or behavior intervention plan. D. Adult prompted early intervention to prevent escalation to aggression	**Door Status:** Open Closed Held	Reason for Door Status: A. Student distracting others B. Student attempting to leave C. Student preference D. Other (Specify)	Total Minutes	Staff Initials
1								
2								
3								
4								
5								
6								
7								
8								
9								
10								

This log should include codes only. Keep a separate anecdotal log with more detailed information.

E-mail a copy to your building administrators, special education coordinator, and building behavior specialist at the end of each month.

You must contact your building administrator and building behavioral specialist by phone or e-mail immediately if a student is in the safe/quiet room for longer than twenty minutes.

Figure 18.2 Example Seclusion Documentation Form

- As of May 2009, only twenty-four states had established policies or provided any type of guidelines to school districts regarding the use of restraint or seclusion, the content was varied, and the policies were not necessarily legally binding in all cases.

- Approximately 65 percent of teachers of students with emotional and behavioral disorders enter the field without being fully certified, and their burnout is highest among groups of teachers.

- Little research has been conducted to determine the efficacy, appropriate applications, or prevalence of seclusion or restraint in educational settings.

- Public schools are the only entity legally obligated to provide services for students with disabilities who exhibit high levels of aggression, yet they do not always have the resources and staff with the needed skills to deal with complex and dangerous behaviors.

- Teachers of students at risk for exhibiting dangerous behaviors need to be aware of district and state policy on the use of physical restraint and seclusion, be trained in crisis prevention and intervention, commit to positive behavior support practices, and take data on any use of physical restraint and seclusion.

Discussion Questions and Activities

1. What are the physical restraint and seclusion guidelines in your district and state?

2. You work with a student who has exhibited dangerous behavior frequently. Your district has not provided training in crisis prevention and intervention. You are meeting with your special education director to discuss the need for training for all staff who work with this student. Outline your argument.

3. You observe a teacher who consistently uses physical restraint or seclusion to gain compliance, and not necessarily only when safety is a concern. What would be your course of action?

thispagestyleplain

Part Eight

Reproducible Tools

Reproducible 1: Positive-to-Negative Ratio Data Sheet

Directions: Each box is for a different day. Choose a certain time period and record how many positives and how many negatives the teacher gave to the students. The goal is for the final number to be greater than four.

Date:	
Positive	**Negative**

Total positives =
Total negatives =
Total positives/ Total negatives =

Date:	
Positive	**Negative**

Total positives =
Total negatives =
Total positives/ Total negatives =

Date:	
Positive	**Negative**

Total positives =
Total negatives =
Total positives/ Total negatives =

Date:	
Positive	**Negative**

Total positives =
Total negatives =
Total positives/ Total negatives =

Date:	
Positive	**Negative**

Total positives =
Total negatives =
Total positives/ Total negatives =

Date:	
Positive	**Negative**

Total positives =
Total negatives =
Total positives/ Total negatives =

Reproducible 2: Break Pass

This pass can be used when the student is given a task to complete, not during instruction or when the teacher is lecturing.

Break pass

(can be used when given a task to complete…
NOT during instruction or when a teacher is lecturing)

I need to take a break. Please allow me to go to

_____ with _____ for
(location)   (supervising adult)

____ minutes before returning to my work.

Break pass

(can be used when given a task to complete…
NOT during instruction or when a teacher is lecturing)

I need to take a break. Please allow me to go to

_____ with _____ for
(location)   (supervising adult)

____ minutes before returning to my work.

Break pass

(can be used when given a task to complete…
NOT during instruction or when a teacher is lecturing)

I need to take a break. Please allow me to go to

_____ with _____ for
(location)   (supervising adult)

____ minutes before returning to my work.

Reproducible 3: Countdown Strips

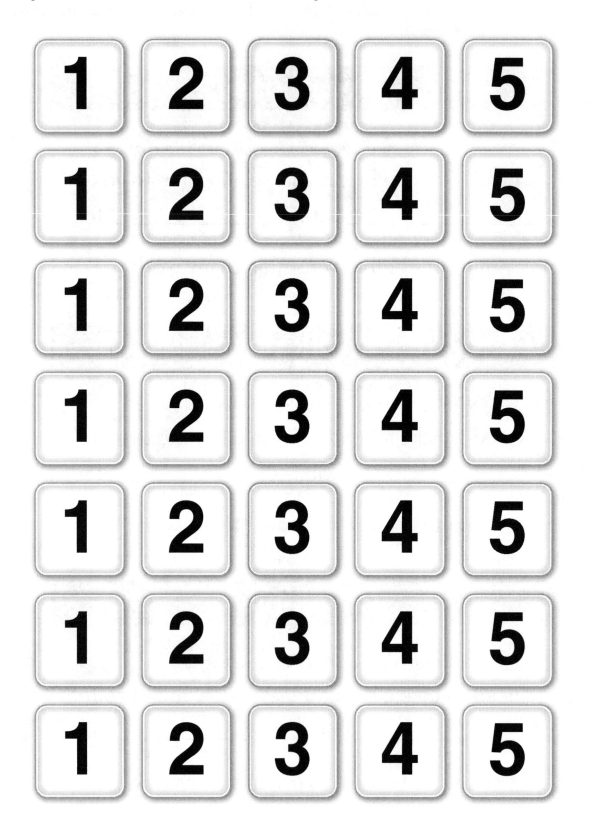

Reproducible 4: Chart Moves Frame

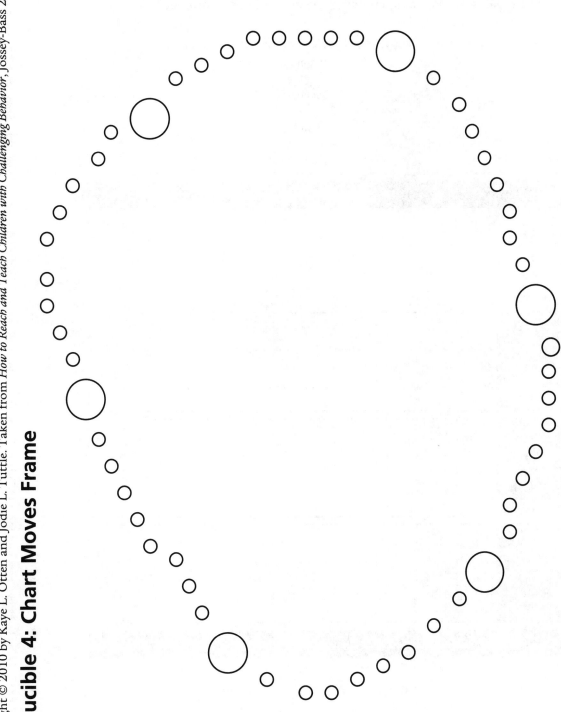

Reproducible 5: Peer Comparison Direct Observation Form

This form is divided into fifteen-second intervals for a total of a fifteen-minute observation. If the target student or peer exhibits the problem behavior any time during the fifteen seconds, the interval is marked as such using the created behavior codes.

Student Name:	Gender:
Grade:	School/Teacher:
Date:	Time:
Observer:	Class Activity:

Description of Setting:

Target student																				
Peer																				
Comments																				

Target student																				
Peer																				
Comments																				

Target student																				
Peer																				
Comments																				

Behavior codes: (Create codes for specific behavior you are observing)

Reproducible 6: Consequence Map Template

What might happen if . . . ?

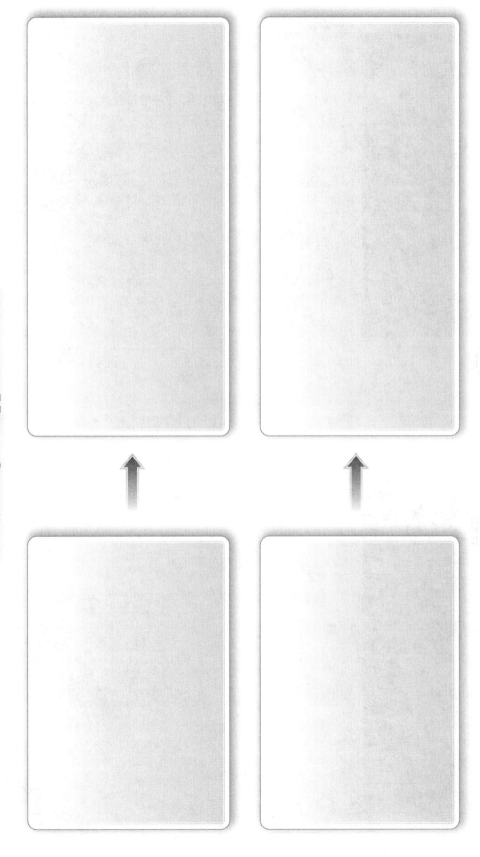

Reproducible 7: If-Then Chart Template

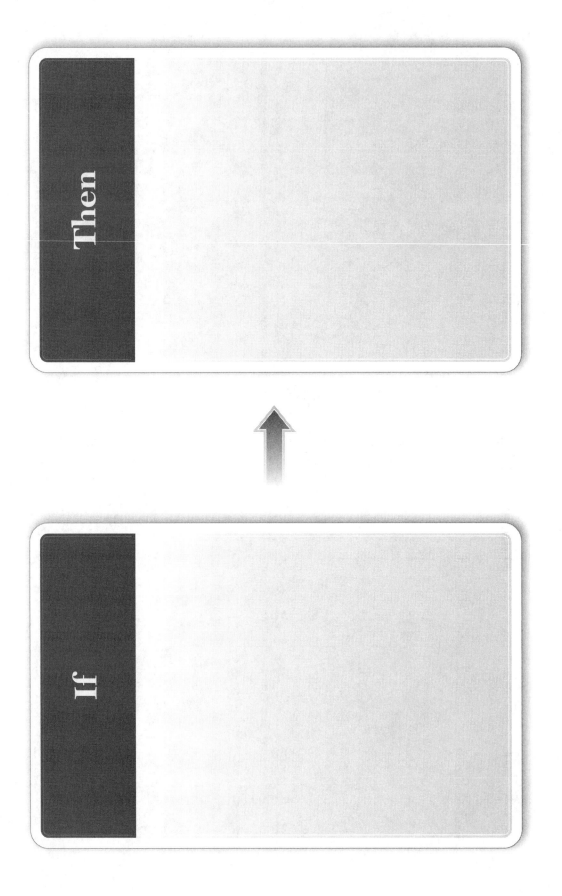

If

Then

Reproducible 8: Notes Template for Functional Behavioral Assessment

Strengths/Interests	Setting Events	Triggering Antecedents	Maintaining Consequences

Reproducible 9: Functional Behavioral Assessment Summary Worksheet

Background information Include any information helpful in designing the behavior plan that does not fit into another category	
Strengths and interests To be used throughout the behavior intervention plan for reinforcers, interest-based curriculum, and so on	
Problem behaviors Operationally define to pass the stranger test, and provide baseline data if possible	

Setting events and triggering antecedents You know it's going to be a bad day . . . The straw that broke the camel's back	
Maintaining consequences What is the naturally occurring payoff?	
Hypothesized functions	

Reproducible 10: Behavior Intervention Plan Worksheet

Target and replacement behaviors	
Direct instruction of replacement behavior: Include what, who, when, and how	
Prevention strategies: Remove or modify the influence of each identified setting event or triggering antecedent or provide additional support	

Remove or reduce naturally occurring maintaining consequences	
Positive reinforcement system	
Natural and logical undesirable consequences	
Progress monitoring plan	

Glossary

ABCF chart: Charts that collect baseline levels of problem behavior and information on possible setting events, triggering antecedents, and maintaining consequences to assist in determining the function of the problem behavior. ABCF stands for antecedent, behavior, consequence, and function.

Applied behavioral analysis: The breakdown of skills into small, discrete tasks, taught in a structured, hierarchical manner. As skills are taught, performance of desired behaviors is differentially reinforced, and antecedent and consequence strategies are evaluated. Data on the student's learning are recorded regularly, and teaching programs are adjusted dependent on student progress.

Baseline: Data collected prior to implementation of a behavior intervention plan that accurately represents the student's current level of functioning.

Behavior prompt: A visual representation of the replacement or appropriate behavior.

Behavioral burst: Temporary increase in problem behavior after limits are put in place or a new intervention is implemented. This is part of the limit-testing process and actually shows that limits and interventions are working.

Behavior-specific praise: Feedback given to a student that gives positive feedback on a specific behavioral skill ("I love the way you raised your hand when you had something to say").

Bribery: An inducement for an illegal or unethical act or the presentation of a reward to an individual to stop an inappropriate behavior or misbehavior.

Chart moves: An individual reinforcement system that shows a visual of a desired reinforcer surrounded by small dots, with larger dots interspersed for the student to connect when he or she meets specific behavior criteria. When students connect to a bigger dot, they earn a small or quick reinforcer such as a short break. When they connect all the dots around the chart, they earn a larger reinforcer.

Class meetings: A regularly scheduled, structured portion of the school day where students and teachers are provided a forum to discuss issues, set goals, and participate in peaceful conflict resolution.

Cognitive behavioral theory: Focuses on the interdependent relationship of the environment, behavior, and thinking and is based on the belief that one's thinking affects one's behavior, that one's patterns of thoughts can be changed, and that desired behavior can be achieved through these changes in thinking.

Consequence map: A visual where the student and teacher map out the connection between positive and negative choices and their subsequent positive and negative consequences.

Contract: A written agreement between two or more parties that stipulates the responsibilities of each party.

Dependent group-oriented contingency: Reinforcement for the entire group is contingent on one student's behavior.

Differential reinforcement of incompatible behavior (DRI): Students are reinforced for behaviors that are incompatible with the desired behavior.

Differential reinforcement of lower rates of behavior (DRL): Students are reinforced for exhibiting progressively lower rates of the undesired behavior.

Differential reinforcement of zero rates of behavior (DRO): Students are reinforced when they do not exhibit the problem behavior at all during a set period of time.

Differentiated instruction: An approach to planning so that one lesson is taught to the entire class while meeting the individual needs of each child.

Direct data source: A data source where someone is observing the student and recording the behavior as it is happening or as soon as possible after it happens.

Duration data: Data that record how long a behavior lasts.

Escalation cycle: The stages that a person goes through when escalating to dangerous behavior and returning to a calm state.

Executive functioning: A term used to describe a set of mental processes that helps us connect past experience with present action. We use executive function skills when we perform such activities as planning, organizing, strategizing, and paying attention to and remembering details.[1]

Fair pair rule: A rule that states the replacement behavior must be desired by or acceptable to the teacher and serve the same (or similar) function as the problem behavior, or the student will just come up with a new (and most likely still inappropriate way) to meet that function.

Fluency deficit: The student knows how to perform the skill and performs it at acceptable levels but is awkward and unpolished when exhibiting the skill.

Frequency data: Data that record how frequently a behavior occurs.

Functional behavioral assessment: A systematic process for understanding problem behavior and the factors that contribute to its occurrence and maintenance.

Group-oriented contingencies: Refers to when an entire class is reinforced based on the behavior of one student, a number of students, or the entire class.

Incidental teaching: Providing direct instruction during the "teachable moments" that happen naturally throughout the day.

Independent group-oriented contingency: Each student earns a reward based on his or her own behavior.

Indirect data source: A data source that provides hearsay, or information reported by someone who has interacted with the student in the past (even the very recent past) rather than observing the behavior in real time.

Individuals with Disabilities Education Act (IDEA): A federal law ensuring services to children with disabilities throughout the nation. It governs how states and public agencies provide early intervention, special education, and related services to more than 6.5 million eligible infants, toddlers, children, and youth with disabilities.

Interdependent group-oriented contingency: Reinforcement of the group is contingent on the behavior of the whole group.

Level systems: An organizational framework for managing student behavior where students earn more privileges and responsibilities as they demonstrate more control over their behavior.

Logical undesirable consequences: Consequences that do not naturally occur as a result of behavior, but are intentionally planned and applied by educators, such as doing missed work during recess.[2] Logical consequences are related to the behavior.

Lottery systems: Independent group-oriented contingency where students are given lottery tickets when they are randomly "caught" exhibiting positive behaviors. They write their name on the ticket, and turn it in to be part of a lottery drawing for various reinforcers at the end of the day or week.

Matching rule: A rule that states that the replacement behavior has to deliver the same amount of reinforcement as the problem behavior for the replacement behavior training to be effective.

Mini-lessons: A brief social skills instruction that is embedded in an academic lesson where the teacher teaches or reviews a behavioral skill at the beginning of the lesson, gives feedback on that skill during the lesson, and reinforces for use of the skill at the end of the lesson.

Momentary time sampling: Data that tells whether a behavior occurred at the exact end of a set interval.

Natural undesirable consequences: Unplanned or uncontrolled outcomes that occur as a result of behavior, such as one student being hit after having hit another student.[3]

No Child Left Behind: A federal law enacted in January 2002 to expand choices for parents, focus resources on proven educational methods, and provide accountability for results.

Performance deficit: The student knows how to perform the skill and can discriminate which skills to use when, but fails to do so at acceptable levels.

Physical restraint: Any method of one or more persons restricting another person's freedom of movement, physical activity, or normal access to his or her body. It is a means of controlling that person's movement, reconstituting behavioral control, and establishing and maintaining safety for the out-of-control individual, other individuals, and school staff.

Positive behavior supports: An application of a behaviorally based systems approach to develop the capacity of schools, families, and communities to design effective environments that improve the link between research-validated practices and the environments in which teaching and learning occurs.

Potato or dead man's rule: A rule that states the replacement behavior in terms of action. It should be stated in a way that tells the student what to do instead what not to do. If a potato or dead man can do it ("Don't shout out"), it is not appropriate. If a potato or dead man can't do it ("Raise your hand"), this rule has been followed.

Precorrection: Reminders by providing students with opportunities to practice or be prompted concerning expected behavior immediately before they enter situations in which displays of problems behaviors are likely.

Premack's principle: First doing something less desirable to earn the privilege of doing something more desirable.

Problem solving: A series of questions a student answers following an undesired behavior where the student identifies the choice made, connects it to the consequences in his or her environment, and makes a positive plan for future choices.

Punishment: The contingent presentation of a stimulus immediately following a response, which decreases the future rate or probability of the response.[4]

Reinforcement: The contingent presentation of something that is valued or desired by an individual after a behavior and results in an increase or maintenance of the behavior.

Reinforcement menus: A menu of items a student has indicated as desirable that he or she can choose from following performance of desired behaviors.

Replacement behavior: A positive behavior that serves the same function and replaces a negative behavior.

Response cost: Losing or having limited access to privileges or reinforcers.[5]

Seclusion: The involuntary confinement of a child or youth alone in a room or area from which he or she is physically prevented from leaving. This includes situations where a door is locked as well as where the door is blocked by objects or held closed by staff.

Self-management: Achieved when an individual possesses internal cues and reinforcement needed to engage in appropriate social behavior.

Setting events: Things that exist in the environment that exaggerate the likelihood that problem behavior will occur ("You know it is going to be a bad day . . .").

Skill deficit: Lack of a behavioral skill or lack of understanding of what skills to use in a situation.

Social skills instruction: Direct instruction of desired behaviors.

Target behavior sheets: Individual reinforcement systems that allow students to earn points for performing desired behaviors and tracking performance across school settings and class periods.

Think time: A logical consequence where a student sits in a designated place away from the group for a short time in order to break the chain of behavior or eliminate class disruption and gives the student time to think.

Time interval data: Data that tell whether a behavior occurs in a set interval.

Time-out: A consequence where a student sits in a designated place away from the group for a short time to minimize reinforcement.

Token economies: Independent group-oriented contingencies that mirror the real-life system of paying money (tokens) to get the things that reinforce us. Token economies can be set up as a reinforcement system for groups of students or individual students.

Transition helpers: Interventions used with students during transitions by providing structure and predictability, in addition to giving them all the information about what is going to happen and time to process it and become cognitively and emotionally ready to handle the change. Common transition helpers are countdowns, timers, and transition objects. *See also* transition object.

Transition object: Highly preferred objects that a student can carry during transitions to make the transition itself more reinforcing and to distract him or her from the not-so-reinforcing task that is coming next.

Triggering antecedents: Events that happen immediately before the problem behavior ("the straw the broke the camel's back").

Visual schedule: Schedules that use words and/or pictures to represent each activity. These schedules help students anticipate and plan their day by allowing them to view the order of activities and what they should prepare for next.

Visual supports: The use of pictures to make verbal communication visual.

Notes

Preface

1. Maag (2004).
2. Rhode, Jenson, and Reavis (1993); Jenson, Rhode, and Reavis (1994).
3. Carr et al. (2002).

Chapter One

1. National Center for Education Statistics (2007).
2. Centers for Disease Control and Prevention (2009).
3. Smith (1990).
4. Nelson (2006).
5. Sutherland, Lewis-Palmer, Stichter, and Morgan (2008).
6. Muscott, Mann, and LeBrun (2008); Zins, Weissberg, Wang, and Walberg (2004).
7. National Center on Positive Behavioral Interventions and Supports (2006).
8. Kauffman (2001); Sprague and Walker (2000).
9. Strain and Odom (1986).
10. Howell, Fox, and Morehead (1993); Maag (2004).
11. Neel (1988); Maag (2004).
12. Mayer (1995).
13. Skiba (2002, p. 90).

Chapter Two

1. U.S. Department of Education (2009).
2. Sugai, Horner, Dunlap, Hieneman, Lewis, and Nelson (1999, p. 7).
3. Maag and Katsiyannis (2006).
4. Carr et al. (2002).
5. Carr et al. (2002).
6. Nelson et al. (2009).
7. Scott, Meers, and Nelson (2000); Stichter, Shellady, Sealander, and Eigenberger (2000).
8. Nelson, Roberts, Mathur, and Rutherford (1999).
9. Scott and Kamps (2007).
10. Sugai, Lewis-Palmer, and Hagan-Burke (1999).
11. Scott et al. (2004).
12. Alberto and Troutman (2008).
13. Umbreit, Ferro, Liaupsin, and Lane (2007).

14. Gresham, Quinn, and Restori (1999); Eiser (1986).

15. Carey and Bourbon (2004).

16. Walker, Schwartz, Nippold, Irvin, and Noell (1994).

17. American Speech, Language, and Hearing Association (2010).

18. Myles and Southwick (2005).

Chapter Three

1. Gresham, Cook, Crews, and Kern (2004).

2. Gresham (1996).

3. Maag (2005).

4. Mathur, Kavale, Quinn, Forness, and Rutherford (1998); Quinn, Kavale, Mathur, Rutherford, and Forness (1999).

5. Kauffman (2001); Maag (2005).

6. Walker, Ramsey, and Gresham (2004).

7. Gresham, Sugai, and Horner (2001).

8. Dobson and Block (1988); Maag (2004).

9. Maag (2004); Cooper, Heron, and Heward (2007).

Chapter Four

1. Smith and Rivera (1993).

2. McEwan-Landau and Gathercoal (2000).

3. Larrivee (2002).

4. Strain and Joseph (2004); Sutherland and Wehby (2001); Sutherland, Wehby, and Copeland (2000).

5. Flora (2000); Loveless (1996); Walker, Ramsey, and Gresham (2004).

6. Feldman (2003); Weinstein (2003).

7. Colvin, Sugai, and Patching (1993).

8. Baker (2003).

Chapter Five

1. Kaplan (1995); Maag (2004).

2. Kaplan (1995); Maag (2004).

3. Sinclair, Christenson, Lehr, and Anderson (2003).

4. Colvin, Sugai, and Patching (1993).

5. Baker, Lang, and O'Reilly (2009); Kern-Dunlap et al. (1992); McCoy and Hermansen (2007); Walker and Clement (1992).

6. Gray (2000).

Chapter Six

1. Sutherland, Wehby, and Copeland (2000); Sutherland and Wehby (2001).

Chapter Seven

1. National Center for Learning Disabilities (2005).
2. National Center for Learning Disabilities (2005).
3. Keeley (2003).
4. Jaime and Knowlton (2007).
5. Hodgdon (1995).
6. Quill (1995).
7. Savner and Myles (2000).

Chapter Eight

1. Lane and Menzies (2002); Scott, Nelson, and Liaupsin (2001).
2. Moes (1998).
3. Bambura, Ager, and Koger (1994); Vaughn and Horner (1997).
4. Kern, Mantegna, Vorndran, Bailin, and Hilt (2001).
5. Kern and State (2009).
6. Kern and State (2009); Kern, Bambara, and Fogt (2002); Hinton and Kern (1999).

Chapter Nine

1. Maag (2004).
2. Walker, Shea, and Bauer (2004).
3. McConnell (1987).
4. Vaughn, Lancelotta, and Minnis (1988).

Chapter Ten

1. Cooper, Heron, and Heward (2007); Maag (2004).
2. Litow and Pumroy (1975); Maag (2004).
3. Collaborative for Academic, Social, and Emotional Learning (2005).
4. Barrish, Saunders, and Wolf (1969).
5. Maag (2004).
6. Sprague and Golly (2005).
7. Mitchem, Young, West, and Benyo (2001).
8. Sprick, Garrison, and Howard (1998).

Chapter Eleven

1. Kaplan (1995); Maag (2004).
2. Bauer and Shea (1988); Bauer, Shea, and Keppler (1986); Cruz and Cullinan (2001); Kerr and Nelson (1989).

Chapter Twelve

1. Alberto and Troutman (1995, p. 500).
2. Maag (2004); Rutherford and Neel (1978).
3. Pryor (1999).
4. Pryor (1999).
5. Nelsen (1985).

Chapter Thirteen

1. Cooper, Heron, and Heward (2007).
2. Nelson and Carr (1996).
3. Rhode, Jenson, and Reavis (1993).
4. Miller (1986).
5. Walker, Colvin, and Ramsey (1995).

Chapter Fourteen

1. Sugai, Lewis-Palmer, and Hagan-Burke (1999–2000, p. 152).

Chapter Seventeen

1. Walker, Colvin, and Ramsey (1995).
2. Myles and Southwick (2005).
3. Crisis Prevention Institute (2006).
4. Goldstein (1999, 2000).

Chapter Eighteen

1. Council for Exceptional Children (2009, p. 1).
2. Council for Exceptional Children (2009, p. 1).
3. Weiss (1998).
4. Alliance to Prevent Restraint, Aversive Interventions, and Seclusion (2005, p. 2).
5. The National Disability Rights Network (2009).
6. U.S. Government Accountability Office (2009).
7. Duncan (2009).
8. Miller (2009).
9. Billingsley, Fall, and Williams (2006).
10. Billingsley (2001).
11. George, George, Gersten, and Grosenick (1995).
12. American Academy of Child and Adolescent Psychiatry (2000); Masters et al. (2002).
13. Couvillon, Peterson, Ryan, Scheurmann, and Stegall (2010).

Glossary

1. National Center for Learning Disabilities (2005).
2. Pryor (1999).
3. Pryor (1999).
4. Alberto and Troutman (1995).
5. Cooper, Heron, and Heward (2007).

References

Alberto, P. A., & Troutman, A. C. (2008). *Applied behavior analysis for teachers* (8th ed.). Upper Saddle River, NJ: Prentice Hall.

Alliance to Prevent Restraint, Aversive Interventions, and Seclusion. (2005). *In the name of treatment*. Retrieved from www.tash.org/publications/parentguide/index.htm

American Academy of Child and Adolescent Psychiatry. (2000). *Policy statement on the prevention and management of aggressive behavior in psychiatric institutions with special reference to seclusion and restraint.* Washington, DC: Author.

American Speech, Language, and Hearing Association. (2010). *Social language use*. Retrieved from http://www.asha.org/public/speech/development/pragmatics.htm

Baker, J. (2003). *Social skills training: For children and adolescents with Asperger syndrome and social-communication problems.* Shawnee Mission, KS: Autism Asperger Publishing Company.

Baker, S. D., Lang, R., & O'Reilly, M. (2009). Review of video modeling with students with emotional and behavioral disorders. *Education and Treatment of Children, 32*(3), 403–420.

Bambura, L. M., Ager, C., & Koger, F. (1994). The effects of choice and task preference on the work performance of adults with severe disabilities. *Journal of Applied Behavior Analysis, 27,* 555–556.

Barrish, H. H., Saunders, M., & Wolf, M. M. (1969). Good behavior game: Effects of individual contingencies for group consequences on disruptive behavior in a classroom. *Journal of Applied Behavior Analysis, 2,* 119–124.

Bauer, A. M., & Shea, T. M. (1988). Structuring classrooms through level systems. *Focus on Exceptional Children, 21*(3), 1–12.

Bauer, A. M., Shea, T. M., & Keppler, R. (1986). Level systems: A framework for the individualization of behavior management. *Behavioral Disorders, 12,* 28–35.

Billingsley, B. S. (2001). *Beginning special educators: Characteristics, qualifications, and experiences.* Rockville, MD: Westat. Retrieved from http://ferdig.coe.ufl.edu/spense/Results.html

Billingsley, B. S., Fall, A., & Williams, T. O. (2006). Who is teaching students with emotional and behavioral disorders? A profile and comparison to other special educators. *Behavioral Disorders, 31*(3), 252–264.

Carey, T. A., & Bourbon, W. T. (2004). Countercontrol: A new look at some old problems. *Intervention in School and Clinic, 40*(1), 3–9.

Carr, E. G., Dunlap, G., Horner, R., Koegel, R., Turnbull, A., & Sailor, W. (2002). Positive behavior support: Evolution of an applied science. *Journal of Positive Behavior Interventions, 4,* 4–16, 20.

Centers for Disease Control and Prevention. (2009). *Autism information center*. Retrieved from http://www.cdc.gov/ncbddd/autism/faq_prevalence.htm

Collaborative for Academic, Social, and Emotional Learning. (2005). *Safe and sound: An educational leader's guide to social and emotional learning programs.* Retrieved from www.casel.org/pub/sel.php

Colvin, G., Sugai, G., & Patching, B. (1993). Precorrection: An instructional approach for managing predictable problem behaviors. *Intervention in School and Clinic, 28*(3), 143–150.

Cooper, J. O., Heron, T. E., & Heward, W. L. (2007). *Applied behavior analysis* (2nd ed.). Upper Saddle River, NJ: Pearson.

Council for Exceptional Children. (2009). *CEC's policy on physical restraint and seclusion procedures in school settings*. Retrieved from www.cec.sped.org

Couvillon, M., Peterson, R., Ryan, J., Scheuermann, B., & Stegall, J. (May/June 2010). A review of crisis intervention training programs for schools. *Teaching Exceptional Children, 5*(4), 6–17.

Crisis Prevention Institute. (2006). *Nonviolent crisis intervention training program*. Brookfield, WI: Author.

Cruz, L., & Cullinan, D. (2001). Awarding points, using levels to help children improve behavior. *Teaching Exceptional Children, 33*(3), 16–23.

Dobson, K. S., & Block, L. (1988). Historical and philosophical bases of the cognitive-behavioral therapies. In K. S. Dobson (Ed.), *Handbook of cognitive-behavioral therapies* (pp. 3–38). New York: Guilford Press.

Duncan, A. (2009). *Key policy letters signed by the education secretary or deputy secretary*. Retrieved from www.ed.gov/policy/elsec/guid/secletter/090731.html

Dunn Buron, K. (2007). *A 5 is against the law*. Shawnee Mission, KS: Autism Asperger Publishing Company.

Dunn Buron, K., & Curtis, M. (2003). *The incredible 5-point scale*. Shawnee Mission, KS: Autism Asperger Publishing Company.

Eiser, R. J. (1986). *Social psychology: Attitudes, cognition, and social behaviour*. Cambridge: Cambridge University Press.

Feldman, S. (2003). A place for praise. *Teaching PreK-8, 33*(5), 6.

Flora, S. R. (2000). Praise's magic reinforcement ratio: Five to one gets the job done. *Behavior Analyst Today, 1*, 64–69.

George, N. L., George, M. P., Gersten, R., & Grosenick, J. K. (1995). To leave or stay? An exploratory study of teachers with emotional and behavioral disorders. *Remedial and Special Education, 16*, 227–236.

Gibbs, J. *TRIBE*. Windsor, CA: Center Source Systems.

Goldstein, A. P. (1999). *Low-level aggression: First steps on the ladder to violence*. Champaign, IL: Research Press.

Goldstein, A. P. (2000). Catch it low to prevent it high: Countering low-level verbal abuse. *Reaching Today's Youth, 4*(2), 10–16.

Gray, C. (2000). *Writing social stories with Carol Gray*. [Videotapes and accompanying workbook]. Arlington, TX: Future Horizons.

Gresham, F. M. (1996). *Best practices in social skills training*. Bethesda, MD: National Association of School Psychologists.

Gresham, F. M., Cook, C. R., Crews, S. D., & Kern, L. (2004). Social skills training for children and youth with emotional and behavioral disorders: Validity considerations and future directions. *Behavioral Disorders, 30*(1), 32–46.

Gresham, F. M., Quinn, M. M., & Restori, A. (1999). Methodological issues in functional analysis: Generalizability of other disability groups. *Behavioral Disorders, 24*, 180–182.

Gresham, F. M., Sugai, G., & Horner, R. H. (2001). Interpreting outcomes of social skills training for students with high-incidence disabilities. *Exceptional Children, 67*(3), 331–354.

Hinton, L. M., & Kern, L. (1999). Increasing homework completion by incorporating areas of student interest. *Journal of Positive Behavior Interventions, 1*, 231–241.

Hodgdon, L. Q. (1995). Solving social-behavioral problems with the use of visually supported communication. In K. A. Quill (Ed.), *Teaching children with autism: Strategies to enhance communication and socialization* (pp. 265–286). Florence, KY: Cengage.

Howell, K. W., Fox, S. L., & Morehead, M. K. (1993). *Curriculum-based evaluation: Teaching and decision making* (2nd ed.). Pacific Grove, CA: Brooks/Cole.

Jaime, K., & Knowlton, E. (2007). Visual supports for students with behavior and cognitive challenges. *Intervention in School and Clinic, 42*(5), 259–270.

Jenson, W. R., Rhode, G., & Reavis, H. K. (1994). *The tough kid tool box*. Longmont, CO: Sopris West.

Kaplan, J. S. (1995). *Beyond behavior modification: A cognitive-behavioral approach to behavior management in the school* (3rd ed.). Austin, TX: Pro-Ed.

Kauffman, J. M. (2001). *Characteristics of emotional and behavioral disorders of children and youth*. Columbus, OH: Merrill.

Keeley, S. P. (2003). *The source for executive function disorders*. East Moline, IL: LinguiSystems.

Kern, L., Bambara, L., & Fogt, J. (2002). Classwide curricular modification to improve the behavior of students with emotional and behavioral disorders. *Behavioral Disorders, 27*, 317–326.

Kern, L., Mantegna, M. E., Vorndran, C. M., Bailin, D., & Hilt, A. (2001). Choice of task sequence to increase engagement and reduce problem behaviors. *Journal of Positive Behavior Interventions, 3*, 3–10.

Kern, L., & State, T. M. (2009). Incorporating choice and preferred activities into classwide instruction. *Beyond Behavior, 18*(2), 3–11.

Kern-Dunlap, L., Dunlap, G., Clarke, S., Childs, K. E., White, R. L., & Stewart, M. P. (1992). Effects of videotape feedback package on the peer interactions of children with serious behavioral and emotional challenges. *Journal of Applied Behavior Analysis, 25*(2), 355–364.

Kerr, M., & Nelson, C. M. (1989). *Strategies for managing behavior problems in the classroom* (2nd ed.). Columbus, OH: Merrill.

Lane, K. L., & Menzies, H. M. (2002). The effects of a school-based primary intervention program: Preliminary outcomes. *Preventing School Failure, 47*(1), 26–32.

Larrivee, B. (2002). The potential perils of praise in a democratic interactive classroom. *Action in Teacher Education, 23*, 77–88.

Litow, L., & Pumroy, D. K. (1975). A brief review of classroom group-oriented contingencies. *Journal of Applied Behavior Analysis, 3*, 341–347.

Loveless, T. (1996). Teacher praise. In H. K. Reavis, M. T. Sweeten, W. R. Jenson, D. P. Morgan, D. J. Andrews, & S. L. Fister (Eds.), *Best practices: Behavioral and educational strategies for teachers* (pp. 59–64). Longmont, CO: Sopris West.

Maag, J. (2004). *Behavior management: From theoretical implications to practical applications*. Belmont, CA: Wadsworth/Thomson Learning

Maag, J. (2005). Social skills training for youth with emotional and behavioral disorders and learning disabilities: Problems, conclusions, and suggestions. *Exceptionality, 13*(3), 155–172.

Maag, J. W., & Katsiyannis, A. (2006). Behavioral intervention plans: Legal and practical considerations for students with emotional and behavioral disorders. *Behavioral Disorders, 31*(4), 348–362.

Masters, K. J., Bellonci, C., Bernet, W., Arnold, V., Beitchman, J., Benson, R. S., et al. (2002). Practice parameter for the prevention and management of aggressive behavior in child and adolescent psychiatric institutions, with special reference to seclusion and restraint. *Journal of the American Academy of Child and Adolescent Psychiatry, 41*, 4S–25S.

Mathur, S. R., Kavale, K. A., Quinn, M. M., Forness, S. R., & Rutherford, R.B.J. (1998). Social skills interventions with students with emotional and behavioral problems: A quantitative synthesis of single-subject research. *Behavioral Disorders, 23*, 193–201.

Mayer, G. R. (1995). Preventing antisocial behavior in schools. *Journal of Applied Behavioral Analysis, 28*, 467–478.

McConnell, S. R. (1987). Entrapment effects and the generalization and maintenance of social skills training for elementary school students with behavioral disorders. *Behavioral Disorders, 12*, 252–263.

McCoy, K., & Hermansen, E. (2007). Video modeling for individuals with autism: A review of model types and effects. *Education and Treatment of Children, 30*, 183–213.

McEwan-Landau, B., & Gathercoal, P. (2000). Creating peaceful classrooms: Judicious discipline and class meetings. *Phi Delta Kappan, 81*, 450–452, 454.

References

Miller, D. E. (1986). The management of misbehavior by seclusion. *Residential Treament of Children and Youth, 4,* 63–73.

Miller, G. (2009). *Preventing harmful restraint and seclusion act (H.R. 4247).* Retrieved from www.wrightslaw.com/info/restraint.bill.hr4247.pdf

Mitchem, K. J., Young, K. R., West, R. P., & Benyo, J. (2001). CWPASM: A classwide peer-assisted self-management program for general education classrooms. *Education and Treatment of Children, 24*(2), 111–140.

Moes, D. R. (1998). Integrating choice-making opportunities within teaching-assigned academic tasks to facilitate the performance of children with autism. *Journal of the Association for Persons with Severe Handicaps, 23,* 319–328.

Muscott, H. S., Mann, E. L., & LeBrun, M. R. (2008). Positive behavioral interventions and supports in New Hampshire: Effects of large-scale implementation of schoolwide positive behavior support on student discipline and academic achievement. *Journal of Positive Behavior Interventions, 10*(3), 190–205.

Myles, B. S., & Southwick, J. (2005). *Asperger syndrome and difficult moments.* Shawnee Mission, KS: Autism Asperger Publishing Company.

National Center for Education Statistics. (2007). Children 3 to 21 years old served in federally supported programs for the disabled, by type of disability. Retrieved from http://nces.ed.gov/programs/digest/d04/tables/dt04_052.asp

National Center for Learning Disabilities. (2005). *Executive functioning.* Retrieved from www.ncld.org./ld-basics/ld-aamp-executive-functioning

National Center on Positive Behavioral Interventions and Supports. (2006). *Talking points on school-wide positive behavior support & school-based mental health.* Retrieved from www.pbis.org/common/pbisresources/presentations/gstalkingpoints0107.doc

National Disability Rights Network. (2009). *School is not supposed to hurt: Investigative report on abusive restraint and seclusion in schools.* Retrieved from www.napas.org/sr/SR-Report.pdf

Neel, R. S. (1988). Classroom conversion kit: A teacher's guide to teaching social competency. In R. B. Rutherford Jr. & J. W. Maag (Eds.), *Severe behavior disorders of children and youth* (Vol. 11, pp. 25–31). Reston, VA: Council for Children with Behavioral Disorders

Nelsen, J. (1985). The three R's of logical consequences, the three R's of punishment, and six steps for winning children over. *Individual Psychology, 42,* 161–165.

Nelson, J. (2006). *Positive discipline.* New York: Ballantine Books.

Nelson, J. R., & Carr, B. A. (1996). *The think time strategy for schools: Bringing order to the classroom.* Longmont, CO: Sopris West.

Nelson, J. R., Hurley, K. D., Symhorst, L., Epstein, M. H., Stage, S., & Buckley, J. (2009). The child outcomes of a behavior model. *Exceptional Children, 76*(1), 9–30.

Nelson, J. R., Roberts, M. L., Mathur, S. R., & Rutherford, R. B. (1999). Has public policy exceeded our knowledge base? A review of the functional behavioral assessment literature. *Behavioral Disorders, 24,* 169–179.

Pryor, D. (1999). Applications of Adlerian principles in school settings. *Professional School Counseling, 2*(4), 299–304.

Quill, K. A. (1995). Visually cued instruction for children with autism and pervasive developmental disorders. *Focus on Autistic Behavior, 10,* 10–20.

Quinn, M., Kavale, K. A., Mathur, S. R., Rutherford, R.B.J., & Forness, S. R. (1999). A meta-analysis of social skills interventions for students with emotional or behavioral disorders. *Journal of Emotional and Behavioral Disorders, 7,* 54–64.

Rhode, G., Jenson, W. R., & Reavis, K. (1993). *The tough kid book: Practical classroom management strategies.* Longmont, CO: Sopris West.

Rutherford, R. B., Jr., & Neel, R. S. (1978). The role of punishment with behaviorally disordered children. In R. B. Rutherford Jr. & A. G. Prieto (Eds.), *Severe behavior disorders of children and youth* (Vol. 1, pp. 69–76). Reston, VA: Council for Children with Behavioral Disorders.

Savner, J. L., & Myles, B. S. (2000). *Making visual supports work in the home and community: Strategies for individuals with autism and Asperger syndrome.* Shawnee Mission, KS: Autism Asperger Publishing Company.

Scott, T. M., Bucalos, A., Liaupsin, C., Nelson, C. N., Jolivetter, K., & DeShea, L. (2004). Using functional behavioral assessment in general education settings: Making a case for effectiveness and efficiency. *Behavioral Disorders, 29*(2), 189–201.

Scott, T. M., & Kamps, D. M. (2007). The future of functional behavioral assessment in school settings. *Behavioral Disorders, 32*(3), 146–157.

Scott, T. M., Meers, D. T., & Nelson, C. M. (2000). Toward a consensus of functional behavioral assessment for students with mild disabilities in public school contexts: A national survey. *Education and Treatment of Children, 23*(3), 265–285.

Scott, T. M., Nelson, C. M., & Liaupsin, C. J. (2001). Effective instruction: The forgotten component in preventing school violence. *Education and Treatment of Children, 24,* 309–322.

Sinclair, M. F., Christenson, S. L., Lehr, C. A., & Anderson, A. R. (2003). Facilitating students engagement: Lessons learned from Check & Connect longitudinal studies. *California School Psychologist, 8*(1), 29–42.

Skiba, R. J. (2002). Special education and school discipline: A precarious balance. *Behavioral Disorders, 27*(2), 81–97.

Smith, D. D., & Rivera, D. M. (1993). *Effective discipline* (2nd ed.). Austin, TX: Pro-Ed.

Smith, T.E.C. (1990). *Introduction to education* (2nd ed.). St. Paul, MN: West.

Sprague, J., & Golly, A. (2005). *Best behavior: Building positive behavior support in schools.* Longmont, CO: Sopris West.

Sprague, J., & Walker, H. (2000). Early identification and intervention for youth with antisocial and violent behavior. *Exceptional Children, 66*(3), 367–379.

Sprick, R., Garrison, M., & Howard, L. (1998). *CHAMPs: A proactive and positive approach to classroom management.* Longmont, CO: Sopris West.

Stichter, J. P., Shellady, S., Sealander, K. A., & Eigenberger, M. E. (2000). Teaching what we do know: Preservice training and functional behavioral assessment. *Preventing School Failure, 44*(4), 142–146.

Strain, P. S., & Joseph, G. E. (2004). A not so good job with "good job": A response to Kohn 2001. *Journal of Positive Behavioral Interventions, 6*(1), 55–60.

Strain, P. S., & Odom, S. L. (1986). Peer social initiations: Effective intervention for social skills development of exceptional children. *Exceptional Children, 52,* 543–551.

Sugai, G., Horner, R. H., Dunlap, G., Hieneman, M., Lewis, T. J., Nelson, M. C., et al. (1999). *Applying positive behavioral support and functional behavioral assessment in schools: Technical assistance guide.* Retrieved from http://works.bepress.com/mruef/2

Sugai, G., Lewis-Palmer, T., & Hagan-Burke, S. (1999–2000). Overview of the functional behavioral assessment process. *Exceptionality, 8*(3), 149–160.

Sutherland, K. S., Lewis-Palmer, T., Stichter, J., & Morgan, P. L. (2008). Examining the influence of teacher behavior and classroom context on the behavioral and academic outcomes for students with emotional or behavioral disorders. *Journal of Special Education, 41*(4), 223–233.

Sutherland, K. S., & Wehby, J. H. (2001). The effects of self-evaluation on teaching behavior in classroom for students with emotional and behavioral disorders. *Journal of Special Education, 35,* 161–171.

Sutherland, K. S., Wehby, J. H., & Copeland, S. R. (2000). Effect of varying rates of behavior-specific praise on the on-task behavior of students with emotional and behavioral disorders. *Journal of Emotional and Behavioral Disorders, 8*, 2–8.

Umbreit, J., Ferro, J. B., Liaupsin, C. J., & Lane, K. L. (2007). *Functional behavioral assessment and function-based intervention: An effective practical approach.* Upper Saddle River, NJ: Pearson.

U.S. Department of Education. (2009). *American Recovery and Reinvestment Act of 2009: IDEA recovery funds for children and youth with disabilities.* Retrieved from ed.gov/policy/gen/leg/recovery/index.html

U.S. Government Accountability Office. (2009). *Seclusion and restraints: Selected cases of death and abuse at public and private school and treatment centers.* Retrieved from www.gao.gov/new.items/d09719t.pdf

Vaughn, B. J., & Horner, R. H. (1997). Identifying instructional tasks that occasion problem behaviors and assessing the effects of student versus teaching choice among these tasks. *Journal of Applied Behavior Analysis, 30*, 299–312.

Vaughn, S., Lancelotta, G. X., & Minnis, S. (1988). Social strategy training and peer involvement: Increasing peer acceptance of a female LD student. *Learning Disabilities Focus, 4*(1), 32–37.

Walker, C. J., & Clement, P. W. (1992). Treating inattentive, impulsive, hyperactive children with self-modeling and stress inoculation training. *Child and Family Behavior Therapy, 14*(2), 75–85.

Walker, H. M., Colvin, G., & Ramsey, E. (1995). *Antisocial behavior in school: Strategies and best practices.* Pacific Grove, CA: Brooks/Cole.

Walker, H. M., Ramsey, E., & Gresham, F. M. (2004). *Antisocial behavior in school: Evidence-based practices.* Belmont, CA: Wadsworth/Thomas Learning.

Walker, H. M., Schwartz, I. E., Nippold, M. A., Irvin, L. K., & Noell, J. W. (1994). Social skills in school-age children and youth: Issues and best practices in assessment and intervention. *Topics in Language Disorders, 14*(3), 70–82.

Walker, J. E., Shea, T. M., & Bauer, A. M. (2004). *Behavior management: A practical approach for educators.* Upper Saddle River, NJ: Pearson.

Weinstein, C. S. (2003). *Secondary classroom management: Lessons for research and practice.* New York: McGraw-Hill.

Weiss, E. (1998). *Deadly restraint: A Hartford Courant investigative report.* Retrieved from www.charlydmiller.com/LIB05/1998hartfordcourant11.html

Zins, J. E., Weissberg, R. P., Wang, M. C., & Walberg, H. J. (2004). *Building academic success on social and emotional learning: What does the research say?* New York: Teachers College Press.

Index

Q

Quiet rooms, 256
Quill, K. A., 80, 167, 169
Quinn, M. M., 19, 28
Quinn, M., 28

R

Rage cycle, *See* Escalation cycle
Rainbow Fish and the Big Blue Whale (Pfister), 53
Rainbow Fish to the Rescue (Pfister), 53
Rainbow Fish, The (Pfister), 55
Ramsey, E., 28, 37, 178, 247
Rat and the Tiger, The (Kasza), 49, 52
Reasonable consequences, 170
Reavis, H. K., xxv, 90
Reavis, K., 178
Red schedule, 184–186; defined, 184; directions, 187; social story text, 186; troubleshooting, 185
Red/green game, 135
Reinforcement journals, 121
Reinforcement menus, 121–126, 284; classwide and larger, 125; at home and larger, 125; at home and smaller, 125; larger and longer, 125; quick, 124; simple tracing systems, 126; small and quick, 124; smaller classwide, 125
Reinforcement schedules, 123–128
Reinforcement, 284, *See also* Individual reinforcement systems; appropriate criteria, setting, 128–129; bribes, 119; deprivation, 129–130; of desired behavior, 117–131; interviews/surveys, 120; observations, 120; pairing educators and school with reinforcers, 129; rewards vs., 117–120; student specific nature of, 120–121; teaching peers to reinforce appropriately, 130
Reinforcers: defined, 118; pairing educators and school with reinforcers, 129
Related consequences, 169–170
Replacement behavior, 284; identifying, 60–61; overlooked, 65–66; and punishment, 166
Reproducibe tools, 267–278
Research, lack of, 259
Residential Child Care Project, 261
Respectful tone of voice, 170–171
Response cost or fines, 176, 284
Responsible Rascal (Schwartz), 54
Restori, A., 19
Rewards, reinforcement vs., 117–120
Rhode, G., 90, 178
Rivera, D. M., 37
Roberts, M. L., 15
Rosie and Michael (Viorst), 52
Rumor and Revenge (Boulden), 54
Rutherford, R. B., 15
Rutherford, R. B., Jr., 167
Rutherford, R.B.J., 28
Ryan, J., 261

S

Safe rooms, 256
Sailor, W., xxvi, 13, 14
Sassafras (Cosgrove), 53
Saunders, M., 135
Savner, J. L., 84, 88
Saying No (Berry), 49
Schedule of reinforcement, 123–128, 126; differential reinforcement of incompatible behavior (DRI) schedule, 127–128; differential reinforcement of incompatible behavior (DRO) schedule, 126–127; differential reinforcement of lower rates of behavior (DRL) schedule, 127
Scheduling academic instruction: example schedule, 110; inflexible items, 108–109; major core academic areas, 109; paraprofessionals, use of, 109–111; planning time, 111; teacher preparation, 108; word processing program, making a table in, 108–109
Scheuermann, B., 261
School and classwide social skills instruction, 36–42; and basic skill deficits, 36; class meetings, 37; expectations or rules, 38–39; frequent positive feedback, 37–38; important lessons, 41–42; mini-lessons, 37; routines, 39–40; teaching the expected skills, 36–37
School Is Not Supposed to Hurt: Investigative Report on Abusive Restraint and Seclusion in Schools (National Disability Rights Network), 257
Schwartz, I. E., 20
Scott, T. M., 15, 16, 17, 99
Sealander, K. A., 15
Seclusion and Restraints: Selected Cases Of Death And Abuse At Public And Private Schools and Treatment Centers (GAO), 257
Seclusion Documentation Form (example), 264
Seclusion, 284; defined, 256; monitoring use of, 262
Second Step: Violence Prevention curriculum, 43, 45
Self-evaluation, 34
Self-graphing, 34
Self-management, 33–34, 284; types of (table), 34
Self-monitoring, 34
Self-reinforcement, 34
Sentence length in writing tasks, 105
Setting events, 17, 284; targeting, 71–72
Shea, T. M., 120, 151
Shellady, S., 15
Sinclair, M. F., 62
Sit Still! (Carlson), 48
Skiba, R. J., 7
Skill deficits, 30, 285
Skill streaming curriculum, 43, 45
Small group social skills instruction, 43
Smith, D. D., 37
Smith, K., 4
Smith, T.E.C., 4
Social and behavioral skills: and academic achievement, 5; proper, problems in selecting, 6

Turnbull, A., xxvi, 13, 14
Turnip, The (Morgan), 55
Two Is Company (Delton), 52

U

U.S. Department of Education, 13
U.S. Government Accountability Office (GAO), 257
U.S. Government Accountability Office (GAO), 257
Umbreit, J., 19
Undesirable consequences, 188; continuum, 174; logical, 169; natural, 167–168; punishment, problems with, 165–167; using, 165–173

V

Vaughn, B. J., 101
Vaughn, S., 130
Verdi (Cannon), 50
Vernon, A., 46
Very Lonely Firefly, The (Carle), 52
Very Noisy Night, The (Hendry), 51
Video modeling, 64
Visual schedules, 84–85, 93, 285; format of, 85; icon, 85; picture, 85; written, 85–86
Visual supports, 80–88, 93, 285; beginning-of-day checklist, 82; calm down visual prompt, 84; how to follow directions visual prompt, 82; how to treat others nicely visual prompt, 83; not sitting properly visual prompt, 84; organizational helpers, 81; organized desk checklist, 81; sitting properly visual prompt, 83; transition helpers, 85–88; visual schedules, 84–85
Visual timer, 87
Volcano in My Tummy, A (Whitehouse), 48
Vorndran, C. M., 101

W

Waiting to be called, 89–90
Walberg, H. J., 5

Walker, C. J., 64
Walker, H. M., 5, 20, 28, 37, 178, 247
Walker, H., 5
Walker, J. E., 120
Wang, M. C., 5
Wasted time strategy, 175, 176–177, 188
We Share Everything (Munsch), 55
Wehby, J. H., 37, 76
Weinstein, C. S., 38
Weiss, E., 247, 256
Weissberg, R. P., 5
Wemberly Worried (Henkes), 50
West, R. P., 136
What Are Friends For? (Grindley/Dann), 52
What Was I Scared Of (Dr. Seuss), 51
What Would You Do? (Schwartz), 54
What Would You Think? (Schwartz), 54
When Sophie Gets Angry—Really, Really Angry (Bang), 48
White, R. L., 64
Why Am I Different? (Simon), 50
Wilfrid Gordon McDonald Partridge (Fox), 53
Williams, T. O., 258
Win or Lose by How You Chose (Judge Judy), 54
Wolf, M. M., 135
"Won't do," 31, 33
Writing strategies, 102–1065; chunking and checking, 106; handwriting help, 106-7; long tasks, providing structure/assisted practice with, 104; paper-and-pencil tasks, 103; required sentence length, 105; starting small and building, 104–105; talking through the idea first, 105; technology, using, 103; writing alternatives, providing, 102–103
Written visual schedules, 85–86

Y

Young, K. R., 136

Z

Zins, J. E., 5